SEEKING SERENITY

Outdoor Adventures in the Lake Superior Region

John Highlen

Artwork by Julie Highlen

NATURAL CONNECTIONS
Deerton, Michigan

Grateful appreciation to the Listening Point Foundation. Portions of the chapter Listening Point first appeared in their publication, *The View from Listening Point*.

Grateful appreciation to *The Boundary Waters Journal*. The chapters Quiet Adventure and Painting the Boundary Waters were first published in a slightly different form in that magazine.

Published by Natural Connections 2026

ISBN 979-8-9900307-2-5 (soft cover)

Printed in the United States of America

Also by John Highlen

Touching the Wild U.P.

Porkies Wilderness Wanderings

Chasing Traver's Magic

To everyone who is seeking serenity in this crazy, chaotic world.

We must learn to reawaken and keep ourselves awake, not by mechanical aids, but by an infinite expectation of the dawn…

Henry David Thoreau – Walden

In the end, our society will be defined not only by what we create, but by what we refuse to destroy.

John Sawhill

Wilderness to the people of America is a spiritual necessity, an antidote to the high pressure of modern life, a means of regaining serenity and equilibrium…I have found that people go to the wilderness for many things, but the most important of these is perspective. They may think they go for the fishing or the scenery or companionship. But, in reality, it is something far deeper. They go to the wilderness for the good of their souls.

Sigurd Olson – The Meaning of Wilderness

CONTENTS

ACKNOWLEDGEMENTS

I am certainly indebted to my wife, Julie, for once again lending her artistic talents to my writing project. I'm incredibly fortunate that, so far, payments have only needed to come in the form of chocolates.

A special Thank You to our friend, Barb Osbon, for keeping an eye on me by diligently applying her proofreading talents to this book. I appreciate her honest insights and attention to detail. This is the third book that she has worked on with me, so she obviously has the patience of a saint.

Many thanks to Teena Walenga for allowing Julie to use a photograph of hers from Isle Royale as a reference for the painting that adorns the front cover of this book. Also, Thank You to Sonya Harshman for facilitating the connection between Julie and Teena. I looked at many photographs during the planning of this book and just kept coming back to that picture for its feeling of serenity.

Also, a special Thank You to the Listening Point Foundation for allowing me to be an artist-in-residence to do some writing with them while I was working on this book. In addition, portions of the *Listening Point* chapter were first published in a slightly modified form in the LPF newsletter, *The View from Listening Point*. The LPF is dedicated to preserving Listening Point and advancing Sigurd Olson's wilderness philosophy. Sigurd Olson's Listening Point on Burntside Lake and his Writing Shack in Ely, Minnesota, are both listed on the National Register of Historic Places at the national level of significance.

Thank You to Stu Osthoff and the *Boundary Waters Journal* for publishing some of my Boundary Waters Canoe Area Wilderness adventure stories. The chapters in this book titled, *Quiet Adventure* and *Painting the Boundary Waters* were first published in a slightly different form in the *Boundary Waters Journal*.

Most importantly, I thank God for giving me the desire and ability to pursue His serenity in the wild places of this world. Those places that are still much like I imagine they were in the beginning.

SEEKING SERENITY

Introduction

I've been roaming the wilds in various forms and to various degrees most of my life. It started with family vacations, along with short expeditions into the fields, forests, and waterways near the rural subdivision where I grew up. Home-made backpacks and Boy Scout canteens eventually gave way to higher-level equipment and higher-level aspirations. Initially, I don't recall searching for or striving for, anything in particular. I just wanted to see what was out there and quench my thirst for outdoor adventures. Over the years, one of the things I've discovered about this thirst is that it's never really satisfied. As I'm returning home from one expedition, I'm already planning the next one, and maybe even the one after that. Some people would call it a way of life. Others would probably call it more of a passion. A few may even refer to my inclination with somewhat derogatory comments. To me, it's just life. So, even though the majority of the adventures chronicled in this book span the past twenty years or so, the book has realistically been in the making for more like sixty years.

When I began writing the stories for this book, my initial inclination was to title it, *SEEKING SOLITUDE*. I liked the sound of it, and I thought it described what I've basically been searching for. But the more I thought about it, I began to realize that maybe that catchy title doesn't properly describe my motivation. When I finally resorted to pulling my old beat-up dictionary off the shelf, trying not to drop any of the loose pages, for *solitude* I found descriptions like *being solitary*; *alone*; *without companions*. My chosen title quickly lost its appeal, because those were not good descriptions of what I'm after or striving for when I venture out into the wilds. I am often alone, but that is certainly not what I'm striving for or what motivates me. Solitude is fine, but with too much solitude, a person tends to become a hermit or recluse, whether they are out in nature or not. On the other hand, with too little solitude, especially natural solitude where you have the atmosphere to truly think, a person runs the risk of being sucked into the mind-numbing ways of the modern world, where most of the things around them are artificial, and encounters are virtual. Balance is the key. The key to both survival and sanity. Regardless, solitude is not my primary motivation.

Then I began mentally kicking around the word *serenity*. When I looked up the word *serene*, I found descriptions such as *calm and cheerful*; *placid*; *tranquil*; *clear and unclouded*. Those descriptions more closely fit what I've really been seeking — and what I continue to seek. It may not be a complete or thorough explanation of what I'm out there looking for, but a complete and thorough description of what I'm looking for likely wouldn't fit on the cover of a book. So, *serenity* is what I settled on to convey the idea of what I'm searching for. The idea that I want to get across to people. *SEEKING SERENITY*. That calm, cheerful feeling of tranquility, where thoughts are clear and unclouded. That state of mind where the world seems good, like it started out. Days are exciting, and the future is bright and welcoming. Sometimes even when it's pouring rain or snow is blasting you in the face.

So the obvious question is, can serenity only be found in the wilderness? Well, probably not, but in my experience, wild and natural areas are some of the best places to look. Even if you don't truly experience serenity on any given outing, you're still usually having an enriching adventure, and it's certainly better than spending time in the city. Any city.

That being said, I'm sure some people wonder why I love getting out into the wilderness, whether I'm consciously seeking serenity or not. Well, I love getting out into the wilderness to get away from the crowds, allowing me to enjoy the natural world, including the sounds. To experience the world as it once was, unpolluted by trash and noise. Where my thoughts and interactions with the natural world can be uninterrupted. To answer the call of the wild and be an active participant in the natural community. To think uncluttered thoughts and ponder things that don't stand out amid man-made clutter. To live simply, within the natural flow of life. Or maybe to simply live within the natural flow of life. To be a kid again, feeling the exhilaration of a true adventure. Living in the moment without the concerns or burdens of grown-up responsibilities. To feel alive and unfettered. To go and see what is out in that vast expanse of forest, over the next hill, at the other end of the lake, or around the next bend in the stream. To see what exists out there in the open areas between roads and even trails. To shuck the responsibilities and tethers of civilization and have the freedom to roam and explore. To have the opportunity to see and do things that most people don't. To live out big adventurous dreams and to be the adventurer I've dreamed about being all my life. Because I enjoy it, and I would be miserable if I didn't do it. Roaming and exploring the wilds, hunting, fishing, hiking, camping, canoeing, snowshoeing…it's who I am.

Those natural areas where I often find serenity feel like home to me. Quiet waterways, forests, meadows, mountains, and bogs. When I'm in the city, I feel like a misplaced foreigner who doesn't belong there. I feel lost and out of touch. People there don't speak my language, and I often don't speak theirs. So, I try to keep those visits short, and even when I'm there out of necessity, I seek refuge. Parks, ponds (even man-made ones), gardens, and sometimes sporting goods stores. Anything to connect with something that is familiar to me. Something or someplace that is more in sync with who I am.

Over the years, my wanderings have not been limited to just the Lake Superior region, but growing up in Michigan and now living in Michigan's Upper Peninsula, this area has certainly been a major focus. I have enjoyed the privilege of spending time in wilderness areas and near-wilderness areas across the country, but the north woods have always held a special allure for me. Not only do I live here, but my heart is here as well, and probably always has been.

Seeking serenity in wild places tends to provide much more than just serenity. Wildlife encounters—sometimes up close and personal—gorgeous scenery, and time to honestly think are all part of the mix as well. Sweat, dirt, unexpected weather, and bugs tend to be prevalent at times, too. It's all part of the stuff that interesting experiences and stories come from. As I have searched the north woods and waterways in the Lake Superior region over the years for this elusive thing we call serenity and the adventures involved in that pursuit, life has certainly been filled with interesting, sometimes surprising, experiences.

This book is a collection of the stories of those Lake Superior area wanderings and adventures. I certainly hope that you enjoy the journey. I hope, too, that these adventures that I've experienced will somehow inspire and enhance your own journey. Whatever that journey may be, and wherever it may lead you. Just make sure to take along a notebook and a camera.

MICHIGAN'S UPPER PENINSULA

I have been in and out of Michigan's Upper Peninsula most of my life. Family vacations. Two stints at Michigan Tech. Building a rustic log cabin in the Tahquamenon area thirty-plus years ago. Then, becoming a full-time resident at the end of 2016. The chapters in this section cover U.P. adventures from the past few years. Many of my other U.P. adventures are chronicled in my first three books.

Rock River Canyon

A few years back, I spent opening day of the firearm deer season hunting in the Rock River Canyon Wilderness. At first, I couldn't find the beginning of the old trail in the dark, but after about ten minutes, I finally located it in the brush. It took me about an hour to sneak into my planned location just past Silver Creek, where I waited until it was good daylight before venturing any farther. At that point, I continued along the old logging trail that follows Rock River about sixty feet or so above the floodplain. I hunted along the old trail well past Ginpole Lake to where the river turns north, with my only wildlife sighting — besides squirrels and songbirds — being a bald eagle.

From there, I bushwhacked through the woods about a half mile south to Silver Creek. Partway there, I jumped a trio of does out in the open woods, which caught me by surprise because I expected deer to be in thicker cover. All I could do was watch them bounding away, hoping they didn't scare any other deer. Down in the Silver Creek canyon, the woods looked too thick to be able to get a shot, even if I saw a deer, so I stayed up on a bench about sixty feet above the bottom, where I at least had a little bit of a view down into the thick cover. Another eagle soared past, looking like it was keeping an eye on me. Once the bench became too thick with brush, I climbed up onto the ridge and continued following the creek as I hunted. That was where I bumped into another doe in a thick stand of oak brush. She was big but still lacked the bones on her head to make it a legal deer. My trek along the creek seemed long, probably because of having to quietly negotiate several stands of thick brush and areas of big deadfall trees. Shortly before I reached the area where I had crossed the creek that morning, I spotted the tail-end of a deer walking off into the brush. It could have been a buck, but I had no way to tell, and trying to sneak up on it would have been futile at best.

When I got back to where I started my hunt near the creek crossing, there was a new buck scrape fifteen feet from the tree I had been leaning against that morning. Based on the slightly dry soil at the top of the antler marks, I assumed that the scrape was made shortly after I left. With the odds against me, I hung around there until it was dark just in case the buck returned. The odds prevailed.

On my way back out of the wilderness, I jumped four different grouse in the dark. The last one was only about ten feet away when it flushed, which gave my heart a quick stress test. I didn't shoot a deer that day, but I did finally get back out into the wilderness to hunt, so I called that my success.

A couple of weeks later, to wrap up the season, I was back out in the wilderness, still looking for a legal buck. The temperature was right about at freezing that morning. On the way into Silver Creek, I crossed or followed a few sets of deer and coyote tracks, which at least gave me some hope, even though I knew from experience that tracks in the snow can be fickle. When I reached the creek about thirty minutes before daylight, I found that the flow patterns had changed due to the weather. Much of the stream was covered with ice or snow, forcing the flow into channels that were about a foot deep. Between channels were sections of snowy ice of questionable thickness, covering the unknown. I looked for a better crossing location, which can be difficult in the dark with perception being thrown off by the headlamp beam, but could not find one. So, I finally just crunched my way through the bank ice, which was covering eight inches of water, and stepped over the first channel onto more crunching ice. The center of the main icepack held me for three steps until a large section broke off and tipped me into the deeper channel. I had no choice but to step into the channel and hop out onto the far bank. There was a lot of noise involved, but I didn't fall, so I considered it a successful crossing. Not clean or completely dry, but at least I wasn't lying in the stream.

A short distance past the creek crossing, I leaned against a tree along the old logging trail until about an hour past full daylight. I thought I had heard something crunching across the creek right about daybreak, but nothing ever showed up near me. With nothing going on around me, I was ready to roam, so I took two careful steps away from the tree to get a better view along the trail. That was when I saw a deer coming through the oak brush down the hill across from me. I just froze and watched. The deer turned out to be a buck, but it was only a three-point with a small fork on the left side and a spike on the right, which was not a legal deer. He spotted me as he stepped into the trail, but with my camo mask on, he couldn't seem to make a positive identification. He was obviously nervous, nonetheless, and trotted back up the hill. During his retreat, he stopped and rechecked me a few times, then trotted off to the southwest. Once he was out of sight, he blew at me a few times just to put everything else in the woods on alert — probably also the equivalent of telling me off. After that encounter, I only ventured a quarter mile west and stood for a couple of hours to let everything calm down. Then I cut south and made another slow loop around to where I started, stopping at a few good vantage points just to watch and listen.

I waded back across Silver Creek and waited there until it was nearly dark. That last hour of daylight is often a mental seesaw. Part of me is optimistic, knowing that deer often move around during that time. But part of me also can't help but think that time is running short and my window of opportunity is quickly closing. On my slow hunt back to the road, I found a few areas where there were fresh deer tracks on top of my boot prints from the morning. The tracks didn't look large enough to be from a legal buck, so I decided not to bother racking my brain with what-if questions and just quietly continued on. At the road, I stood and listened to the river for a few minutes before getting in my truck. On the way home, I began optimistically considering future Rock River Canyon explorations. What else could I do?

Two years later, I returned for a pre-hunting recon tour on a cool October morning. I parked partway up the north side of the wilderness and set out along the only trail into the heart of the wilderness about 9:00 am. It's getting fainter and more undefined each year, but it's technically still a trail. There wasn't much color in the forest leaves, but the sun was out, making the woods feel bright and cheery anyway. The forest was quiet except for occasional bird calls and my footsteps crunching in the leaves.

The first mapped stream crossing was dry, so there was no waterfall tumbling over the ledge just below the trail crossing, like there usually is. From there, I started bushwhacking. Instead of trying to follow the canyon rim, which is often not well defined, I navigated by compass, cutting through the flatter woods farther back from the edge. The second mapped stream crossing was wet, but not very wide. As I worked my way across the top of a mucky area beyond the crossing, I flushed a pair of ruffed grouse that went crashing off through the brush. After crossing another mucky area, I found myself at a deep north-south canyon that was bigger than I was expecting for the third stream crossing. I could see a stream at the bottom of the canyon, so I ventured down to investigate. The stream was about four feet wide, which seemed too big for the third stream, so I wondered if I had missed the third stream while I was above the two swampy areas, and maybe I was at the fourth stream. Maps and reality sometimes don't match up precisely.

There were deer tracks in the exposed sand where I crossed. It was a pretty stream, tempting me to stay and play, but I had other areas to explore. After the crossing, I found a small flat area adjacent to the stream. Just upstream was an open, swampy section of the creek that looked like it included a small pond. So, it was indeed the fourth stream, because I recognized the area from hunting there sometime in the previous few years.

Having my bearings again, I climbed into new territory in a forested flat well above the stream. Then, I dropped over the other side and followed the Rock River valley to my wilderness fishing area, flushing another lively grouse along the way. I reached the accessible area of the river, where thick tag alders gave way to hardwoods, late in the morning, and found that the water was low. Maybe even lower than when I last fished there a couple of months earlier. With river music in the air, colored leaves were floating in the water and collecting on exposed riverbed rocks. New leaves trickled down with each mild puff of breeze. I relaxed for a few minutes in the autumn tranquility.

Before moving on, I couldn't resist eating an early lunch at the river, watching the sunshine sparkling on the water and listening to the small riffle in front of me singing in the amber morning light. I wanted to be fishing, just because the river was so inviting, but the time for chasing trout in this water was done for the year.

When I later left the river, heading south, I followed a line of six-foot-tall limestone cliffs that were composed of thin layers, oriented at about a thirty-degree angle. As I went to jot down a few notes, I realized I had somehow lost my black pen out of my pants pocket. Instead of spending time trying to precisely backtrack to find it, I switched to the red pen that was still in my pocket and made a mental note to be extra careful keeping track of it because I didn't have a second backup. I felt a little guilty basically leaving trash in the woods, but my chances of finding a dark pen in the leaves on the jumbled forest floor were probably pretty slim.

As I climbed up toward the south canyon rim, working around mucky seepages and deadfalls, I ran into a line of cliffs that were thirty to fifty feet tall and consisted of thickly layered limestone. I climbed to the base of the cliffs and followed them eastward, looking into small caves and crevasses as I went. There were ferns growing from the limestone powder on some of the ledges, which caught me by surprise because I didn't expect anything to be growing in pure lime. In addition to the little close-up details, all along the cliff base, I enjoyed a commanding view of the sunlit autumn forest below.

Wanting to explore more of the cliffs, I passed by the first exit ramp that led to the top and continued along the bottom of the cliff face. As I crossed the exit ramp, I found it to be a wide seepage, covered with wet mossy rocks. The muck beneath the rocks didn't hold them in place well, making for a precarious crossing due to the steepness.

Farther along the cliffs, I explored into a cave about twenty feet deep and found a considerable collection of porcupine droppings at the back of the cave. Nobody was home at the time, so I didn't have an encounter with an agitated resident. The cave brought back memories of a cave in the base of the Lake Superior cliffs, where I used to ice climb in the Keweenaw when I was in college. A friend and I would sometimes spend the night in that cave so we could ice climb for a couple of days without the inconvenience of going home. That was back in the days when sleeping on a floor of ice with a thin, stiff foam pad didn't cause me any lack of sleep.

Not far from the Rock River Canyon cave, I crossed a swath of lime powder on the ground that turned out to be a six-inch-deep wet mire due to another seepage. My boots came out white, but at least I didn't slip and get my entire backside whitewashed. At that point, the ground at the cliff base was getting steeper and more difficult to traverse, so I opted to take the next exit ramp, which was basically a small gully, up to the top, where walking was much easier. When I had hunted along the top of the canyon during the November deer season, the bare snowy forest looked cold and harsh. On this sunny early October day, there was little resemblance. The forest felt warm and inviting.

After about thirty minutes of hiking along the canyon rim, I entered the area where I had previously explored while hunting and began recognizing familiar features. Soon, I was at Silver Creek, searching for a shallow crossing location. Once across, I followed the creek down to its confluence with the Rock River, making mental notes of potential fishing locations. The creek still contained a considerable amount of sand, which I assumed was a remnant of the sand dump that filled in most of my Rock River fishing holes a few years prior. At the confluence, there was a swath of bright sand making the bend, following the flow out of the creek and into the river. Above the Silver Creek entrance, there was no sand at all visible in the river. Below, the river bottom was primarily sand, just like the creek.

On my way out to the road, I spotted a large whiteish object in the woods, which I assumed was trash. To my surprise, it turned out to be a bowling-ball-size puffball mushroom. Looking around, I readily spotted three others, one of which was more the size of a basketball. I understand that they are good to eat, but not knowing much about mushrooms, I just left them for the rodents that had already been nibbling on them and continued on my journey back to the road.

About a month later, I spent the better part of another day deer hunting within the wilderness, which was getting more familiar with each visit. When I arrived before daylight, it was raining. Not hard. Just a steady sprinkle. I was thankful for the rain because the moisture would take the crunch out of the dry leaves that covered the ground. It would have been nicer, though, if the rain had finished for the day so that the dampness was limited to the leaves and not spreading through my clothes.

Quietly, I snuck into the woods along what was once an old two-track but is now a swampy remnant of a trail. After about thirty minutes of stealthy progress, I carefully waded across Silver Creek and slipped up into the edge of the hardwood forest, right where it transitioned to the evergreen-dominated river floodplain. There, I found a tree to lean against while I waited in the continuing rain for daylight to seep into the wilderness. In fact, at that point, it was more of a rain than a sprinkle, making time pass even more slowly than usual.

After a couple of hours of watching squirrels, birds, and raindrops, I slowly worked my way a little farther into the wilderness, still following what was left of the old logging trail. Then I lingered in the protection of a small group of hemlocks for about thirty minutes, trying to decide on my next move. Protection, meaning that the hemlocks blocked probably ten percent of the rain.

At that point, I decided to hunt someplace I had not hunted, or even explored, before, just for the adventure of it. So, I carefully descended into the floodplain to explore and hunt near the Rock River in hopes of finding a buck lurking about somewhere in the cover of the cedar and hemlock swamp. Once I made my way out to the river, I found that there was a relatively high and dry strip of land paralleling both sides of the waterway. Turning upstream, I slowly hunted my way farther into the wilderness, keeping an eye on both sides of the river, figuring that if I got an opportunity to shoot a deer on the other side, I would just have to find a place to cross, even if it meant wet feet to go with the rest of my slowly saturating clothes. In addition to hunting, I was taking in the new scenery and looking for potential fishing locations as well. However, fishing opportunities didn't look very promising because the river was flowing over a bedrock riverbed, with virtually no features that fish could use for cover. Squirrels and woodpeckers were abundant, as were chickadees in some locations, just no deer. In fact, I wasn't even seeing any signs of deer having been there. Tracks, droppings, rubs, scrapes. Nothing. I did come across a small tributary with an eighteen-inch tall waterfall that was working on wearing down a section of bedrock streambed, but I was hoping for more than just scenery.

After a couple of hours of following the river, I found myself at the eastern end of Ginpole Lake, watching a light fog mingling with the shoreline trees. There, I parked myself beneath a semi-protective pair of large hemlocks and indulged myself in lunch, while I watched a pair of red squirrels squabbling over property rights.

After lunch, I slowly followed the river back downstream all the way to Silver Creek. Still no sign of a deer. Rain was still falling steadily, with no reprieve in sight. My hat was soaked to the point of excess water dripping from the bill. Much of my upper body was beginning to feel the wetness seeping through my four layers of clothes, as were my knees. My pants were entirely wet, but so far I could only feel the dampness at my knees. With my outer fleece jacket, enough water had wicked down the sleeves so that I could wring water out the cuffs like wet sponges.

Taking stock of the situation, I decided it was time to head out of the wilderness before I was completely soaked and started getting chilled. And it was still raining. I was glad I came out to explore and hunt a new area, but I was certainly a little disappointed with the lack of deer. That evening, there was a small buck eating apples under the trees in our backyard. It was not a legal buck, but still a live deer on the hoof, so I took that as my deer sighting for the day. Dragging a deer out of the Rock River Canyon Wilderness would have to be for another day. Hopefully. In the meantime, I decided more scouting expeditions were in order. Maybe spending more time hunting there and hoping to find a legal buck was like throwing coins down a dry wishing well, but at least it was an interesting place to store my spare change. Besides, I was looking at it as more of an investment.

BEAVER BASIN WILDERNESS

Our original plan was to hike the Chapel Rock-Mosquito Beach-Mosquito Falls loop within the Pictured Rocks National Lakeshore, but when we arrived at the forty-vehicle parking lot, it was overflowing, with vehicles parked along the road for a couple of hundred yards before the formal parking lot. In addition, eight more cars followed us in. We opted to skip the circus and try someplace that we thought would be a little less crazy. So, we headed over to the Beaver Basin Wilderness. Even though it's still part of the Pictured Rocks National Lakeshore, it's a little more remote, which usually makes it a little less busy.

Our hike started at the Little Beaver Lake Campground, which is not part of the wilderness, but it's a convenient place to park to access the west side of the wilderness. On the trail around Little Beaver Lake, I couldn't help noticing the little creek that entered the west side. All I can say is that it looked trouty with its sandy bottom and ample supply of woody debris. So, as with many creeks that I encounter, I made a mental note to investigate it later.

Around the north side of Little Beaver Lake, the trail winds around a collection of rock outcroppings that are worn and pockmarked just like the nearby cliffs along Lake Superior. Based on the arrangement, weathering, and sculpted caves, those outcrops were obviously once a Superior wave-worn shoreline. Likely an island. Now, they're half a mile inland, hidden in the forest, causing me to wonder what the lake once looked like.

Toward the east end of Little Beaver Lake, the forest contains a large concentration of red pines, making it feel up north woodsy for a guy born and raised downstate. I loved the aroma of the pine-filled woods. As we reached Beaver Lake, within the formal wilderness boundary, there was a whitetail fawn splashing around in the sandy shallows, sending ripples out from the shoreline brush that screened it from view. Sneaking in closer to investigate, we could see that it still carried faint white spots in its fur. Once it saw us, we were involved in a waterside stare-down for a few minutes before it slipped off into the brush, probably looking for mom.

While we were standing on a hill overlooking Beaver Lake, a pair of blue herons circled the lake. One of them flew past at eye level, only about twenty yards away. I saw it look at us as it methodically flapped by in its ancient-looking flight pose. We then followed Beaver Creek up to Superior, where there was a bridge to cross. The creek is only about a half mile long, but there was a massive logjam near the river mouth, creating fantastic trout habitat. I couldn't see any trout, but I was sure they were there. From the Superior beach, which is part of Twelve-Mile Beach, we could see the east end of the Pictured Rocks cliffs. According to our map, Spray Falls was right there somewhere, but we couldn't make out the details to be able to see it.

After crossing the bridge, we hiked down the east side of the creek back to Beaver Lake again. From there, we continued over to Trappers Lake just to see it, then out into the middle of the wilderness area south of Beaver Lake. The interior of the wilderness area was mostly a maple-beech mixed hardwood forest with some maples reaching between two and three feet in diameter. I suspected that area would provide a brilliant autumn color display sometime in October and made a mental note to come back then to see the show. It was three and a half miles from Trappers Lake to the Lowney Creek Campground, which is where Lowney Creek enters the south side of Beaver Lake, right across the lake from Beaver Creek. With Beaver Creek being so short, I'm not sure why they are considered two different creeks. To me, Beaver Creek is simply the culmination of Lowney Creek, so I would consider it to be part of Lowney, but I don't have the authority to make decisions like that, so they're two different creeks. At least by name. Being an avid trout fisherman and a lifelong lover of moving water, it was difficult to tear myself away from the creek and continue our hike around the lake back to the trailhead. I consoled myself by promising we would return. I didn't know exactly when, but I knew that we would.

A couple of years and many excursions later, we continued our Beaver Basin Wilderness exploring. This time it was by kayaking instead of hiking. We met our friends Barb and Tim at the Little Beaver Lake Campground launch site. Even though Little Beaver is outside the formal wilderness boundary, the lake was quiet. A sunny sky, mild summer temperature, and a light breeze made for a gorgeous UP day for kayaking, or anything really. Now I love hiking and have for most of my life, but there is something special about being on the water in a quiet, manually powered watercraft, and experiencing the world from that perspective. Whether by canoe or kayak — and these days, by paddleboard, although I have never personally been on a paddleboard — there is a personal connection with the water body that you just cannot get with a larger motor-powered craft. That being said, we were enjoying our peaceful connection with the lake as we entered the wilderness through the short creek connecting Beaver and Little Beaver lakes.

Just before we reached Beaver Lake, we encountered a school of what appeared to be small bass, some of them up to eight or ten inches in length. They were readily visible in the clear-running creek and didn't seem to be bothered much by our intrusion. I also thought I heard a faint loon call when we first entered Beaver Lake, but I never heard it again, so I couldn't be sure. Dragonflies and damselflies in a variety of color variations were abundant out on the open lake. We also found a large array of clams in the shallows of the lake, leaving trails in the silty bottom. A clump of wild blue flag flowers stood at the water's edge. Most of the flowers were withered from their June glory, but one blossom was still holding its beauty well into the heat of July.

After following the north shoreline over to Beaver Creek, we found quite a few dazzling damselflies with iridescent dark blue bodies and black wings gathered at the inlet to the creek. Looking down the sandy stream, it reminded me of a smaller version of the Au Sable River near Grayling. I felt a pull to go explore, but with all the logs and other wood in the water, exploring by kayak certainly wouldn't be the best option. The creek looked like it needed to be carefully explored with a light fly rod. Another day. Another visit. As I quietly floated near the creek entrance, I reached into the shallow water and rubbed the algae covering off a section of a submerged log, revealing a beautifully vibrant straight grain pattern. I couldn't tell for sure what kind of wood it was, but I would have loved to be able to incorporate that log into our home somehow.

On the opposite side of the lake, we weren't able to get a close look at Lowney Creek, which made its entrance directly across from Beaver Creek, because of a sandbar extending out into the water, created by sand filtering in from the creek. Regardless of our lack of access, I could still picture the little sandy creek flowing through the wilderness. Even though I had wanted to try fishing that creek when Julie and I first saw it a couple of years earlier, I still hadn't done it. The only reason was that there were too many other inviting explorations on my list, so it remained on my list as something I needed to pursue in the future. Just one of many somethings that I needed to do. Sometime.

On our way back through the connecting creek to Little Beaver, the school of bass was still hanging out at the Beaver Lake end, along with a twelve-inch sucker holding still in a spotlight of sunshine, giving us a clear look at its every detail. As we quietly floated past, part of me was admiring the fish and the way they were calmly finning in the faint current. The other part of me was looking at the fish and thinking about dinner.

Overall, the pace of the day was slow and relaxed, allowing us time to truly take in the scenery and experience the moments as they came. Just like wilderness exploration really should be.

We ended the day by borrowing an unoccupied campsite at the Litter Beaver Campground and cooking brats over a small campfire. As we were just relaxing and talking by the fire, a young couple approached us, looking a little lost and confused. They were looking for the Mosquito-Chapel parking lot, where their vehicle was parked. They were really perplexed when we informed them that their vehicle was at least seven or eight miles west of where we were. As it turned out, they had somehow made a wrong turn when returning to the trail from a short lakeshore overlook and ended up hiking east instead of west. At that point, Barb suggested that they just join us for a brat, with the promise that she and Tim would drive them back to their vehicle afterward, instead of them having to make an even longer unexpected hike, partially in the dark. They relaxed a bit then and gladly joined us.

Our next Pictured Rocks wilderness area visit started out promising, with us seeing two deer and three ruffed grouse along the gravel road on our way to the Beaver Basin Overlook. When we arrived at about 9:00 am, our car thermometer showed the temperature to be a nippy thirty-one degrees Fahrenheit, even though the sky was sunny and clear. At the overlook, autumn was stretching out in front of us across the Beaver Basin, enticing us to come and explore.

Two dark green bands of trees ran east-west across the basin, likely indicating the locations of drainages. As we began our hike down the trail into the heart of the colorful basin, we were surprised to be walking into a world of green, finding that most of the vibrant color was limited to the forest canopy. Near the bottom of the trail's descent, we emerged into an open maple forest to the east, with a green hillside remaining to the west. That was about where we had our first Lowney Creek encounter of the day. As we crossed the bridge, the creek was flowing cheerfully through the amber morning light. Like the other portions of the creek we had seen before, it looked like a trout stream. Then again, to me, most streams look like trout streams. It's been that way for most of my life. Exploring that little stream has been on my list for several years — ever since we first hiked by it. And it's still on my list for exploring with a light fly rod. Again, one of these days.

Shortly after the stream crossing, we saw three large puffball mushrooms near the creek. Being so visible, I was surprised that nobody had picked them. From there, we continued a short distance to the first old dam impoundment that Trout Unlimited is working with the Park Service to remove in an effort to return the wilderness area to a more natural state. As we explored, sunlight was slowly penetrating the forest, igniting leaves, as well as my imagination, as I was thinking about potential investigations and explorations.

The second creek crossing was down in what I believe was one of the green belts that we saw from the overlook — most likely the closest belt. Instead of colorful maples, the nearby forest along that section of the creek was dominated by hemlock, fir, spruce, and cedar. Then, not far past the creek crossing, we were back out into the maple forest again.

The third creek crossing was especially picturesque. It was surrounded by a mix of evergreens and small amber maples. Two tiny waterfalls were within sight of the trail, urging me to go off-trail to explore, which typically doesn't take much urging. Julie had a commitment that afternoon, though, so I pushed aside my bushwhacking impulse and continued along the trail. Off-trail creek explorations would be saved for springtime fly fishing.

Shortly after turning onto the trail to Trappers Lake, I could see water in the valley off to our right from several places where I strayed off the trail to take a peek over the rim. I put off making the descent for a closer look because I was hoping we would eventually get into an open section of mostly mature sugar maples in the forest, where the combination of sunlight and amber leaves makes the entire forest glow with autumn. I had experienced it many times before in other predominantly sugar maple forests where the saturation of color was mesmerizing.

With another half-hour of trail hiking behind us, we still had not found the glowing conditions I was searching for. Time was ticking away, and there were predictions for afternoon clouds, so I began to be concerned that my search might be in vain that day in that particular forest. The autumn color extravaganza I was hoping for might be a bust. With most of the understory leaves still primarily green, we turned around and backtracked to the dam ponds that were down in the valley, hoping more autumn colors would be visible around the ponds and on the slopes of the valley sides.

The first area where there appeared to be a wide-open valley view didn't pan out. Partway down, I got a good enough peek to see that the valley in that vicinity was filled with drab brush and dead spruce tangles. Visibility and colors would be limited at best. I climbed back out to let Julie know that we needed to move on, because I really wanted a colorful open pond view.

A little farther along, I ventured off-trail again to peer into the valley. It looked like we were at the end of the upper pond, so I ventured down the steep slope for a closer look. It appeared that I was correct about where we were. Near the very upper end of the pond, by a small island of long marsh grass, was the bow of an old, rusted rowboat angling up out of the water and muck. Somehow, the aluminum rope eyelet at the top of the bow was still bright and shiny, like it was still regularly being used. Along the hillside, there was color on lower sugar maple branches and a collection of butter-yellow striped maples. Still, it wasn't the vibrant autumn picture I was searching for. That scene that makes you feel like you're bathing in autumn. So, back up to the top I climbed, through a slippery carpet of straw-colored white pine needles, to report my findings.

After a few more peeks from the top of the valley, I found my way down to the old dam we had visited with the Park Service the previous summer. Autumn colors ended abruptly where the tag alders began. I put my fingers in the water. It was good and cold, even after passing through two warming ponds. Trout water. In fact, brook trout water. Taking another step, I spooked something in the shallows of the stream below the dam. At first, I thought it was a large fish, but with a better look, it turned out to be a big muskrat swimming underwater. I watched it swim away as I stood there in the sunshine, with chickadees chattering pleasantly at the edge of the brush along the creek. Then, back up I climbed to let Julie know what I had found.

On our way out to Beaver Lake, we saw a white pine not far from the trail that was about four feet in diameter. It looked huge amongst the other trees. As we stood there for a minute, looking at that tree, I had a difficult time imagining a time when a tree of that caliber would have been just an average tree. It was difficult to fathom a seemingly endless forest filled with trees like that.

Near the lake, the creek contained a lot of sand that was not apparent farther upstream. The water, though, still felt cold like a good trout stream should. The north side of Beaver Lake was mostly pine green. The most colorful area was the west side of the lake, where it was primarily a maple forest. At the rustic campground, we stopped for a few minutes for a long, cold drink of water and to get out some snacks to eat on our way back to the overlook. Then, we began the long climb back up to the overlook parking lot, which surprisingly didn't take all that long or seem very strenuous. In fact, we were at the overlook close to thirty minutes sooner than I expected. Several people were there when we arrived, apparently content with a brief glimpse from above. I thought about sharing some of the details from our explorations within the valley, but then I decided to just let them be content with their brief overlook summary of the Beaver Basin Wilderness. We'll continue our in-depth study. Year by year, tree by tree, fish by fish.

BIG ISLAND LAKE

We left the car in an otherwise empty parking lot a little before 9:00 am. Our vehicle thermometer had indicated twenty-seven degrees Fahrenheit just before I shut it off, which caused a little difficulty removing our canoe from the car racks because the straps were frozen to the canoe. With the parking lot and portage trail cloaked in shade, we portaged into a lake bathed in sunshine. I was glad to see that there was no ice at all on the water. Mist was rising from the lake in the morning glow across vivid reflections of shoreline trees. Rusty orange lakeside brush and ferns were glowing brightly in the morning light. It was a dreamscape lake shrouded in a dancing mist, making me realize that this time of year, any day could be the last gorgeous autumn day. You need to appreciate those gifts as they come, because autumn is fleeting at best.

At first, we just stood and stared. Then, when Julie attempted to take a picture, the camera didn't want to work. Not wanting to lose the opportunity to capture the tranquility of the scene, I jogged back up to the parking lot to get Julie's cell phone from the car. Once we were able to capture the moment, and I was good and warmed up, we launched our canoe into a sunlit bay filled with red oval lily pads with yellow-green starburst centers. First, we paddled over to a large beaver lodge to see if we could hear any of its residents inside. From there, the sun was peeking through a misty point with a tall white pine skeleton highlighted in the morning radiance. That was when I noticed my toes were beginning to feel the cold through my warm-weather boots. They're built for wet, sloppy conditions, but they don't offer much protection from the cold.

Just around the point, paper birches were highlighted on a hillside of rusty ferns. Some autumn color still lingered in the treetops, but most of it was on the ground. As we paddled, the sun, still low in the sky, projected our shadow onto the hillside. We could clearly see two people paddling a canoe through the hillside trees.

While we were getting ready to cross the portage to Mid Lake, I looked back across to one of the islands on Big Island Lake to see a small group of maples still ablaze after most of the rest of their kind had already shed their leaves to begin their winter slumber. The portage to Mid Lake was short enough that we didn't even take our day packs out of the canoe. We just picked it up from each end and carried it across. The paddle across Mid to the Townline Lake portage wasn't much longer than the portage because we saved our exploration of Mid Lake until later so we could reach Townline earlier, while the early morning sun and morning mist were still on the water.

As we stood at the other end of the portage, looking out over Townline Lake, a pair of swans flew over us with heavy wingbeats and loud honking echoing across the water. We slowly cruised around the lake, trying to take in every moment. A flock of ducks took flight from the north end of the lake. I'm not very adept at duck identification, especially at the distance they were, but the white of their undersides flashed with each beat of their wings. One of the features we admired about the lakes in the Big Island Lake Wilderness was the abundance of birch trees with their trunks glowing white against the backdrop of dark evergreens and late-season ferns.

Paddling back to the south, we saw a large fish jump clean out of the water just off the campsite point. The fish and splash both were bright flashes of silver. The campsite itself looked inviting, nestled at the base of its little evergreen point. Directly across the narrow arm of the lake was a hillside covered with birch trees mingled with a smattering of pines. I could imagine it as an extravagant peak-color display if we had been there a couple of weeks earlier.

Most of Townline was dark and murky, but paddling through the narrow connector to Upper Lake, we paddled into gin-clear water. That came as a surprise due to Upper Lake being a small, marshy-looking lake. We passed through to a narrow waterway exiting the southeast end of the lake and winding through a large swath of reeds and grasses. A relatively short distance down the creek, we encountered a beaver dam that created about a four-foot drop to the sprawling marsh beyond. We just quietly sat for a few minutes, steeped in the wilderness serenity, surveying the marsh and listening to the sounds of water continually trickling over and through the dam.

After steeping ourselves in the tranquility of Upper Lake, we quietly returned to the trail and portaged back to Mid Lake. There, we ate our lunch while gazing across at tamarack gold. Lunchtime entertainment was provided by a pair of pileated woodpeckers busily working over a nearby white pine skeleton like a couple of feathered jackhammers.

Going by memory, I knew the portage from Mid Lake to Coattail Lake was on the west side of the lake near the south end. I also knew from experience that portage locations on Forest Service maps are not always shown in their precise location. So when we found a formal trail heading west off Mid Lake, we went ashore, pulled our packs out of the boat, and prepared for the portage. Just as I was getting into position to hoist the canoe onto my shoulders, Julie came back from her short jaunt up the trail to announce that we were at the campsite, not the portage trail. We called it a rest break and moved on to the actual portage, which was a little farther down the shoreline, tucked inconspicuously into the lakeside brush right where the map showed it to be.

The portage trail climbed to the top of a low ridge, where we walked into a brilliant stand of understory maple and beech still in prime autumn attire. It was finally getting warm enough for me to shed the wool shirt I had put on as an outer layer just before we left our vehicle. On Coattail, a mild breeze was rippling the lake. The early afternoon sun that would have pushed temperatures into the uncomfortable zone only a month ago now felt good. Our only notable experience on Coattail Lake was that something relatively large swirled at the surface of the water right near us. Neither of us was looking in that direction at the time for a visual clue, but based on the sound and the fact that nothing resurfaced anywhere farther from the canoe, I'm pretty confident that it was a large fish. They always seem to do that when I'm not fishing.

McInnes Lake has a collection of tamaracks scattered around the shoreline, which added golden highlights to the evergreens and gray maple trunks. We stopped at the lake's only campsite to see what we could recall from our few-day stay there several years earlier. I remembered our evening exploration hikes along the wooded ridge that parallels the lake. I also found that I vividly remembered the view of the lake from the ridgetop campsite. Looking out through the thin veil of white pine branches at the lake below, I could visualize all of the pockmark rings from fish hitting the surface while we were camped there without a fishing rod. And on a more somber note, I recalled hearing about the guy who lost his life there a year or two after our stay. It reminded me that wilderness adventures are not without risk. It also reminded me to savor each day that God gives us because we don't know how many days that will be, or which one will be our last.

The portage to Klondike Lake climbs up and runs along the same ridge that the McInnes camp is on. It's an open forest of maple and birch that was carpeted with fallen leaves, even though many of the birch tree crowns still held colorful leaves as well. When we reached the swampy north end of Klondike, we could see that, like many of the area lakes, it too supported a collection of smoky gold tamaracks, or larch, as they are also known. The portage trail remained on the ridge instead of dropping down to the lake in order to bypass the boggy northern lakeshore and to access the water from more stable ground a little farther down the shoreline.

After first exploring the swampy north end of Klondike once we launched our canoe, we followed the eastern shore down to a large bay that looked interesting on the map. As we approached, it didn't appear to be all that big, but as we paddled into it, the bay seemed to expand into a huge bay with a slow creek snaking out even farther through a brushy bog. We followed the winding creek out farther, past multiple dead-end offshoots. Twice, I thought we had hit a barricade, only to see a way around just before we hit it. Shortly after passing a beaver lodge that probably belonged to the keeper of the surrounding channels, we came to a long beaver dam with no significant channel beyond it. Much like we encountered over on Upper Lake earlier in the day. Water could be heard trickling over or through the dam, but it simply disappeared into the brushy bog beyond. Backtracking out to the lake, we made one temporary wrong turn into a dead-end channel, but quickly realized our error and got back on track.

As we completed our tour of Klondike, we noticed the quaint little camp and commented on its attribute of facing north so you could see the northern lights if they were out. As we talked about the site, I realized that all of the campsites we had seen in that wilderness were nice in one way or another. The other thing that came to mind was the fact that most of the lakes only had one campsite, which was a great blessing for peace and quiet, allowing the people at each camp the opportunity to truly experience the wilderness on a personal level, without unwanted noise from other campers.

On our way back to McInnes Lake, we noticed fresh deer tracks in the portage trail. I'm always on the lookout for inhabitants of the wilds and appreciate seeing signs of wildlife in the wilderness, if not the animals themselves. Out on the lake, we could feel the temperature dropping as the north breeze increased. Clouds were moving in as well. So, we paddled on to the next portage, made the mild crossing, then worked our way back up to Mid Lake.

As we made the short carry-over portage back to Big Island Lake, it dawned on me that we had not experienced any muddy or mucky trails within the entire northern half of the wilderness. Apparently, between the sandy soil and relatively light traffic, even damp areas of the trails didn't get churned to a muddy mess like most trails we've experienced across the Upper Peninsula.

Back on Big Island Lake, we paddled over for a closer look at the maples we had seen earlier that were still retaining most of their leaves and found that one was incorporated into a large beaver lodge that was built around its base. We then continued around the west side of the islands, where the water was shallow, just to take a closer look at the side of the lake we had missed when we passed through in the morning. As we paddled, I was already beginning to miss the wilderness, and we hadn't even reached the final portage yet. Even with the sound of the increasing breeze and the small choppy waves it was causing, we could periodically hear random manmade noises from beyond the wilderness telling us we were nearing the end of our journey.

We lingered at the final portage out of Big Island Lake, enjoying a snack as we savored one last view of the eastern shoreline illuminated by the early evening sun. I said a quiet farewell to the Big Island Lake Wilderness, probably until autumn returns once again, and took a mental picture of white birch trunks and puffy white pines against a backdrop of russet ferns to carry with me as I hoisted the canoe and set off up the trail.

PORKIES PONDERINGS

In 2020, my wife Julie and I were both blessed with an artist-in-residence with the Porcupine Mountains Wilderness State Park, allowing us to spend a little more than a month living in a rustic cabin in the Porcupine Mountains woods — two weeks in January and two-plus weeks in October. During our October stay in the park, one of the entries in my notebook of outdoor adventures read, "Besides a collection of adventures, pictures, and memories, in addition to assembling a mass of notes, what has emerged from this artist-in-residence experience is a head full of dreams and plans. The more adventures I have here in the Porkies, the more I realize this relationship is just beginning." The Porkies had certainly proved to be a great place for big dreams and adventurous explorations. Regardless of good intentions, life gets busy. And complicated. As a result, the few years following our motivating residencies, we only managed to visit the Porkies for a couple of one-day stints. Finally, in the spring of 2025, we returned with the opportunity to spend at least a few consecutive days in the park.

We had been wanting to stay in the Union River Cabin ever since we saw it during one of our artist-in-residence ventures. We had only seen it from a distance, because we weren't sure if it was vacant or not, but its location caught my attention and imagination. The cabin is nestled in a maple and hemlock grove, right on a big bend in the Union River. Being only a stone's throw from the water, I could imagine lying in bed at night with the windows open, listening to the music of the flow. Not to mention evening campfires within reach of the river's song.

When we planned our visit, I noted the date for the maximum six months in advance reservation window. On that date, I made our cabin reservation for fear of losing the opportunity if I procrastinated. The day we arrived, overflowing with high hopes and expectations, it was hot and sunny. Way too hot for early May in the Upper Peninsula. We were told to park and access the cabin by way of the Union Spring Trail. However, I recalled a back way into the cabin from the Union Mine Interpretive Trail that seemed much shorter. A couple of quick hikes showed that the recommended access route took about fifteen minutes. The alternative route only took about five minutes. Knowing we were in for multiple trips to haul in our gear and supplies for four days of hiking, fishing, and painting, we opted for the five-minute route. Four trips later, everything we needed was at the cabin. I was happy to find that not only could we hear the river with the cabin windows open, but we could also actually see the river from most of the windows as well.

Once we toured the cabin vicinity, I rigged up my 4-weight fly rod and hiked out to South Boundary Road and began fishing my way back to the cabin. As I entered the river just upstream from the big twin culverts at the road crossing, it brought back memories of the kid in me just having to wade through one of those culverts during our autumn residency visit.

About a hundred yards upstream, I found the first of what I considered fish-holding water. There was a pair of small waterfalls illuminated by the early afternoon sun. The left fall was about a five-foot drop into a plunge pool. The right side cascaded down a mossy rockslide into another smaller plunge pool. Both pools tapered into short runs. A small rainbow trout came thrashing out of each of the runs with a pheasant tail nymph in its mouth. After that, nothing else seemed interested in my fly offering. I considered changing flies but decided that covering more new water was more important than trying to catch every fish in any given location, so I continued upstream through the rocks and shining water, casting and exploring.

By the time I reached the cabin, the pheasant tail had only brought out one more trout, two if you count a quick hit-and-run where the hook never got set. Photo opportunities of water, rock, and forest had been plentiful, but Julie had our only good camera, so I stored away what I could in my head, knowing that the images weren't necessarily secure for any great length of time.

I found Julie painting a plein air scene of the river near the cabin. Even though the painting wasn't complete, I was happy, and a little relieved, to find that she was pleased with how it looked so far. We both took a brief snack break before Julie finished her painting. And it did indeed turn out looking nice.

Later, we went down to the Union River Outpost Campground so that I could fish that stretch where I had fished during previous visits. Though I had caught both rainbows and brook trout in that area before, nothing was interested in the nymph that I was offering. The water looked a little low for mid-May, so I pulled out my thermometer and found the water to be sixty-two degrees Fahrenheit. Not terrible, but not great for trout that time of year, either. I began thinking that either the trout were a bit lethargic or maybe they had moved to colder water elsewhere. I had the evening to ponder things by a campfire. Technically, we were not camping, but I still always refer to a fire as a campfire. Even at a cabin or in our backyard.

We awoke the next morning, our first full day in the Porkies, to sunshine and warmth. Our plan — okay, my plan — was to start at Lake of the Clouds and follow the Escarpment/Big Carp River Trail out to Superior and back. It would be a solid sixteen miles and include four river crossings. I honestly wasn't sure if Julie was up to the challenge or not, especially considering the heat, but she was willing to try. I knew that I was up to the challenge because I've been doing things like that most of my life and simply haven't acquired the sense to mellow out as I get older.

Lake of the Clouds was shimmering in the morning sun. Trees and shrubs in the cherry family were in full bloom. As we headed west along the escarpment, the air was alive with bird songs. Even relatively early in the morning, the heat made any uphill climb feel draining. Just two days prior, we experienced temperatures in the forties at home. With temperatures in the seventies, direct sun exposure was already beginning to feel downright oppressive. To add to the discomfort, Julie's hiking boots were causing hot spots on her feet. The rugged terrain certainly didn't help. At one of the escarpment campsites, Julie changed into her Muck Boots to lessen her foot discomfort. That, of course, added to the heat for her.

Shortly after passing the campsites, we could see Lake Superior, our destination. In a way, it felt good because our goal was within sight. But, then again, it looked like it was a long way away. We kept hiking, although I could tell the heat and foot issues were beginning to wear on Julie.

At the end of the main escarpment, the trail descended into the darkened coolness of a large hemlock grove. Trilliums began showing up along the trail, in full bloom. The relative coolness was refreshing. Quietly strolling through the hemlocks, it truly felt like we were in the wilderness.

As we neared the edge of the shadowed hemlocks, near the path was a large sugar maple with a sizeable, charred hole all the way through the base, yet the tree was alive and budding for yet another spring. I was amazed at how sometimes the plant world can be so hearty and yet at other times be so fragile. Within sight of the big maple stood the skeleton of a large hemlock, with the lifeless bark peeling off under the forces of the elements. Long after death, it still stood, providing homes, perches, and food for the local community.

At that point, we left the hemlock grove and reentered the brightness of the spring maple forest. The brightness was short-lived, though, as the trail soon leveled out along the talus slope at the bottom of the west end of the escarpment, where the forest was again dominated by hemlocks. As we walked the shadowed path through mossy boulders and decaying logs, I thought back to the last time we explored that area during my October artist-in-residence. Early snow had whitened the landscape and prematurely pulled much of the autumn colors from the maples and birches. Instead of feeling cool, the shelter of the hemlocks provided the warmth of security and respite from the chilling wind. That's one of the reasons why I love hemlock groves. Regardless of the season, they provide feelings of safety and security, protection from the elements. In the shade of the hemlocks that morning, we passed a decaying log that had four small conks growing on a larger conk, reminding us that even in decay, there can be beauty and new life.

When we reached the Carp River crossing, we took a break in the shade to have a quick snack and drink. We rested on a large horizontal maple log, surrounded by spring beauty flowers and bird songs. The river was a little too deep for our boots, and there were no good logs available to provide a bridge, so our only real option was to remove our boots and socks and wade wet. The sting of the water felt refreshing, but the rocks and gravel in the riverbed were painful to walk on with bare feet. As usual, I just grunted and grimaced my way across so I could deposit my boots and daypack, then wade back across to help Julie.

Unfortunately, the gravel proved to be too rough for her, causing her to turn back about a third of the way across. Once she was back on the sandy bank, I hobbled back across the river to retrieve my pack and boots.

With the decision being made for us that we were not going to be able to explore the section of Carp River Trail that we had not experienced before, or make it out to Lake Superior, we went back to our shady maple log to finish our full lunch and think about other options. Julie was struggling with the heat and foot pain. Regardless of how much I wanted to reach Superior, I needed to accept the fact that even if we found a way to cross the river and made it to Superior, Julie would likely seriously struggle to make it back out to Lake of the Clouds. The risk certainly outweighed the gain. Even though Julie offered to hold tight and wait for me at the nearby campsite while I made the trek out to Superior by myself, I decided to do the right thing and turn back.

On our way back out, we surprised a garter snake that was taking advantage of the warmth in a spot of sunshine on the forest floor. When it suddenly moved, it surprised me as well. In the shelter of the hemlocks along the talus piles, we marveled at a three-inch-diameter, twenty-foot-tall maple growing from a small bowl of moss and soil atop a six-foot-diameter boulder. One root extended along the side of the boulder down to the nourishment of the forest floor. The rest of its roots were simply secured into crevices in the boulder. Nearby was a twenty-inch-diameter basswood tree with a thick ring of shoots just above ground level. Some of the roughly thirty shoots were probably twelve feet tall. The main tree appeared to be alive and budding, so I was perplexed as to what would cause such a profusion of shoots. What I took away from both the ring of new shoots and the maple perched atop the boulder is how adaptive and resilient nature is designed to be.

After a few sit-down rest breaks for Julie, we made it back to Lake of the Clouds mid-afternoon. I was glad that I didn't push the hike any farther than I did, otherwise it may not have ended well. Julie found a shady spot at the overlook while I hiked down to the Carp River bridge, which is just downstream from Lake of the Clouds. The flow was slow due to a loosely packed beaver dam on the upstream side of the bridge, where the bridge was actually part of the dam structure. I noticed that even with the dam holding back some of the river, the water upstream still looked low. Especially for springtime. The river looked more like I would expect it to look in August, not mid-May. I hoped that it wasn't a preview of the summer just ahead, and I especially hoped it wasn't an indication of climate fluctuations in the years to come. Even though I felt a tinge of concern, the frogs and birds didn't seem to be concerned. They were still singing and going about life as usual.

After my climb back up to the overlook, we headed back to our cabin with a short stop at the Lake Superior beach just east of the Union Bay Campground. Even though we live only a few minutes away from Superior, it's still difficult for me not to poke around on a Superior beach whenever I have an opportunity to. I found a small agate. Even though it was insignificant as agates go, finding it satisfied the rockhound in me.

About 7:00 that evening, I felt a need to play in the river, so I hiked back out to our car from the cabin to get my fishing gear. Just for fun, I fished a yellow stimulator dry fly upstream from the cabin. I hadn't fished in that area yet, so I decided that I had better do it while I had the opportunity, because opportunities seem to quickly fade away.

I caught one small rainbow trout and had one other trout hit my fly, but I was too slow on the hook set. When I came to a stretch of water that contained a considerable amount of protective wood, otherwise known as snags, I switched to a small streamer and went back downstream to a deep hole just down from the cabin. When I had fished there the previous day, I thought it looked like a good place to feed a streamer in from above the fast chute feeding into the hole, where it was protected from above by a rock overhang. I imagined catching a nice trout out of there. Even though I was certain that dark water held trout, I couldn't seem to entice any of them to bite.

Later, I sat by our campfire looking straight up at the Big Dipper for the second night in a row. Biting bugs died down at dark, allowing us to fully relax, sitting near the dancing flames while we listened to the music of the river. Cares and concerns from the outside world felt distant.

Compared to the draining heat of the previous two afternoons, the next morning was pleasantly cool. Birds were cheerfully singing, as was the river. Road noise from South Boundary Road was nonexistent. As for people, the only sounds were our own, which we kept to a minimum. The afternoon heat was not what we expected or hoped for, but the early-season serenity of the cabin and the overall park was certainly to our liking. My plan for the day was to hike in and fish the Upper Big Carp River below Trap Falls. I had no idea what the fishing would be like, and it really didn't matter much. I had been wanting to fish in that area ever since I first saw it several years earlier. The beauty of the location and the fun of the anticipated adventure were what drew me in and inspired me. I wasn't concerned as much with the caliber of the fishing.

When we reached the backcountry campsites at the bottom of the collection of falls, Julie began setting up to paint. I rigged up my fly rod and ventured downstream a quarter mile or so. Before I began fishing my way back up to Julie, I stuck my hand in the river. It felt cool, but not cold, so I pulled out my thermometer and checked the temperature. The river was running about sixty-six degrees Fahrenheit. Not very good from a brook trout standpoint. If it were just a few degrees higher, I would have considered it to be too stressful for the trout and just packed up my gear and called it a hike.

As I fished up through the maple and hemlock forest, I came across a beautifully fishy hole in one of the river bends. The dry fly I was using was getting a bit waterlogged, so I probably should have applied some flotant, but I didn't. Often, I've had good success with my fly floating just below the surface instead of riding high and dry. On the third or fourth cast, I hooked a small fish. As I was bringing the fish in, several larger fish followed in hot pursuit, like when a gull finds something to eat and the other gulls rush in to try to snatch the food. The taker turned out to be a creek chub, and I highly suspected the pursuers were as well.

Moving on, I caught a second creek chub, but that was the extent of my catch. It looked like a beautiful trout stream, and I didn't doubt there were trout in it. Somewhere. Maybe I was using the wrong fly. Maybe that stretch of water was fished frequently. Maybe the water was just too warm. I could ponder things over lunch, which I ate while sitting on a boulder in the river. Pondering the water flowing through the rocks and boulders upstream held my attention enough that I didn't focus on my lack of fish-catching success. Although, I did fish the Carp River below Trap Falls, which was my ambition for the past few years, so from that point, the day was a success. And as a bonus, we had the entire area to ourselves with no interruptions, which was a pleasant surprise.

After lunch, Julie continued painting while I hiked up past three sections of falls to check the water temperature upstream and to look for trout. On the way, I checked the three small tributaries that I crossed as well. One was a little cooler than the river, but the other two were not. I wasn't surprised to find the temperature above the falls area to be about the same as below. I fished a few prime-looking locations on my way back down to Julie simply because I couldn't resist. One shadowed hole bordered by a cliff looked particularly inviting. I fished the foam line that ran along the edge of the hole, where there was one quick hit-and-run by a small fish, but that was the extent of the action.

At some point on my way back downstream, I realized that the day had become overcast and pleasant feeling instead of oppressively hot. That was about the time that a dead branch dislodged and fell from a tree, sounding like an animal crashing through the brush. Startled, I looked to see what was making the ruckus and to make sure it wasn't running toward me. It wasn't. The branch just lay there on the ground.

When I returned to Julie, the sun was back out, and Julie had finished up a nice plein air painting of the river. We took our time hiking back to the car, enjoying the tranquility of being the only people in the area.

We debated having a fire that evening because it was back to being overcast, and we could hear distant thunder. Our discussion didn't last long, as we came to a quick agreement that we had nothing to lose if we gave it a try. Our fire was rain-free for an hour or so. Then, we began feeling a few light drops now and then, which led to a light falling mist. We held out for another twenty minutes before moving our chairs under the cabin porch roof, where we watched the rain for a while before I finished extinguishing the fire for the night.

The next day, we took advantage of the early morning coolness to pack up and haul our gear out to the car. Then we concluded our time in the Porkies near the mouth of the Presque Isle River. When we arrived, nobody else was there, so we enjoyed the falls and Lake Superior beach on our own, much like we had done during our January time in the park several years prior. Once again, we were able to experience the piece of creation we call the Porcupine Mountains Wilderness as it likely was prior to modern civilization. I was thankful for the refreshing experience, which is an opportunity most people don't get in busy places like the Porkies. That peacefulness felt like a fitting way to conclude our adventures in the park, along with our Porkies ponderings.

McCormick Wilderness

It had been cold and gusty all night, with temperatures in the single digits. As a result, State Highway M-28, the road we live on, had been closed all night. My wife, Julie, and I needed to leave by about 8 am to make it up to Big Bay for the Yellow Dog Watershed Preserve snowshoe hike and cross-country ski trek along part of the old Bently Trail, which connected the old McCormick camp with the Huron Mountain Club property. At 7:30 am, they finally reopened M-28, so Julie and I were on our way to Big Bay for the snowshoeing event fifteen minutes later. Fortunately, the roads were not nearly as bad as I suspected they might be, making me wonder what all the road closure fuss was about.

According to our vehicle thermometer, it was eight degrees Fahrenheit when we hit the trail from the AAA Road with our informal guides, Wade and Dan. They had been researching, finding, and re-marking the old Bently Trail for quite a while so that people could begin using it again. The trail traversed through primarily snow-covered evergreens, with the normal host of north woods deciduous trees like birch, maple, and alder intermingled. With the overall planned route being about three miles, it was a decent trek for snowshoes and backcountry skis on an unpacked trail. The snow, which was deeper than I expected compared to our property at home, consisted of packed powder atop a crystallized base layer. I was using a pair of aluminum-frame snowshoes for the first time because I was concerned about the crystallized snow being too abrasive on my traditional wooden snowshoes that I normally wear. The aluminum snowshoes worked okay, but I found that they sank in deeper than my other snowshoes, and they were considerably noisier. Coming from a hunting background, I hate being noisy in the woods, but I had to live with it. At least for that outing.

The scenery wasn't anything noteworthy, just a normal, gorgeous snow-covered UP forest. In addition to the scenery, it was interesting to wander through a new area that I had never visited before with people who could share insights into the history of the trail as well. That history included the old halfway cabin where folks trekking along the trail could get out of the elements for a rest stop. As we were standing there admiring the cabin, one of the things that amazed me was that people of higher means once considered trekking through the wilds, and spending time in a rustic cabin, to be an acceptable activity. I certainly couldn't see that happening today.

Our turnaround point was Bently Lake, which is a small, nondescript marshy lake that's only about a half mile from the northeast corner of the McCormick Wilderness. On the far side of the lake, there is still an old Bently Trail sign. It was lying on the ground because the large white pine it had been nailed to was now just a decaying skeleton. Wade brushed off the sign and found a way to reattach it to what was left of the tree.

The sky was overcast for most of the day, but when the sun occasionally appeared, the landscape was bathed in warm light for a brief time. It also pushed the temperature up to fifteen degrees. On the hike back out to the road, I had an opportunity to talk with Wade and Dan about some of their ventures out in the nearby McCormick Wilderness. As part of those conversations, I mentioned my desire to portage a canoe the three-and-a-half miles into White Deer Lake and paddle into the upper reaches of the Yellow Dog River. It turned out that they had done that before, which boosted my confidence in following through with my plan. In fact, I pretty much made the commitment to go ahead and do it that upcoming summer. It wasn't a verbal commitment, just a mental one, but I considered it to be a binding agreement that I would hold myself to.

Well, for a variety of reasons, summer came and went without my McCormick plans being fulfilled. Instead, later in October, we crossed the Pesheeke bridge into the McCormick Tract about 8:30 am. I could see my breath, which wasn't surprising since our car thermometer had noted the temperature to be twenty-five degrees Fahrenheit just before we turned it off. Trees and grasses wore a coating of frost, as did most everything else. My main temperature indicator was that when I hoisted our canoe onto my shoulders to embark on our three-and-a-half-mile portage, the aluminum gunnels made my fingers sting, causing me to need to support the canoe one-handed and change hands every minute or two. Tamaracks were frosty gold, but not yet to their full autumn radiance.

We had only hiked the trail once before, several years earlier, so the scenery was still new and engaging. At least what I could see of it from beneath the canoe. Not far into the portage, we passed an open-water marsh surrounded by frosty trees and filled with frosted grass and reeds. In the most protected areas, a faint layer of skim ice covered the surface. The morning sun was just beginning to illuminate spruces across the marsh, adding a splash of warmth to the chilly scene.

About the time I began thinking about setting the canoe down for a short break, the trail crossed a significant creek. Significant meaning that it was too wide to just jump across and too deep to wade without getting wet. The logs others had placed in the water as a crossing aid were either rotted or icy, and in some cases, both. The larger rocks that were there for the same reason wore an icy coating as well. Julie brought up the possibility of using the canoe for the crossing about the same time that I started thinking about the same thing. So, I placed the canoe across the creek just upstream from the rocks, allowing the rocks to keep it in place. I crossed partway on the rocks, then held the boat stable near the middle while Julie climbed through the canoe. Before hoisting the canoe back onto my shoulders, I peeled off my pullover fleece to keep from overheating. At that point, my fingers were warm enough to counteract the earlier sting of the aluminum gunnels, so I was feeling pretty good.

Now and then, the sounds of water trickling through mossy rocks and logs could be heard along the trail, which kept me busy part of the time, looking for the source. Thankfully, with the temperature already below freezing, there was no detectable breeze to exaggerate the chill. As I was focusing my attention on the surrounding landscape, a red dogwood branch caught on the front of the canoe for a moment. When it pulled free, it slapped me across my right eye. Thank God for quick eyelid reflexes, but my eye still watered for quite a while afterward, making it difficult to watch the scenery.

When we reached the swampy area where the Forest Service had built a boardwalk several years earlier, just after our first visit, we found that the project didn't quite meet the need. The narrow wooden walkway started and stopped multiple times, leaving sections of the trail with two to six inches of mucky water to wade through — or maybe I should say that it was watery muck. I guess I couldn't complain too much, though. The mucky wading was better than trying to climb over the tall rocky ridge that the portions of boardwalk skirt around.

When I took a short break after our wading episode, I was a little concerned about our progress. I had expected the portage to take us about two hours. We were already an hour and a half into it, and our progress seemed slow. I hadn't yet noticed the side trail heading off to Lower Baraga Lake, which was less than halfway to our White Deer Lake destination. That meant that we appeared to be well behind my expected pace, giving me concerns about having enough canoeing time once we reached the lake.

Concerns aside, I hoisted the canoe and continued on, hoping to make up some time now that the swampy slog was behind us. Still, I was thankful that the sketchy boardwalk did keep us from needing to climb up and over the rocky ridge along the trail like we did on our first visit. Doing that climb with a sixteen-foot canoe on my shoulders would have been a little dicey, if not downright stupid. Not that I wouldn't have done it. I was just thankful that I didn't need to.

The next thirty minutes passed by smoothly, allowing us to arrive at White Deer Lake right on the two-hour mark, just as I originally anticipated. So, our progress must have just seemed slower than usual. Regardless, I was happy. I was also excited to finally be standing on the shore of the lake again, this time with a canoe at our disposal instead of wishing I had one.

The lake was calm, except for minor ripples obscuring reflections of the surrounding forest. A faint ghostly mist was rising from the water in the small bay just beyond the old McCormick cabin complex site. A single small white swan feather rested on the water, helplessly entangled in lakeside brush. The world was quiet, except for the calling of a few birds. I had been waiting for an opportunity to explore the surrounding lakes for about eight years, so we launched our canoe filled with anticipation.

As we paddled past the remains of the old Chimney Cabin foundation, I thought of all the cabins and other buildings that once dominated the site and the grand festivities that likely took place, even up into the 1980's. Once again, man's grand plans were slowly being reclaimed by the forest and seasonal elements.

Once we were past the island that had housed many of the cabins, we just floated for a bit, taking in the view from the middle of the lake. I watched a trio of swans that were at the southern end of the lake while Julie took reference pictures of a tiny evergreen island near us in the middle of the lake. I'm sure a painting will come from those pictures in the near future. As I looked around, I thought about the empty parking lot where we parked, which is the only formal access to the entire sixteen-thousand-acre wilderness. It was sobering, yet somehow inspiring, to realize we were likely the only people in that wilderness, enjoying the solitude of the lakes and forest.

While we were paddling along on White Deer Lake, I looked into the water toward the sun and saw some features that I presumed were caused by the sun's rays in the murky water. But as I looked more intently, I realized that the lake was very shallow and I was seeing features of the lake bottom, which surprised me. I had assumed that a lake between rocky hills like that would be deeper. Not that I'm keeping score, but once again, my assumptions were off the mark.

At the far end of White Deer, we entered an enchanting winding creek connecting to Bulldog Lake. Small white cedars, sparse brush, and tanned grasses lined the waterway. Around every bend, I anticipated seeing one of the area's moose. Though the moose remained hidden in the surrounding forest, it looked and felt like wilderness even without their presence.

As we emerged into Bulldog Lake, we could hear a waterfall somewhere to the east. Based on the relatively high pitch of the sound, I could tell that it was a small creek that tumbled into the lake somewhere back in the brush. We found the narrow channel of moving water coming through the grasses along the lake, but we were not able to get the canoe through to the waterfall. Water between the tussocks of grass was too deep for Julie's hiking boots and even my LL Bean boots. So, we left the little stream as a mystery and continued our exploration of Bulldog Lake as a lone Canada goose took flight from the other side of the bay. A cool breeze had picked up as we entered the main part of the lake, giving me a slight chill. Many rock outcroppings were visible around the lake, reminding me of the lakes we've explored far to the north in the Boundary Waters of northern Minnesota. Before my mind wandered too far, I pulled it back to the moment we were in.

Following the eastern shoreline, we passed the faint portage trail to Lake Margaret, saving that trek for a little later, after we finished exploring Bulldog. At the north end of the lake, we paddled through a small opening into a little bay that narrowed to become the Yellow Dog River. The entrance to the bay is hidden from sight until you are very near, giving the feeling that it somehow opens up as you approach.

At the end of the bay is what is left of an old control dam, where a four-foot waterfall pours through the dam opening and continues along its course to Lake Superior. I stood on the old dam wall, turning one of the hand wheels that would have once controlled the flow, thinking for a moment about my many fishing adventures miles downstream on the Yellow Dog River. I also wondered if brook trout were present there in the plunge pool below the dam. I wondered too about what that stretch of river was like before the dam was built, who built it, and why. I would probably never know the answers to all those questions, but an answer to my first question would be available after the opening of trout season in late April, leaving me roughly six months to plan my answer-seeking adventure. It would require a lot of work for a small amount of fishing, but sometimes those are the most memorable fish to catch.

When we re-emerged into the main body of Bulldog Lake, we paddled over to investigate the stream coming into the west side that could technically probably be considered part of the Yellow Dog River. The flow was only noticeable where it trickled over a tiny beaver dam. At least I assumed it was a beaver dam. It could have easily just been a pinch-point in the creek where sticks had naturally collected. After another hundred yards or so, we ran out of readily navigable water, so we backed out to a wider spot where we could maneuver enough to turn around.

After paddling back across the lake and spending some time trying to photograph the sunlight on a twisted and bent white pine on a rocky point, we stopped for a late lunch at the portage to Lake Margaret that we had passed by earlier. Not knowing how difficult the faint trail might be to portage the canoe on, and realizing our afternoon was ticking away, we decided to leave our canoe behind and just quietly hike across the trail up and over the low rise separating the two lakes for a peek at Lake Margaret. The trail follows a tiny stream that trickles through roots and mossy rocks. It was obviously rarely used, making it difficult to follow in some areas.

Lake Margaret was intriguing with its many bays and points, causing me to briefly consider going back for our canoe. It also brought up thoughts of hauling in our camping gear sometime to allow us time to explore for more than just one day. On our way back to Bulldog, I took a side jaunt and climbed to the top of a wooded ridge in hopes of a panoramic view. It was an interesting venture, but the forest proved to be too thick for a view. Panoramic or otherwise.

Back down near the lake, I noticed that the tiny creek held a sizeable collection of acorns. Closer inspection revealed acorns scattered across the forest floor, which I didn't expect due to the abundance of maple and evergreen-dominated woods across the Upper Peninsula. My discovery made me wonder why there weren't any signs of deer in the area. That was something I needed to think about.

We launched our canoe into Bulldog Lake once again and began retracing our route back out of the wilderness. As we did a little more exploring along the northwestern shoreline of White Deer Lake, I found myself wondering more about the past and the history of that wilderness. I also thought more about the future and my potential interactions with this wilderness. Plans began forming in my mind. I kept them to myself, though. Julie often just sighs or rolls her eyes when I begin expounding on ideas for future ventures when we haven't even completed the adventure we're currently on.

As usual, the hike out seemed quicker than the hike in. Even with a canoe on my shoulders. As we crossed the bridge back to our vehicle and the paved road, I realized that one of the benefits of designated wilderness areas and their inherent restrictions on development is that you know they will be there for that next visit you're planning.

Whether you've shared those plans or decided to keep them quiet until a more opportune time.

65

WILDERNESS STATE OF MIND

Around the Lake Superior region, we're blessed to have many wilderness areas where we can immerse ourselves in the natural world and enjoy the wilderness balm for mind and body. Some of those areas are large, sprawling swaths of land and water carrying a formal wilderness title. Other areas, even though they may carry a wilderness name, are much smaller parcels. Many natural areas are not protected by a wilderness designation at all, but they still possess wilderness attributes, regardless of their size. The benefit of those wilderness-like tracts is that they are so numerous that they are often close to home, or at least close to wherever you happen to be, making them easily accessible, without a major time commitment. I often take advantage of that benefit.

I left the trailhead shortly before noon with sunny skies and fifty degrees showing on the thermometer. The surrounding forest in the Elliott Donnelley Wilderness was at peak color. At least I considered it to be peak color, but I can't say what the formal criterion for peak color actually is. Regardless, with sunshine on the multi-colored leaves and a cool breeze stirring, it felt like autumn. There was only one other vehicle in the parking lot, promising an uncrowded, peaceful hike. Ferns were already brown and withered, but sugar maples were in their prime, boasting vibrant shades of yellow. The water level in the Little Garlic River was low, which accentuated the rocky river channel. Colored leaves collecting in the pools and on the rocks made the river look calm and soothing. Fish-holding water was basically non-existent, making me wonder where the fish go in these conditions. Redish layered cliffs along the stream added even more color to the mix. Chickadees were busily chatting amongst themselves as I quietly strolled along the trail, which soon left the river level and climbed to lofty overlooks, providing a bird's eye view of the stream, confined in its guiding canyon. Sugar maples gave way to hemlocks, guarding the river from the heat of the sun. Between the showy maples, somber hemlocks, and a rocky autumn river, it made me wish I had brought a camera. My wife, Julie, is usually in charge of taking pictures, though, so I typically don't even think of packing a camera. Mental pictures would have to suffice.

Still meandering through the forest well above the riverbed, the trail crossed a narrow rocky dry tributary streambed that gave witness to times of rushing water adding to the river's flow. That day, though, it was quiet and dry, except for a minute seepage dripping from the bedrock staircase leading down to the river. Looking around at the saturation of color in the leaves, I realized that this was likely one of my last autumn journeys while it still looked like prime autumn. Soon, after a few more blustery rains, the brightly colored leaves would be doing their part in rebuilding the soil, and the world would look like early winter. That day, though, it exuded autumn glory, making me forget for a time about the coming snows.

I crossed another rocky, dry tributary about halfway through the designated wilderness, which is only about twelve-hundred acres in size. Even though it's not very large by wilderness standards, it certainly has the feel of wilderness, regardless of how big or small it is. Then the trail dropped down and followed the riverbank again. Returning to that more intimate contact with the river felt good, but part of me was missing the grander view from above.

The trail soon climbed again, but not nearly as high above the river as before. At a hairpin bend in the stream, there was a resting bench in the middle of a flat area in the bend. It not only looked like a great place to sit for a spell, absorbed in the flow, but an inviting place to fish as well. So, as usual, I made a mental note. Then I began wondering when my mental notebook would fill up. I doubt I'll have to worry about that, though. Before it fills up, I'll probably forget enough of the earlier stuff to open up more room for new stuff. At some point, forgetting may even outpace the new thoughts, and I'll just have a blank notebook. But I'd rather not think about that now.

Just upstream, there was evidence of an old river bend that once was but is now dry and growing in as part of the forest. I wondered what caused the change and what the fishing was like there before the river rerouted itself. Thoughts like that tend to bombard my brain and hang around there, taking up space until I go ahead and write them down — again, to make room for more thoughts.

A little farther upstream, tag alders began to dominate the riverbanks, and the trail wandered farther away from the water. That was where the shady somberness of the hemlocks gave way to the brightness of the sunny maple forest again. Soon after, I reached the upstream end of the formal wilderness area, crossed the road, and began the mile-long hike to Little Garlic Falls. Not far along that trail, it entered an open, airy stand of sugar maples that were basking in the sunshine. Red maples are certainly eye-catching, but I think it's the amber brilliance of sugar maples that dominates the autumn show.

Just below the falls, the river snakes its way through a boulder garden. Then, the trail ends at a rock face that guards the falls' plunge pool. I remembered the falls being bigger, although our last visit was earlier in the year when the river was fuller, which may have given it a bigger, bolder look. Wanting to assess fishing opportunities above the falls, I crossed the river on some protruding rocks to avoid scaling the rock face and continued up past a collection of cascades and pools. That area is a boulder-strewn streambed running through a canyon of sorts again. The stream was back to being in the shade of a hemlock grove, too, which always seems to give things a wilderness air. It was a beautiful place, but it didn't look like there was much good holding water for trout in the river. Fishing probably wouldn't be very good, but it did look like a pretty place to get skunked, if that's what it came to.

At that point, I was nearing private property, so I lingered on a rocky slab that extended into the river and enjoyed a quick snack, along with a refreshing drink of water. Afterward, I began leisurely retracing my route back to the trailhead with a cool breeze transporting leaves that were slowly drifting back to the soil.

For another wilderness adventure that really didn't involve a large wilderness area, Julie and I stopped at Canyon Falls in late April, on our way home from delivering artwork to a gallery in Calumet. The water there has always been tannin-stained, but that day the color seemed bolder than usual. In its current state, the Sturgeon River near the falls and canyon reminded me of the Tahquamenon. The main falls are only about twenty feet tall, but the power of that churning chisel to sculpt the canyon walls and floor was plainly evident. I could envision rock being removed, minuscule layer by minuscule layer. Maybe even grain by grain. There has to be an impressive plunge pool hole in the riverbed, but what it looks like is left solely to our imaginations. As I stood near the brink of the falls, then above the churning plunge pool, the river looked like foaming fury.

On the top of the far side of the falls, there are a few gentle falls leading into the chaos of churning amber-orange water nearby. Those benign little falls don't even hint at the power being unleashed only a few yards away.

The sculpting of the layered, lichen-covered canyon walls that contain and restrain the torrent testifies to the power of the flow. In one location, I was able to carefully work my way down to water level. Standing on a slab at water's edge, I could feel the power of the river through the rock and, for some reason, felt a slight temptation to take another step and join the flow. I was thankfully wise enough not to proceed, though the pull was there. It likely would have just provided someone with material for a story on the evening news. After climbing back up, we followed the river to the end of the canyon, peeking over the rock ledges here and there to witness the drama below.

Back at the main falls, I was drawn to a rock nose atop the plunge where the tannin water created an amber-orange curtain spilling over the ledge. It reminded me of childhood visits to Tahquamenon. There too I was mesmerized by the curtains of north woods tannin water. I could somewhat see the features underneath the curtains, but I could never see them fully or touch them. The details were vaguely known, but never clearly or fully understood. The mysterious world beneath and behind the curtains, those unknown benthic features, pulled at my imagination. That day at Canyon Falls was no different. I was glad that we stopped for a relatively quick visit. Even though it's a popular place, during most of our time there, we were unbothered by the presence of others, leaving us free to explore with our eyes and imaginations.

Closer to home is Laughing Whitefish Lake. Even though it's not truly wilderness, it puts me in a wilderness state of mind. For several years, I had been looking at it on the map, surrounded by a forest with no indication of access trails. I needed to go there and see it for myself.

For my first expedition there, lingering clouds from a rainy night had finally thinned out to allow partial sunshine by mid-morning. Julie and I left my old truck at the Nature Conservancy parking lot, which had the capacity to hold about one-and-a-half vehicles. From there, it was a flat, easy hundred-yard portage to the footbridge where we launched the canoe. In that area, the Laughing Whitefish River looks wild, snaking through the brush, providing glimpses of only one small stretch at a time, leaving the rest to the imagination. The thermometer was hovering around fifty degrees Fahrenheit, but the north breeze made it feel much cooler, to the point where my life vest, which usually makes me feel too hot, felt comfortable to have on for a change. Old logs in the water created a couple of minor squeeze-through areas before we reached the old Peter White camp. There, an old concrete dam lay in ruins right near the main cabin. Fortunately, the river had found a route around the broken-up structure, so we were able to easily paddle through, gazing at history and wondering as we passed by.

Just upstream was a new, low-profile beaver dam that was an easy pull-over with the canoe. Being mid-October, autumn colors were waning, but it still looked and felt like fall. The sun continued peeking through the clouds here and there as we paddled. Soon, we crossed an older, more established beaver dam, which included a few large trees, now logs. That dam required both of us to get out of the canoe to wrestle it across, then get back in. Even though we had just recently paddled by the Peter White camp, the area looked and felt like we were exploring someplace wild and new.

After the beaver dam and a few more snaking turns in the river, we paddled through a wide area full of reeds and grasses, just before entering Laughing Whitefish Lake. The shoreline was mostly evergreens, with some colorful trees peeking through from the forest beyond. The lake, which was quiet except for the stirring of the north breeze and our paddling, looked to be only about a half mile long and not very wide. A lone bald eagle flew over the middle of the lake with the sun illuminating its white head and tail against a backdrop of dark rain clouds that were rolling in.

Near the south end of the lake, the sun was setting an old yellow birch ablaze along the western shoreline. We spotted a pair of old rowboats overturned on the east shore, just before where the river flows into the lake. The sight of those man-made objects residing at the lake diminished the wild atmosphere for me. I may have been a little naive, but based on the lack of access shown on the map, I didn't expect to see anything like that. Some nearby rock outcroppings in the woods did quickly re-establish some of the lake's wild charm for me, though.

Beyond the lake, we continued paddling upstream through a narrow channel that wound through thick tussocks of tall grass. The winding channel was sometimes barely wide enough to squeeze the canoe through. Before we made it a hundred yards up the channel, we reached an old beaver dam and had to back out, because the waterway petered out and there was no room to either go forward or to turn around. Beyond the dam, I could visualize the river snaking its way up to where it becomes a real trout stream, not far below the Laughing Whitefish Falls. That's where I usually begin fishing when I fly fish the falls area. Typically, I hike in from the falls parking area. Then, as I near where I like to cut into the woods off the trail, I slow down and casually tinker around until the trail is clear and nobody is around to witness my exit — there is no sense in broadcasting the location or inviting company. I'm sure lots of other people know about the somewhat hidden trail, but I like to feel like it's a secret of sorts, ignoring the fact that if it were indeed a secret, there wouldn't be a relatively faint trail at all. From that point, it's about a quarter-mile trek down to the river, passing by limestone formations and some large white pines. I usually begin fishing right where the river transitions from a gravel-bottom trout stream through the forest to a slow-water stream meandering through a tag alder jungle. From there, I slowly fish my way upstream, ending at the plunge pool below the falls. Sometimes I catch rainbows. Sometimes I catch brook trout. Maybe both. Maybe neither. I have thought about portaging a canoe in and trying to float the river down to the lake, but that would certainly draw attention, which I want to avoid. Especially if the float gets halted by a major dam complex, low water, or a section of small, braided channels through a marsh — like what was just above the dam where we had stopped — and I need to backtrack out. The adventure of making the connection between the falls and the lake is still enticing to me. I haven't done it yet, but I can see it happening one of these days. Or maybe one of these years.

The sun re-emerged just before we paddled back into the lake, where we bumped into a couple of small flocks of wood ducks. Twice, something relatively large swirled at the lake's surface. I didn't actually see it happen. I just heard the sound and turned to see the disturbance, so I don't know what the creature was. Based on what I saw, I suspected that they were fish. I just didn't know what kind.

We stopped to look at the old, overturned rowboats on our way back. They obviously hadn't been used in quite a while. One had a registration sticker from 1974. We also stopped to take a closer look at the rock outcroppings in the eastside forest. When I walked around the main outcrop where there was a big undercut, I ran into a camp of some sort. It was constructed with log poles, some new-looking plastic tarps, and sheets of clear plastic. I wasn't sure if it was intended as a makeshift deer camp or if someone was living there. Either way, I decided to mind my own business and not investigate, so we cut our shoreline visit short and got back in our canoe. As we paddled away, I had the strange feeling that we were being watched. I couldn't help looking back over my shoulder a couple of times, but all I saw were rocks and trees.

Along the west shoreline, we saw another overturned rowboat in the woods. That one looked much newer and in better condition than the others. Apparently, the lake was not nearly as wild and unvisited as I had imagined.

Back in the river, just before the smaller beaver dam, a lone duck sat motionless on the water and let us paddle by like we were nothing to worry about. We were back at our launching point shortly after noon, finally accomplishing what I had been wanting to do for several years. Accomplishments like that are always satisfying. Even if they don't turn out exactly as you had envisioned.

When I need a breath of fresh air, or I just need to get out and make personal contact with the wild, I'm blessed not to always have to travel somewhere. If time is short or I just don't feel like driving anywhere, I can just walk out the door and start wandering. Our home property includes a hardwood forest, aspen groves, evergreen sanctuaries, hills and valleys, streams, swamps, and even a few rock outcroppings, where I can wander at will. Deer hunting isn't the greatest, but there are just enough of them around to keep me trying. Bears, bobcats, pine martens, and even an occasional moose also roam the neighborhood.

Sometimes, in order to expand our hundred-and-sixty-acre yard, I'll venture off onto neighboring timber company (CFR) land and explore my way north up to the state land where the Tyoga Historical Trail resides. If time isn't a constraint, I'll oftentimes veer farther east and follow a pretty little creek north. I don't recall ever hearing or seeing a formal name associated with the creek, but it's big enough to hold a few steelhead now and then in the spring. I've never seriously fished it, but I should. My intentions to fish the creek have always been good. I just tend to spend my time fishing other, more significant streams until there isn't any trout season left. So, it's typically late autumn, during deer hunting season, or winter, during snowshoeing season, that I wander the CFR land next door and dabble in our neighborhood creek.

That creek I sometimes follow pours over a three-foot waterfall up near the road, then winds its way north past a collection of huge mossy boulders and through a couple of marshes, before spilling into the Laughing Whitefish River near the Tyoga Trail south bridge. Besides mingling with the river and creek, the trail also crosses a few other smaller creeks and meanders through hardwoods, meadows, swamps, and hemlock groves. Farther north — beyond the state land — CFR lands and Michigan Nature Association properties also include some beautiful rocky Lake Superior shorelines.

Between our home property, state land, and connecting CFR lands, the few-thousand acres around our house provide me access to most everything the UP has to offer other than tall cliffs. And those are less than an hour away. It's not true wilderness, but when I'm sitting quietly in a shadowed hemlock grove, roaming a maple-beech-birch forest, or meandering with a north woods stream, I can still genuinely feel wild at heart, like I felt when I was a kid. Ultimately, that's plenty wild.

ISLE ROYALE

My wife and I first ventured out to Isle Royale for two backpacking trips in the 1980's, shortly after college. Those early adventures are combined into the first chapter of this section. We returned with our two young daughters in 1999, to do some canoeing in the island's interior lakes. That visit is covered in the second chapter. Then, in 2024, Julie and I spent two weeks on the island, living in a cabin, which was our base for daily backcountry excursions. That venture provided the stories for five consecutive chapters in this section. In 2025, we returned again, intending to paddle and portage a big loop covering the eastern portion of the island. That visit is chronicled in the last two chapters.

First Impressions

As we passed the rocky guardian islands on our way into Rock Harbor for the first time, I could feel that the island held a certain mystique. Our true introduction to Isle Royale, though, started out as anything but peaceful and serene. Since everyone arrives on the island at the same time on the ferry, once you get through the mandatory group orientation, it's a footrace to the Three Mile and Daisy Farm campgrounds. Some people, like us, push through to Daisy Farm, while others try to find a place right there around the Rock Harbor dock area. But it seems like the bulk of the backcountry folks getting off the boat make the dash to Three Mile. It's a shame because there is some beautiful scenery that a lot of people miss as a result. During our dash, we did notice a pair of loons in Rock Harbor, which was a novelty for us at that point in our lives. Most people likely just passed them by, unnoticed. The downside was that we were participants in the dash. The upside was that we were young and in good condition for backpacking, so we arrived at the campground early enough to get a campsite. In fact, looking back at our collection of slides from that mid-August trip, it's hard to even recognize the younger, leaner us.

From there, we shifted into backcountry mode and slowed things down to more of a purposeful, take-in-the-scenery pace for the rest of the trip. Other than keeping an eye out for the neighborhood red fox that frequented the campground, our first evening was spent in anticipation of the next day, when we would leave the boat traffic and busyness behind and enter the true backcountry of the island. The wilderness. As with most first-time visits to someplace special, we were still at least a little in awe of even being there.

The next morning, during our couple-mile trek to Moskey Basin, we had the pleasant surprise of seeing a pair of moose roaming through the woods along the trail. One was a small bull. The other one never gave us a good enough look to tell. All I knew was that at that point, our first Isle Royale experience was a success, regardless of what happened during the rest of our visit. Still, we were wide-eyed and hungry for more as we reached the end of Moskey Basin and embarked on the roughly two-mile hike to Lake Richie. Somewhere along that wooded trail, we heard a relatively large branch break somewhere back in the trees, not far off the trail. We both froze in stride, intently watching and listening. Soon, a large dark form became visible through the trees. As the moose neared the trail, we could see that it was a large bull. When it crossed the trail, barely fifteen yards in front of us, my brain went on high alert, not knowing if we should just quietly stand there and watch or if we should quickly shed our packs and find the nearest climbable tree. The disinterested casual glance the bull directed our way gave me my answer. As the bull was stepping back into the trees on the other side of the trail, we heard another stick snap. That was about the same time that we noticed the second, slightly smaller bull, approaching the trail, following the same route as the first one. That bull followed suit, slowly crossing the trail as it gave us a casual glance. We just stood there, somewhat stunned, as the two bulls strolled out of sight back into the forest. We managed to take several pictures, but I didn't even recall going through the thought process of manually focusing the 35MM camera and releasing the shutter. A few moments later, the forest was quiet, except for the pounding of two hearts in the middle of the trail.

We reached Lake Richie, still excited from our encounter, and watched several mergansers cruising the shoreline while we took a short rest break. The islands, bays, and peninsulas that defined Lake Richie looked like a wildlife paradise as well as an explorer's paradise. I would have loved to have access to a canoe, but we were committed to our backpacks, so we continued along the trail toward Lake Lesage, Lake Livermore, and the Greenstone Ridge. Our eventual destination for the day was the west campground at Chickenbone Lake, on the other side of the Greenstone Ridge. After Lake Richie, our only wildlife sightings along the way were red squirrels and an assortment of songbirds. But every step was taken in anticipation.

When we reached Chickenbone and found a vacant campsite, Julie wrapped herself up in the tarp that we use under our tent and took a short nap in the late afternoon sun before we got the tent set up. As I was exploring near camp, I took a picture of her while she slept amid all our gear. After setting up our tent and eating dinner, we spent the evening relaxing around camp while keeping an eye on the lake in anticipation of another moose sighting.

Our next sighting came in the morning with a cow and calf wading in the marshy shoreline grass across the lake, highlighted in the morning sun. A little later, we were enjoying open panoramic views from up on the Greenstone Ridge. During a short rest break along the rocky ridgeline, a butterfly chose Julie's bright red sleeping pad strap as its rest spot in the sun. During that break, I also caught a three-inch-long red-bellied snake in the grass amongst the rocks. It felt like my senses were on high alert, looking for everything the island had to show us, large or small.

Dropping down from our Greenstone views to Hatchet Lake, we continued north to Todd Harbor. Along the way, we didn't encounter any more moose, but we did get a sweet introduction to a colossal patch of thimbleberries. Even though they are extremely difficult to save or transport without destroying them, thimbleberries are my favorite wild berry because they are the sweetest, most delicate berry I have ever tasted. You don't even need to chew them. I always simply just crush them with my tongue and squish them around in my mouth while I'm savoring their flavor, which I would describe as hyper-raspberry. They're at the top of my berry list. In my mind, summertime on Isle Royale will always be associated with thimbleberries.

As we were searching for a campsite at Todd Harbor, we talked with another camper who told us about a camp jay incident that he recently experienced. He was breaking off small pieces of a bagel and holding them out for a camp jay to come down and take them from his hand. After feeding a few pieces to the bird like that, he set the bagel down on the picnic table while he held out another small piece for the bird. The jay hovered near the small offering in the guy's hand for a few seconds, then quickly dropped down to the table, grabbed the entire remainder of the bagel, and flew away, leaving the guy standing there still holding out the small bagel morsel. I didn't bother mentioning to him that you're not supposed to be feeding animals on the island anyway, but he and the bird apparently both learned something from the experience.

Once camp was set up, we enjoyed a brief rinse-off "swim" in the harbor, followed by some time playing on lakeside rocks. I say "swim" because in the icy waters of Superior, a swim is usually a brief, exhilarating experience. Since I have always been attracted to moving water, we also spent some time exploring and playing in a small waterfall that was tumbling into the harbor. When it comes to moving water, I'll always be a kid.

The next day, on our way through McCargo Cove, a small group of hen mallards caught my attention. Especially one particular hen that was standing on shore, apparently sleeping. Whether or not she was truly sleeping, I don't know, but her eyes were closed, and she seemed oblivious to our presence. I was playing with a new zoom lens at the time, so I have a picture that consists mostly of just her head with her eye closed, looking like she's peacefully sleeping. Shortly after leaving the ducks, we saw a cow moose wading in the shallows at the very end of the long, narrow cove. She was too preoccupied with eating aquatic vegetation to be bothered by our presence. A little farther along the trail, we spotted what I believe was an osprey on a large dead branch that extended into an opening in the forest canopy. We watched each other for several minutes until the osprey either decided that we were not all that interesting or it had more pressing things to do with its time. It slowly raised its wings and, a few wing-beats later, was gone from sight.

We returned to Chickenbone for the night, finding a campsite in the east campground, then moved on to a shelter at Moskey Basin the following day. On our way across the two-mile hike between Lake Richie and Moskey Basin, we encountered a cow moose, accompanied by her mostly grown calf. They moved around to get a better look at us from various locations and positions. At one point, they were broadside, tail-to-tail, with their tails hidden behind a large tree. It made them look like mirror images of each other, with the tree being the reflection line. After several pictures, we moved on and left them to their foraging.

Once we reached the shelter and got our gear unpacked, we did a little foraging of our own and found a double handful of blueberries.

I don't recall if we incorporated them into a meal or just ate them on their own. Not that it really matters, because fresh wild blueberries are good pretty much any way with anything. Especially in the backcountry. While we were foraging, we also captured some pictures of a gangly-looking snowshoe hare in its late summer attire and a frisky red squirrel just being its frantic self. On our way back to the shelter, we spied a lone cow moose peeking at us through a stand of small aspen trees. I'm sure I didn't make note of all the moose we saw on our first Isle Royale adventure, and we certainly didn't get pictures of all of them, but Julie and I both recalled seeing seventeen moose overall. Of course, that was when the island's moose population was in the neighborhood of twenty-five-hundred animals, so sightings were common. Even expected. The population has since declined significantly due to multiple factors. I'm thankful we were able to experience the island and its lofty moose population when we did.

By dinner time, clouds rolled in, accompanied by fog and rain, which made us thankful to have a picnic table partially protected by the shelter roof overhang to cook and eat on. During the rain, a flock of mallards strolled over from the lake and joined us at the shelter. I assumed they were accustomed to people sharing food with them. For their own good, though, we did not. And they didn't look pleased.

Overcast transitioned to darkness as the last full day of our first Isle Royale visit slipped by. The last picture in our collection of slides commemorating our first visit is of a young Julie sitting on the edge of the Moskey Basin dock, with the surrounding water barely visible through the fog. She's looking at the water contemplatively. Probably wondering when we would be able to return.

The return trip happened two years later, after I had finished up at Michigan Tech and we had moved back downstate in Michigan for work. We made the roughly ten-hour drive to Copper Harbor, then made the ferry crossing on an overcast day when the water was a bit agitated. I could not find any notes from that visit, nor could I lay my hands on the slide deck. Maybe we had switched to photographic prints by then. If so, I have not been able to locate those either. Regardless, it was mid-September, when the bull moose are somewhat crazed from their mating rut, so some of the events from that trip are vividly etched in my mind. No notes or pictures needed.

My first recollections are from when we were camping at the west Chickenbone campground. In the evening, we took a quiet walk along the west side of the lake, hoping to see a moose. When we were about halfway down the side of the lake, we heard a bull grunting off in the brush, maybe sixty or seventy yards away. Based on the commotion and lack of antlers clashing, I assumed that the bull had turned his pent-up hormones loose on the local landscape and was making a scrape. If you're not familiar with the term, a scrape is where they use their hooves and antlers to tear up a patch of ground and urinate in it to inform other moose that they are around, with the hope of warning other bulls and attracting cows to stick around until he returns. The mayhem that ensued off in the brush sounded intense. I wanted to sneak over for a look, just for the first-hand experience of it. Julie was wise enough to stay out of the potential harm's way and opted to leave the area. Not wanting us to get separated with a rut-crazed bull crashing around, I followed Julie back to camp, looking over my shoulder in hopes of getting at least a glimpse of the bull, but he never gave me the privilege.

The next morning, we were lying in our tent, thinking about actually getting up. It was decent daylight, but still relatively early. While we were lying there relaxing, we heard a bull grunt not far away. We quietly got out of our sleeping bags and up on our knees so we could look out the window of our small mountain tent. Just as we began spying out the small window, a large bull crossed the path leading to our camp, stopped about ten yards away, and stared intently at our tent. I began trying to picture if there were any nearby trees we could climb, and wondering how quickly I could unzip the tent door. Or if I should even bother unzipping the tent door if the bull started heading our way. Before I was able to come to any conclusions, the bull casually sauntered off into the woods. About the time I was exhaling my sigh of relief, the bull started shredding the woods, sounding like someone had turned a bulldozer loose. We got out of the tent in time to see the top of a tall maple sapling shudder and then go down. The forest then suddenly went quiet. I stood there wondering where exactly the bull was and if he was leaving or coming back our way. Whether or not it was the same bull from the previous evening, I didn't know and honestly didn't care. Regardless, we didn't see him again.

The following day, over on the west side of Siskiwit Lake, we came across a fresh moose scrape near the trail. It consisted of a torn-up area about ten feet in diameter — torn-up meaning everything inside the circle, ground cover, ground, and trees, were completely shredded. I thought it would be interesting to watch a bull making an impressive scrape like that. From a distance.

We didn't see a lot of moose during that mid-September visit to Isle Royale, but the moose encounters we did have were certainly exciting, again raising the question of when we could return for another visit.

CANOEING WITH THE KIDS

Shortly after lunch, we were packing up our gear and loading our canoe for a six-day, mid-summer, paddle and portage tour of central Isle Royale. This would be a different kind of trip for us. In addition to paddling and portaging instead of limiting our explorations to the main backpacking trails as we had done on our previous visits, Julie and I were also accompanied by our two young daughters. Amy was nine years old, and Megan was six. This was not their first expedition, as we had backpacked a portion of the Pictured Rocks National Lakeshore trails the previous summer. But it was the first time that we all shared a single canoe for a backcountry venture.

Our fourteen-and-a-half-foot Old Town Kingfisher canoe was extra wide, so the girls were able to sit side-by-side on folding seats near the middle of the boat. The wider boat didn't allow for great paddling speed, but it certainly felt stable, which gave me peace of mind for our kids. Our gear was stowed behind them and behind my stern seat. It wasn't exactly roomy, but it wasn't uncomfortably tight either. Julie and I provided the primary propulsion, but the kids each had a paddle sized for them that they could use or not whenever they pleased, which helped keep everyone happy.

As we began our paddle to Daisy Farm Campground, the freedom of open water without the weight of our belongings on our shoulders felt exhilarating. Without roots and rocks and winding trails, we easily outpaced most of the backpackers that were engaged in the usual foot race to Three Mile and Daisy Farm. Within about an hour, we happily glided past Three Mile campground. After not much more than another hour, our canoe was beached at Daisy Farm, and we were selecting a campsite. Our paddling time included doing a brief pass-by of the lighthouse, but we didn't want to linger so as not to risk missing a good campsite opportunity. We hadn't seen any wildlife as I had hoped for, but our packing and paddling systems seemed to be working fine. We considered that to be our first-day success story. That and the fact that nobody got wet.

After dinner, other than a brief tour of nearby trails, we mostly just relaxed around camp. The girls seemed happy just to be on a big adventure. With our previous visit being ten years in the past, Julie and I were excited to be back on the island and enjoying some wilderness freedom. We had no special expectations other than hopefully seeing a moose or two and introducing our kids to Isle Royale.

The next morning, refreshed and ready to explore, we packed up and made the next ninety-minute paddle into Moskey Basin, with plans to camp on Lake Richie. During our voyage, we were entertained by three loons that approached our boat, calling loudly and diving. Being out on the water instead of on the trails was proving to have its benefits. It was also just plain fun.

After a brief snack break, I left Julie and the girls to explore the rocky shoreline and surrounding area near the end of the basin while I made the first two-mile trek to Lake Richie with our canoe. Being new to portaging a canoe and not even knowing anyone with that experience, I flipped the seventy-five-pound canoe up onto my shoulders without the cushion of a portage pad and embarked on my first real portage. I soon found that simply walking around our yard a few times with the canoe perched on my shoulders had not prepared me at all for the real thing. The experience proved to be exciting, but painful. Being athletic and still in my thirties, I just endured and pressed on, glad to be back on the island to explore some new territory. The pain would eventually go away.

After leaving the canoe at Lake Richie, during the hike back to Moskey Basin, unencumbered by extra weight or pain, my steps felt light and bouncy, giving me a slight urge to run. Fortunately, I had the sense to conserve my energy and just stay with a safe brisk walk.

On the return trip to Lake Richie, my backpack, though probably just as heavy as the canoe, felt much more comfortable to carry. It also felt good to be reunited with my family so I knew they were safe and we could enjoy the adventure together.

Once we all reached Lake Richie, we enjoyed a small celebration snack — with young kids, you tend to do a lot of snacking. Shortly after launching into Lake Richie, we watched a cow moose swimming across the lake. The choppiness of the water didn't seem to bother her at all. It bothered us a little as we had to paddle directly into it on our way to find a campsite. My current map shows three canoe campsites on the lake, but I only recall two. One of the sites was already occupied, but the other, we felt, must have been reserved for us. So, we gladly accepted it and set up our home for the next few days.

After the familiar routine of dinner preparation and clean-up, we spent a couple of hours just cruising the lake, looking for whatever there was to see. Those sightings included several loons, four of which were calling within twenty yards of our boat. Just before returning to camp, we watched a cow moose that came out into the lake to feed. More than satisfied with our wilderness experiences of the day, we returned to camp for a hot chocolate nightcap. I also needed to boil quite a bit of water to refill our bottles after a long, hot, and sunny day. During our evening relaxing and water boiling, we watched the hyper antics of a red squirrel as it was harvesting mushrooms and spreading them out to dry in a nearby fir tree. Later, sleeping bags felt plush, and sleep came easily. Of course, that was back when the hard ground didn't feel all that hard.

Rain had settled in by the next morning, so we ate our breakfast in the tent before embarking on a soggy day. A cow moose at the edge of the lake, not far from camp, raised our spirits and brightened our outlook on this sullen day. As we approached the half-mile portage to Intermediate Lake, a bald eagle soared overhead, further brightening the day. Living downstate at the time, bald eagle sightings were a rare treat limited to up north vacations.

Our explorations on Intermediate Lake were mingled with numerous loon interactions. Being relatively new to north woods canoeing at the time, we were amazed at the number of loons we saw. And not just at a distance. Many of our loon sightings were up-close-and-personal. Nestled somewhere in the mix of loon interactions, a cow moose wandered into the scene as well. We were excited to be experiencing the wilderness connections that we had hoped for, and everyone seemed to be enjoying our big adventure.

As we ate our lunch on a shoreline rock outcrop, it was still raining, causing us to protect our lunch snacks between bites. The quarter-mile portage to the rocky shoreline of Big Siskiwit Lake was uneventful. Siskiwit's waters were well agitated by the rainy wind, so we stuck close to shore, taking advantage of the protection of points and east-end islands wherever we could. We ventured out into the lake just a bit, but I was concerned about the waves getting worse, so we soon turned around and began working our way back to camp. Somehow, about the time we were turning around, we came to realize that Amy and Megan didn't have their life jackets on. They hadn't mentioned it, and, with extra bulky cool-weather clothes under their rain jackets, Julie and I thought they had their life jackets on. Regardless of the reason, the reality was that the kids' life jackets were still in the jumble of sleeping bags back in the tent, and we were two lakes away, paddling through wavy conditions. Of course, that realization heightened my concerns about growing waves. We couldn't realistically get off the water and bushwhack our way all the way back to camp, or even close to it, so we paddled on with extreme caution, not to mention the big knot in my stomach. I remember mentally questioning my parenting abilities along the way as well.

As we made our way back to Intermediate Lake, the wind died down and the sun made its appearance, which made us — or at least me — feel a little better. It still was not a good situation for the kids, but I was at least a little less on edge about the potential of a life-threatening mishap. A pair of playful otters on Intermediate, along with a large collection of tadpoles with legs skittering around in the shallows, helped take my mind off our situation. Being that we were sticking to shallow-water shorelines anyway, we took the opportunity to investigate a few beaver lodges along the way, but nobody was home.

An eagle greeted us as we paddled toward camp on Lake Rickie. I was enjoying the animal interactions and wilderness scenery, but I was greatly relieved to safely reach camp for dinner. As we unloaded our collection of day packs from the canoe, we discovered a small mouse stowaway. Exactly how, where, or when it came to be in our company, we had no idea. I carefully released it, well away from our tent. That evening, we spent the last couple of hours of bright daylight cruising

Lake Richie — with everyone wearing a life jacket! We saw our resident eagle again, along with a parade of loons. Just before returning to camp, we quietly bobbed in the gentle ripples while we watched two blue herons patrolling the shallows. Even though it had been a bit of a nerve-racking day for a while, it ended on a peaceful note. Lying in the tent later that evening, feeling relaxed and content, I'm not even sure that I made it through my evening prayers before falling asleep. I know I made it through the "thank you" part, though, because that came first.

In the morning, we could see a storm brewing in the distance, but Lake Richie was calm and clear. Our camp neighbors had left sometime the previous day, so the lake belonged to us and the loons. For our first portage trip back to Moskey Basin, we all joined in carrying packs, leaving the canoe for my solo second portage. At the top of the first uphill grade, we came across a cow and calf moose. Unfortunately, the forest was too thick for Julie to get a good picture of them. After they continued on their way, so did we. Near Moskey Basin, we found a wolf track in the muddy trail, which was almost as exciting for us as seeing a wolf.

We were thrilled to find an unoccupied shelter along the shoreline when we arrived at the basin. I left Julie and the girls there to settle in as I made the trek back to Lake Richie for our canoe. As an experiment, I cut a couple of strips off my foam sleeping pad to use as make-shift portage pads for the two-mile haul. Unfortunately, it didn't work well. The portaging was still painful, so I just ended up shortening my sleeping pad for no real gain. All I could do was chalk it up as a lesson learned and make plans to find real portage pads before our next canoeing excursion.

When I returned to the shelter with our canoe, the kids, which included me, spent some time playing in the shallows. Not being one to ever completely take off my "dad hat", I was warning the girls to be extra careful because the rocks were slippery. About thirty seconds

after I issued that warning, I slipped and did a header into the lake —
just to prove my point, of course. Now, roughly twenty-five years
later, that incident is one of the highlights of the trip that both our
daughters remember.

Later, we took a cruise around the end of the basin in our canoe.
We found a small waterfall and followed the creek on foot until a large,
downed tree blocked our way. Back at the basin, a pair of otters swam
by and looked us over while we were watching an eagle. The water
was choppy, but not enough to cause us any issues. Being a little
paranoid from the other day, I still made a visual check to make sure
everyone was wearing their life jackets.

Back near our shelter, I found a large leech in the shallows, which
I didn't expect. I just didn't envision leeches in Superior, or even a
sheltered bay of Superior. We were done playing in the water anyway,
but even if we hadn't been, we were done playing in the water. Later
that evening, I found that even though the shelter was more convenient
and spacious than our tent, the wood floor certainly wasn't more
comfortable. Even without any roots or rocks.

Apparently, the shelter floor was comfortable enough, because we
slept in and got a late start the next morning. Heavy fog had settled
in. While Megan was trying to take a picture of the rest of us standing
near the water in front of the shelter, she mentioned a moose. We
thought *Yeah, right*, but when we finally turned around to look, sure
enough, there was a cow moose swimming across the bay behind us.
We saw a variety of eagles and loons as we paddled Moskey Basin
back to Rock Harbor, but the fog continued. In fact, it seemed to get
thicker as morning turned to afternoon. Even though we hugged the
southern shoreline as we paddled, all we could see was a small stretch
of shoreline right near the boat. We stopped at Edisen Fishery and
Rock Harbor Lighthouse, hoping the fog would at least thin out while
we were touring, but it seemed to get even thicker. By the time we
reached the main boating channel at the far end of Mott Island, the fog

was too thick for a safe crossing. I wasn't worried about not being able to see the other side of the channel. I was concerned about a motorboat coming through and not seeing us. As we were considering what to do, a fairly sizeable boat came through the channel faster than I expected for the conditions, heading for the dock at the Park Service headquarters. Its wake sent a couple of waves over our gunnel, wetting not only some of our gear, but Megan, too. That incident made our decision for us. We paddled back along the shore to the far side of the Park Service complex, figuring that most boats wouldn't be going past that point into Moskey Basin. At our intended crossing point, we just sat there for a few minutes, listening. Nothing. We slowly began paddling straight away from shore into the fog. I kept glancing back over my shoulder as I continued to listen for boats. As the shoreline behind us was about to disappear and there was nothing but fog ahead, I told Julie to paddle hard. We both dug in hard with our paddles, propelling us into the unknown. Several strokes later, a hint of the far shoreline came faintly into view. I breathed a sigh of relief as our shoreline view improved with each stroke. We paddled on along the northern shoreline to Threemile Campground, arriving about 6 pm. Our celebration was a big meal of mac & cheese. It may not sound like much of a celebration, but that evening, it tasted like a feast.

The fog finally lifted shortly after dinner, opening up new possibilities for the evening. We decided on a photographic moose hunt and headed up the trail toward Mount Franklin. Along the way, we found a beaver pond that looked like a good moose haunt. A beaver showed itself, but no moose. The end of Tobin Harbor was mooseless as well. When we were almost back to camp, we crossed paths with a red fox that had a red squirrel in its mouth. We stood off to the side of the trail and let the fox trot by with its dinner, then made our way back to camp to relax for one last evening on the island.

The next morning, we enjoyed an easy paddle back to the Snug Harbor docks. It was a bit wavy, but we were paddling with the wind, which rarely seems to happen, so we made good time and managed not to take on any water.

After unloading our boat, we heard reports of people seeing multiple bull moose on higher ground, up near Mount Ojibway. At first, I was just a bit envious. Then I thought about all the things we had seen and done, and the fun our kids had had, not to mention the enjoyment I got out of watching our daughters having a fun wilderness adventure. With our canoe, we finally got to see things that we had dreamed of seeing on previous visits when we were limited to trail travel. Then, I thought of the bulls that we had encountered on those previous visits. At that point, I accepted our visit as a success and headed off with my family to enjoy our last few hours on the island.

Looking back at our photo album of that trip, I smile at how young our now-adult daughters look in the pictures. And I'm especially surprised at how young Julie and I look. I'm glad we took the opportunity to have wilderness adventures like that when our kids were young. Even though I no longer look like I did in those pictures, when I get out in the wilds, I still feel a bounce in my steps, just like I did back then.

RETURN TO THE ISLAND

Standing there on the dock, on a mid-August afternoon, it was hard to believe that twenty-five years had passed since we last visited Isle Royale. With two weeks available to explore and reacquaint ourselves with the island, part of me wanted to just relax and settle in. The other part of me wanted to get busy exploring. The "get busy" side won, so as soon as we were in our cabin and somewhat unpacked, we grabbed our daypacks and cameras and set out on the roughly two-mile hike to Scoville Point. With nearly a year of planning under our belts, there were lots of places on our list to visit, but Scoville Point was someplace new that we had never seen before and the most doable destination with the time we had available that first day. As part of that initial investigation, we were also interested in seeing the official artist-in-residence cabin, which was near Scoville Point. We were curious to see what we were missing by creating our own unofficial artist-in-residence stay on the island instead of just continuing to apply for an official residency through the Park Service.

One of the first things I noticed when we hit the trail was the lack of biting bugs. Later in the hike, a few bugs did show up, but the first thirty minutes or so were refreshingly bug-free. The other thing I noticed while exploring the trail along the sheltered waters behind Raspberry Island was how much the Isle Royale Superior shoreline looks, smells, and sounds like the not-far-away Minnesota Superior shoreline. Regardless of the similarities, one of my goals over the next two weeks was to connect with the uniqueness of the island that I had not visited since we started exploring the Minnesota shoreline and Boundary Waters Canoe Area Wilderness more than twenty years ago.

During our frequent views of the shoreline, we soon noticed a small island out near Scoville Point that consisted of a collection of fractured bedrock. Pillars reaching up out of Superior were covered with orange lichens. Part of what drew our attention was the intensity of its colors illuminated by the afternoon sun. Julie took reference pictures of that island every time the trail exposed a new view of it. Between pictures of that island and photos of miscellaneous items of interest along the trail, I began thinking that Julie just might fill up her camera's SD card before we even completed our first two miles of hiking. Every new view of the small rock island seemed better than the previous views.

Scoville Point itself is a long point of exposed bedrock that reminded me a lot of Artist Point in Grand Marais, Minnesota. Out near the tip was a small swale of trees, stunted from harsh conditions and poor soil. The trees were mostly white cedar and spruce, with a couple of paper birch and tag alder joining the mix somewhere along the line, in addition to a lone ash tree. Across the small bay on the north side of the point is a secondary point that is home to the formal artist-in-residence cabin. Other than having a nice view, the cabin didn't look like much, which is something it had in common with the much more modern cabin we were staying in.

Surrounding Scoville Point, there is a collection of small islands, some supporting vegetation, some not. To the east, the small islands continued into the distance, sheltering Merrit Lane. While I surveyed the area, I took advantage of the breeze on the open point to dry out the back of my t-shirt from carrying my daypack on our sunny hike. With all of the picture-taking, the hike took us about two hours instead of the hour that I had anticipated.

On our way back to the cabin, we took the north side of the Stoll Trail, which partially follows Tobin Harbor. The scenery was a little less than the south loop near the open lake, but we found more thimbleberries to enjoy and a little more cooling shade. It also gave us an opportunity to experience more new territory. We made it back to the cabin later than expected for dinner, but at least we accomplished something worthwhile on our shortened first day.

Besides being a dry place to cook, sleep, and store our gear, the main thing Julie and I both appreciated about the modern cabin we were staying in was the view. Most of the north side of the cabin was actually a window overlooking Tobin Harbor. Even though we were staying for two weeks, I was confident that I wouldn't get tired of that view.

The next morning, we began our first full day at 7:20 am, watching the day begin to unfold outside of our glass portal. Sun and clouds were sharing the sky. A trio of loons flew past our view as they followed Tobin Harbor toward the open lake. One called out what seemed like a greeting as it winged past. Julie was frantically packing for her first day of painting, not knowing exactly what to expect. New ventures always tend to be nerve-racking like that. Being on Isle Royale wasn't exactly new, but it had been well over twenty years since our last visit, and she wasn't an artist at that time. So, the island wasn't really new, but painting en plein air on the island certainly was. I simply waited. Writing en plein air was nothing new for me. Neither was north woods exploring.

Julie decided to paint a mile or so down the trail where a patch of thimbleberries along the path caught her eye. We were following the Tobin Harbor Trail west (mostly), and I was interested in seeing more of the harbor, as well as the trail, so once Julie got set up, I continued down the trail just doing what I do. Exploring. Knowing that Julie wouldn't be done painting any time soon, I opted to take the side trail to Suzy's Cave. I had seen signs to it before. I had also seen it noted on maps. I had just never taken the time to hike the side trail to actually see it.

The trail wasn't anything special. Neither was the cave, which was really a crawl-through portal in a rock outcrop. It was worth the side trip just to see it, though, and know what it was. When it was first discovered in the middle of the wilderness island, I'm sure it was more exciting. An easy access trail and considerable foot traffic tend to diminish the novelty of things. I did find, and eat, several thimbleberries along the trail. That was my bonus for the short side trek.

Back along Tobin Harbor, I was intrigued by the many islands dotting the waterway. They gave the harbor a tranquil feeling. The roar of a seaplane, though, soon shattered the tranquility as well as the wilderness atmosphere. It left me hoping that sometime during our stay we would be able to escape the many man-made distractions that surrounded the Rock Harbor area. Obviously, the west end of Tobin Harbor was not far enough out from the Rock Harbor docks and lodge to make that happen. I knew there was a threshold out there somewhere that would allow us to step away from the modern world, at least for a short time, but we had not yet found that line and crossed it. That gave me a goal to strive for.

I turned around at the trail to Three Mile Campground and headed back to see how Julie was doing with her first painting. As it turned out, she wasn't having the best of times painting. I didn't think it looked bad, but then again, that's usually the case. It typically turns out that the painting is fine. It's just taking longer to shape up than Julie is willing to give it. I was just happy that the cool morning breeze made for perfect hiking conditions. Mosquitoes were present, but not in sufficient numbers to be annoying. Okay, they're always annoying, but they didn't seem to bother me much. Maybe it was because they were so much sparser than at home, or maybe it was just because I was excited to be exploring Isle Royale again. Regardless, the bugs weren't causing me any issues.

During the course of the morning, I noticed several hikers who looked like they had issues walking. Still, they were out on the rocky, rooted trails experiencing the island. Some of them concerned me a little, from the standpoint of their own safety, but I had to give them credit for getting out and hiking — some were even backpacking — instead of sitting it out. I did have to question how much benefit some people were getting out of their time on the trail, though. They were just talking and visiting with their companions instead of taking in the sights and listening to the sounds of the wild. For some of them, their hike might as well have just been a sidewalk stroll through town. They were apparently seeking something, but I highly doubted that it was serenity or solitude. Then again, if they lived in a large city, then some noise along the trail still probably seemed tranquil.

After Julie wrapped up her painting, we both trekked out to the Three Mile Campground Trail, then decided to make the climb up to Mount Franklin on the Greenstone Ridge. Partway up, we passed a pretty view of a large boggy area that grabbed Julie's attention. Painting an island bog was on her list, so she decided to end her climb there and began setting up to paint. I was set on seeing the view from the top, so I continued on my own, leaving Julie to her painting. I considered it to be a recon trip to see if Julie would want to paint the view from the ridge. The twenty-minute climb was pretty gradual, but it was still a climb in the heat of the afternoon. I spent my cool down time at the top, admiring the limited view, which was looking basically south. The ranger station complex on Mott Island was readily visible, as well as the area around Conglomerate Bay and Saginaw Point. The views in other directions consisted of just foreground trees. Out beyond Mott Island, I could vaguely see the rugged mountainous profile of the Keweenaw Peninsula. There was, of course, no detail. Just a gray-green rugged profile along the horizon. It was a beautiful view, but not the wide-open, three-sixty view I was expecting. That's the view I always picture when I think about the Greenstone Ridge. I took a few pictures, discreetly peed in the woods, and headed back down to see how things were going for Julie and her marshy bog painting.

As it turned out, things were going pretty well, and Julie was in a good mood, which meant that I was too. After taking a few pictures of the marsh and Julie painting it, I settled down on a sun-bleached log that sloped slightly into the open water of the marsh. Dragonflies kept me company as I pondered random things and jotted notes. Sun and clouds were still vying for control of the sky. As I gazed out across the marsh, I half expected to see a moose amble into view. To my dismay, it didn't happen. The only large mammal in the scene was a guy on a log. Then again, I wasn't really in the scene. Actually, yes, I was. I just wasn't in the painting. I was spectating off to the east of the scene that Julie was painting.

Julie packed up as dark gray clouds worked in from the west. She wasn't quite done with the painting, but the threatening clouds said she was done for now. We debated putting on our rain jackets when the droplets started falling about fifteen minutes later, but opted to take our chances. The light rain was short-lived, so our gamble paid off. We strolled back to our cabin relatively dry.

The following day, early morning hours were overcast and windy. The sun came out about 10 am despite the forecast for rain. Still, Julie decided to paint a couple of close-by scenes just in case the rain did materialize. First, she painted a fireweed and spruce scene just a hundred and fifty yards from our cabin, along the footpath to the lodge. I roamed and took a few red squirrel pictures, which was difficult because they rarely hold still for more than a second or two. Red squirrels always seem to be on a frantic mission to eat and store up food as fast as they can, every waking moment. I also found a nice fireweed specimen for Julie to paint near the old Smithwick Mine site. Looking down into the old shaft, which was once ninety-six-feet deep but now just a fifteen-foot-deep pit, reminded me of dead end dreams and aspirations. We all have them, some bigger than others, but I think we all have them. It also reminded me of foolish or impulsive exploitations that ended up just compromising the environment with no real gain. There was a lot of that in the 1800's and early 1900's, but it's certainly not limited to that era. We're still making non-intelligent and greedy decisions today in the name of "progress". Get rich schemes that ultimately fail. People as a whole don't seem to learn.

While Julie was still painting mid-morning, I was sitting on a rock in Superior, along the Scoville Point Trail, looking out at Raspberry Island. Even though waves were supposedly up to ten feet high out on the open lake, in front of me, minor undulations were gently caressing shoreline rocks. Boat trips on the Isle Royale Queen IV were cancelled again due to waves, but you wouldn't guess that based on where I was. I watched a small shorebird scampering around on a neighboring rock, eking out a living, eating whatever it was eating. The sun peeked out for a few minutes, just long enough to prompt me to take off my fleece, then it was gone again, leaving me in the overcast gloom. The sullen sky made the small islands in front of me look lonely and desolate. Moods can change quickly on Isle Royale, as with anywhere. Especially the Big Lake.

Later, Julie moved over to the fireweed I had found at the Smithwick Mine. Once she got set up, I planned to do more exploring, which I did, but not for long due to impending rain. As I was standing there watching Julie paint, the noise from the lodge operations — mostly the big generator — reminded me that even though we were on a wilderness island, that particular area was just another resort. The Rock Harbor area around Snug Harbor somehow doesn't seem to fit with the rest of Isle Royale. It's much busier and more developed than I remember from our visits years ago. And I'm pretty sure it's not just my memory.

When Julie finished painting, I checked out the moose antler collection at the park office. Finding a moose antler has long been one of my goals, or at least a strong desire. The biggest one in the collection probably weighed roughly twenty pounds, and it certainly was not huge. Roaming around with a pair of those on your skull would definitely give your neck and shoulder muscles a workout, which is probably why bull moose were designed with such a bulky front end.

Afternoon rains finally materialized late in the day. So, we switched gears to working in the cabin. For a while, working consisted of sitting in a chair in front of the mostly glass front wall, watching the world get a washing. A seaplane — yet another of many seaplanes — took off right in front of our cabin. As that plane took off with a roar, for a moment, the annoyance was replaced by a flashback to Kodiak Island, Alaska. I was standing on a gravel beach on the shoreline of a remote lake, watching the seaplane that had just dropped Julie and me off, lifting off from the water and roaring away, leaving us in a deep silence. Our link to the outside world disappeared into the distance, leaving us to spend the next couple of days in a small cabin that we had rented from the U.S. Forest Service. The corners of the cabin were worn and tattered from Kodiak bears chewing on them. A reminder of our remoteness and vulnerability.

I soon came back to Isle Royale, but the plane was gone, along with its annoying roar. As we continued working in the cabin, Julie took a look at the sky at about 8:30 pm and declared there wouldn't be much of a sunset. I agreed. We assumed it would be blah and accepted it as fact. Then, about an hour later, she exclaimed, "Whoa! Look at the sunset!" I looked up from my writing to see the sky — and especially the clouds — ablaze in an orangish-pink illumination. We quickly turned off the cabin lights so we could snap a picture without the glare. Then, Julie ran outside to snap a few more shots. We nearly missed the whole show because we had dismissed the likelihood earlier, then didn't bother to look up from our work to check. It seems to me that there's a lesson there somewhere.

CANOEING ROCK HARBOR

The day we chose to paddle Rock Harbor and Moskey Basin was sunny and warm, so we decided to get an early start and launched our canoe about 7:40 am from the beach near the lodge grill. Shortly after we started paddling, we wanted to explore the rocky islands just west of Snug Harbor, but we knew there were other adventures waiting and Julie especially wanted to paint at the historic lighthouse farther down the harbor. So, we paddled on, visually investigating the collection of rugged islands from afar as we passed by. There were a few locations, like the lighthouse, where we specifically wanted to spend some time, but in between those locations, our plan was to simply relax and enjoy a day of canoe travel, taking in the sights and sounds of the day. Just east of the park service complex on Mott Island, I watched a trio of otters slip into the water from the rocky edge of the island. They apparently had no interest in coming over for a visit, like most otters seem to do. Maybe because of the area where they lived, they already saw more than enough people to satisfy their curiosity. We soon lost sight of them along the shadowed shoreline. Even though we were certainly interested in having a personal encounter, they apparently were not.

With a steady but casual paddling cadence, we reached the Rock Harbor Light by about 10 am. There was a secluded little gravel cove that looked inviting just around the corner from the building, so that was where we beached our canoe, thinking that it would be an interesting place to see anyway, and we could just walk over to the lighthouse from there. Unfortunately, it turned out to be difficult to reach the lighthouse from there due to thick trees and a rocky cliff in the woods. So, I ended my bushwhacking search for an access route, and we moved our canoe to the open gravel beach right in front of the lighthouse, which actually worked out better because we didn't have as far to haul Julie's painting supplies. In addition, we were better able to keep an eye on our boat during our visit. The lighthouse is located on the Middle Islands Passage. It's now a museum, and the tower is closed to visitors, or at least it was while we were there. When we visited twenty-plus years ago, the building was empty and open, including the tower. I reminisced for a moment about climbing the tower stairs with our kids and enjoying the open access not available at most lighthouses. I tend to think back and reminisce quite a bit these days. Twenty-some years is an easy gap to hop across in your mind. At least at my age it is.

After scoping out several potential vantage points for painting, Julie chose to paint from an exposed rock outcrop right along the water. Spending an extended time on the relatively small semi-level spot atop the tall outcrop made her a little nervous but offered what she thought to be the best painting view. While she painted, I explored, as usual. It's what I do. Up on the outcrop near where Julie painted, I snacked on some sun-dried blueberries that had been growing in a juniper patch. I don't know if it was the fragrance of the junipers in the air or if the berries had actually picked up the juniper flavor, but the taste of the blueberries had a definite hint of juniper. I have heard of that same phenomenon with wine, where if you know what you are doing, you can detect subtle flavors from the environment where the grapes were growing. Now I'm not familiar enough with the growing environment for any wineries, so I can't really test that claim myself, but I'm pretty confident it was true for those Isle Royale blueberries.

When Julie was done painting, we took advantage of an established trail and hiked over to the Edisen Fisheries Museum. Julie wanted to do a plein air painting of the main fish house, but the dock around the building was too small. Unless she painted from out in a boat, she would be too close to the building to get the perspective and proportions right. We, of course, had our canoe available just down the trail, but sitting in a canoe and painting for at least a couple of hours would not have worked well either. So, Julie took several reference pictures instead, hoping she could get a good enough shot to be able to develop a painting in her studio after we returned home.

After going back and taking one more stroll around the lighthouse grounds, we then paddled down the harbor a short jaunt to the wolf-moose research area, where we met Rolf and Candy Peterson. Rolf is a retired professor and researcher from Michigan Tech who spent considerable time spearheading the wolf-moose study on the island. I knew they had been working there for quite a few years, but I was still surprised to find out from Candy that it had, in fact, been fifty-four years. They had an impressive collection of antlers and skulls, as well as other bones, which was what caught my attention when I first saw their cabin many years ago. We ended up visiting for probably forty-five minutes, and had interesting conversations about moose, wolves, Isle Royale, the Park Service, and a bunch of other wilderness-related stuff. Rolf and Candy were both very personable and easy to talk with, not to mention hospitable. It felt like we were having conversations with a couple of old friends, which made it hard to leave. Especially knowing that we may never have another opportunity to visit, because we didn't know how much longer they would continue working there or when we would be able to return.

We paddled away at about 3 pm, heading for the end of Moskey Basin, where Julie wanted to capture some pictures of the shelters. We had fond memories from staying there with our daughters, so Julie wanted to create a painting to celebrate those memories. After about an hour of steady paddling through an array of waterfowl, we reached our destination. It was getting uncomfortably hot, so we took a short break for water and snacks before Julie wandered off in search of photo opportunities. The shelters were unfortunately all occupied and had an array of stuff draped all over around and on them, so Julie wasn't able to get any of the pictures she was hoping for. Up until visiting the wolf-moose research area, Julie's intent had been to do some plein air painting at the end of the basin as well, but time was getting short, and we still had a long return trip back to Snug Harbor, which would require a lot of paddle strokes.

Thinking back on our visit, Moskey Basin was one of the few places that looked pretty much like I remembered from our earlier visits. Either my memory was failing or much of the scenery around Rock Harbor had changed significantly over the years. Of course, we only previously explored the harbor by boat once, so I may have just missed or misplaced some of the details. My mental filing system isn't necessarily as robust as I'd like it to be.

While paddling back toward our cabin, waves were getting choppy near the end of the basin, but they mellowed out as we continued through Rock Harbor. We repeated our interactions with loons, ducks, and geese. Bald eagles, too. Just before we reached the park service complex, we took a butt-break stop, just to stand up for a few minutes, then pushed on toward Snug Harbor. Because of some historic stories I had read, I really wanted to stop for a look at Cemetery Island, but there was no good canoe landing location that didn't involve precarious rocks or a bushwhack through thick brush, so we just paddled on, thinking that maybe we would have more time to attempt a visit another day. About a half hour before we reached Snug Harbor, I watched a lone otter stroll across a narrow strip of beach and slip into the water. It swam parallel to shore for a short distance, then dove. We continued paddling, hoping for another look. Even though we were expecting to see the otter again, we were surprised when it popped up less than twenty feet from our boat. It immediately dove back down as soon as it saw us, obviously as surprised as we were. That's one of the things you can expect when you're exploring outdoors. Surprises.

Shortly afterward, we paddled out amongst the rocky islands just west of Snug Harbor, where we had thought about exploring earlier in the morning. They're the islands that I've always considered to be the guardians of Isle Royale. That collection of rugged rocky islands that always grabs my attention and imagination when we pass by on the ferry just before docking in Snug Harbor. As we passed through a small channel between the islands, which was open to the main lake, two-foot rollers caught us by surprise and made us a little nervous in our open canoe, so we rode them back through the channel into calmer water and decided that was enough rocky island exploring for the day.

We landed back at our starting point about 7:40 pm, roughly an hour earlier than I expected when we left Moskey Basin. Even though we made better progress than I originally expected, it still ended up being a busy, twelve-hour day. We were not able to see and do everything we wanted, but we still felt we accomplished quite a bit. It felt good just spending most of the day on an extended paddling excursion. Meeting Rolf and Candy and getting a close look at the collection of moose antlers around their cabin was something I had wanted to do for quite a while, so that felt like a major accomplishment as well.

As we were thinking about getting ready for bed later that night, which was a little before midnight, we saw the northern lights. We were hoping to see them while we were on the island, but didn't think our chances were very high, so the sighting caught us a little off guard. They were not very bright, but bright enough that we readily saw them. They were primarily red and green. Mostly tall spikes extending up into the sky and small curtains dancing around. They didn't last very long, so I was amazed and thankful that we were able to see them. If we hadn't looked out the window when we did, we would likely have missed the show. Our wall of large windows in the cabin pretty much faced north, so we had front-row viewing without having to fight off the biting bugs. During the light show, we enjoyed a concert of sorts, too, as the loons seemed to be going crazy, frantically calling. Once the lights faded and the loon calls went silent, we waited and watched for another twenty minutes or so, just in case there was an encore. When we finally went to bed, I thought I might have a difficult time going to sleep because of the excitement. Instead, my euphoric mood quickly transitioned to oblivious sleep.

TOBIN HARBOR AND BEYOND

With the previous day being a long day of paddling, we decided to change plans for the day to decrease the amount of time in the canoe. Instead of doing the portage over the Greenstone Ridge into Duncan Bay, then paddling (and fishing) Duncan and the Five Fingers Region, we opted to spend the day exploring Tobin Harbor and the surrounding area. It was on my to-do list for this trip anyway, and it's also known for having some coaster brook trout, so I wanted to fish it, too. The idea was to have a shorter paddling day, with a lot more time out of the boat, before launching into another long paddling day in the northeast region. So, we launched our canoe near the seaplane dock about 8:25 am. For whatever reason, we both agreed we wanted to paddle toward the open lake first. Within thirty minutes, three seaplanes flew right by us and landed. We didn't account for the fact that ferries and planes were working extra to reduce the backlog of people stuck on the island — or somewhere else — due to large waves the past couple of days. Despite the roaring intrusions by the planes, we meandered around some small islands in our canoe as we worked our way out to Scoville Point. We wanted to see if there was a place suitable for landing our canoe, so we didn't need to hike out there with all our gear for Julie to paint. I was also looking for rocky drop-offs around the islands, as I was told that those would be good places to fish. I didn't really find what I would identify as a rocky drop-off around any of the islands, but we did identify a couple of likely canoe landings between Scoville Point and the formal artist-in-residence cabin. My big discovery of the morning was realizing how many private cabins are congregated around the entrance to Tobin Harbor. It seemed like there was a cabin on almost every island in addition to several along the point leading out to the artist cabin. I was surprised and somewhat disappointed. To me, all those cabins took away from the charm and allure of Isle Royale. Its wildness was diminished in my mind. Although, after thinking about it for a while, I guess those cabins are not much different than the twenty-some cabins managed by the park service — the ones we were enjoying staying in. The main difference is that the private cabins are spread out a bit, so they significantly expand the developed footprint. Regardless, to me, it does reduce the wildness of the island. Another new realization for me was the number of small islands between Scoville Point and Blake Point. It's an intriguing collection. They caught my interest, to say the least. Enough that I added that area to my exploration list for later in the trip.

Even though we didn't paddle out through those islands, I did decide to at least take a cruise through Merritt Lane. The water was relatively shallow in some sections, making the bottom clearly visible. The lane felt quiet and secluded. Peaceful. We wanted to linger, so about 10:40 am, we stopped at the Merritt Lane Lakeside Camp, which is near the northeast end of the lane, not far from Blake Point. The shelter and two tent sites were all unoccupied. Perfect. We could relax for an early lunch, and Julie could paint if she wanted to, without interruptions. The first thing I noticed was a moose pelvic bone leaning against the camp sign. When I climbed up onto the dock and turned toward the water, what caught my attention was the view out into the community of small islands. It was enchanting. Enough so that Julie decided that she needed to paint it. It was a sunny day with a mild breeze. A perfect paddling day. A perfect day for most anything. I ate my lunch snacks as I roamed around. With no trails connecting to the camp, my roaming was limited. I mostly sat on a rock, then on the dock, jotting notes and taking in the day. Julie set up her easel and began painting a view of the islands. During my limited roamings, I found wolf scat near the campsites. Grasshoppers were abundant. Occasionally, one would hitch a ride on my shirt, which was fine, but I don't like them on my skin because their feet are very scratchy, and I don't like the feeling. I also noticed during my short stroll that the concrete part of the dock was poured in 1957, the same year my dad graduated from high school.

After exploring the area, while I was sitting pondering things, occasionally taking a peek at Julie's painting, a pair of sailboats slipped through between the islands, without making a sound. All we could see were the sails as the two floated by like ghosts. With loons calling and a light breeze caressing the landscape, the day was feeling more like the Isle Royale I was looking and hoping for.

My wilderness thoughts were interrupted by a third sailboat. This one was closer and moving faster. Then I heard it. The motor. It was under gas power rather than wind power. I wondered if the captain was trying to catch up to the first two boats or if they were just taking the easy way to travel. I decided that it didn't matter. The wilderness spell had been broken. Then I heard voices. Looking down Merritt Lane, I could barely see a pair of kayakers. I couldn't see any details, but I recognized the rhythmic pattern of paddle flashes as they approached, having a constant, loud, non-wilderness conversation. They stopped for a bit just beyond the camp, but the loud conversation continued. Thankfully, they soon moved on toward Blake Point, but their conversation continued until they were out of sight.

As my brain began resyncing with the sunny day and the sound of water, birds, and hoppers, I spotted the silhouette of a canoe coming through the lane. With it came more voices, reminding me that solitude can be and often is a fleeting thing. I started thinking about how most modern people have no idea what solitude is or why it's sometimes necessary. Even yearned for. The canoeists stopped and asked if we were camping . We admitted that we were not staying; just passing through. They decided to stay, which was fine. It just wasn't what I was hoping for. Solitude was gone. To drive that point home, we could hear the motor of the ferry as it left Rock Harbor, some three miles away and on the other side of a ridge. Then I heard the loud squeak of the shelter door as the canoeists stepped inside to survey their new home for the night. It was the first of many door squeaks. I refocused my thoughts on a school of minnows, tiny minnows, that were foraging near the dock. They didn't seem at all bothered by the squeak of the shelter door or the occasional slam.

We eventually met the two other canoeists. They were pleasant to talk with and turned out to be nice people. Julie finished her small painting of the view out into the islands and packed up her art gear. Then we loaded our canoe and departed without any fanfare, other than Julie slipping on the wet rock slab and falling into the edge of the water while we were moving the boat. Fortunately, she didn't get hurt. She just found it to be a refreshing break from the heat.

As we paddled back through Merritt Lane and past the empty private cabins, we regained a little of our feeling of peace and solitude. We stopped to check out the Lookout Louise Trail for future reference. While we were there, we visited Hidden Lake, looking for moose even though we knew that early afternoon on a warm sunny day was not prime time for moose sightings. We also stopped by the portage to Duncan Bay on our tour of the north side of Tobin Harbor, just for a brief preview of our upcoming portage.

Just after leaving the small bay that housed the portage, we saw a trio of loons. One was frantically thrashing and splashing like it was in distress, while the other two calmly watched. After watching for a bit, we realized that it was a pair of adults, watching their adolescent chick trying to learn to fly. It was practicing the long flapping, walking on water, take-offs that loons are known for. Its attempts were just splashier and more spastic than any we had previously witnessed. At one point, the young bird tried to do the high-reaching, wing-flapping stretch, the iconic loon pose that is often captured in photos. Except that the youngster fell over backward and flailed around like it was drowning. Its parents seemed unconcerned. We left the trio to their training session and continued our journey to the end of Tobin Harbor, where we paddled into Tobin Creek. Wildflowers were tall and fragrant along the open creek, mostly milkweed and jewelweed. A couple of bends later, the water level decreased, and we were confronted by a stockade of sticks. As we sat there for a minute, I noticed the same thing that had caught my attention a few days earlier. The creek was flowing in the opposite direction from what I expected. It was flowing out of Tobin Harbor. The current was slow, but it was definitely flowing out of the harbor. I was baffled at first. Then I realized that we were witnessing the effect of a seiche, where Lake Superior basically sloshes around. The Big Lake sloshing to the north was pushing water up into the creek, overpowering its natural flow direction. I had seen it before in other Superior streams. With that mystery solved, we spun our boat around in the bend near the stockade and began our paddle back to where we had started.

After a quick PBJ dinner at our cabin, we launched our canoe again into Tobin Harbor, intent on checking out the evening view from Lookout Louise and seeing if any moose showed up in the boggy surroundings of Hidden Lake. We arrived at the trailhead within about twenty minutes. Hidden Lake was vacant, except for birds, so we began our trek to the lookout. I found myself quietly sneaking along the trail through the thick brush, feeling more like I was moose hunting than hiking.

A majority of the climb was through a relatively recent burn area. The openness, yellowed grasses, and charred timber made the sun feel even hotter than it was. Huge, exposed boulders and the rock pillars of Monument Rock stood defiant to the fire and other elements. They were somewhat changeless pieces of a changing landscape. Along the trail, we stepped over the mostly eaten remains of a young hare, which added to the harshness of our surroundings. Near the top of the ridge, we finally re-entered the relative coolness of the shaded forest.

The view from the lookout was captivating. Even more so than the view from Merrit Lane. The evening sun sparkled off the collection of waterways stretching out below us. The map of the area that I was looking at came alive. Waterways led to waterways. Hills beyond hills beyond hills were layers of greenish gray, fading into the distance. The evening calm was quiet but for the whisper of the breeze and bird melodies. Rock Harbor sounds were non-existent. Again, this was the Isle Royale I was looking for. I just stood there and marveled. The strength of the afternoon sun had waned, and the atmosphere was transforming to a hazy softness known only to late evenings and misty mornings. We quietly turned and headed back toward our canoe. The next time we experienced the Duncan Bay scene, we would be immersed in it, paddling its waters in our canoe.

Just over the ridge from the lookout, I was looking down to check my footing on the trail. When I looked up, I was looking at a large bull moose that had apparently just noticed me as well. I abruptly stopped. He retreated a few steps and just stood there, his face masked by a large tree trunk. I motioned to Julie to stand still. We all waited. Several minutes we waited, three statues in the woods. Then the bull slowly walked off in a semi-circle around us. We slowly moved forward to maintain visual contact. When he stopped, we stopped, pondering each other's next move, like a northwoods game of chess. The fact that he grabbed a mouthful of vegetation now and then told me he was not too disturbed. The size and shape of his antlers took me back a number of years to a similar-looking bull that chased me up a tree out in the middle of the vast Frank Church River of No Return Wilderness in Central Idaho. That bull had been wound up by the mid-September mating rut. Being only mid-August, this bull in front of me wanted nothing to do with people, which is why he just slowly turned and began making a detour around us, sixty or seventy yards away. We quietly moved forward to a sharp bend in the trail where we could watch the bull walking down the trail ahead of us. We cautiously followed, keeping a respectable distance. At one point, that distance shrank to about 30 yards, which probably was not really respectful enough, so we stopped.

The bull quickly tired of our presence and veered left, off the trail, where he encountered a blow-down tree. He jumped the downed tree like a quarter horse and trotted for several steps, widening the distance between us. We stopped where he had left the trail and watched him stroll off through the woods, stopping periodically to look back at us. When he was out of sight, we continued our descent to the water, excited by having finally seen a moose. The encounter made us even more cautious as we neared Hidden Lake and the surrounding marsh. But nobody was out and about — moose or people.

We quietly paddled back to our cabin across Tobin Harbor, enjoying the evening coolness. The western half of the moon was already hanging in the southern sky. A pair of loons winged past us heading west, barely ten feet above the water. At only about twenty yards away, we could see their every detail as they passed. It seemed like a good way to end an adventure-filled day.

The next morning, we caught up on some office/studio work at the cabin — me writing and Julie painting. After lunch, we packed up and paddled out to Scoville Point for Julie to paint on-site. As usual, I roamed and explored. Julie selected a location near the end of the point, looking west down the length of the bare rock and beyond. Her vantage point gave her a line of sight down a cleft in the rock — a valley of sorts. So, besides all the other roaming, I explored the length of the cleft, which was at least a couple hundred yards. Superior reached in fifty yards or so. At the end of that finger of water floated a sixteen-inch-diameter tree trunk that was roughly twenty feet long. It was thoroughly debarked and looked like someone had taken a big wood rasp to it. The log was blocked in by a large rock, so I suspected it was ushered in by stormy waves.

Further into the small valley was a pair of stagnant ponds, complete with minnows. At the far west end of the second pond were two clumps of iris plants. The flowers were, of course, long gone, but the plants held several seed pods. There were also cedars, alders, a spruce tree, and other vegetation I couldn't identify. A mini garden oasis amid a world of rock. I eventually made my way back out onto the open rock. Standing out in the refreshing breeze felt good. Even though the sun wasn't glaring, it was still hazy and hot. Out of the breeze was uncomfortably hot. Even in the shade.

After visiting much of the rocky point as well as the official artist-in-residence cabin, I perched myself on a step in the rock, near the very tip of Scoville Point, looking to the east.

Having the source of heat on my back instead of in my face was a relief. Thankfully, the breeze continued. Sitting there, looking out beyond the surrounding islands to the open lake, the next stop was the horizon. I could have been sitting at the end of the point or the end of the known world. From where I sat, nothing beyond the horizon existed. The crowd of hikers visiting the point had come and gone. No boats were in sight. Again, this was the Isle Royale I remembered.

Looking north across the little bay, the artist cabin didn't look like much. An earlier peek in the windows had validated that impression. It wasn't much for looks or comfort. The location was nice, but not spectacular. I realized, though, that what the cabin provided artists with was a place to begin to connect with the island. A place to think. A Listening Point. An artist-in-residence stay at the cabin would not really be a journey in itself or the culmination of a quest. It would be the beginning of a journey. An initial connection to build upon. That was what this trip was for me as well. I was planning to use this trip and our Minnesota trip the following month to help build a book. This book. About wilderness and near-wilderness adventures around the Lake Superior region. A book about wilderness feelings and the quest I have for solitude and serenity. A quest I know I share with many people. That does not mean that I want to ditch everyone else and be alone all the time. To me, solitude is a rest from daily busyness. From the unnatural and sometimes unreal manmade world, cluttered with stuff. Stuff that clouds our minds and dulls our senses. Solitude is how we can resync ourselves with reality and life and the people we were created to be.

Those thoughts were all fine and good. They were even refreshing, helping me wrap my head around this relatively new project I had embarked on. But the other part of reality was that the day wasn't working well for Julie. As is sometimes the case, her plein air painting wasn't going well. She was struggling and once again disappointed. She threw in the towel at about 6:30 pm. It was time to pack up, completed painting or not. At that point, plein air painting may or may not continue into our future. I wasn't sure what would happen.

The paddle back to our cabin was quiet but, due to our not-so-good-moods because of painting issues, not very peaceful. It was simply a progression of paddle strokes.

THE NORTHEAST

Yet another hot and sunny day was underway when we launched our canoe a little before 8 am. Tobin Harbor was calm and quiet. The only ripples were from waterfowl and fish. As we paddled across Tobin to the Duncan Bay Portage, a loon approached our boat. It got to within about twenty feet of us and started calling. It dove and came right back up, called again, then started doing the routine where they rise up and basically dance on the water while calling. It repeated that routine probably a dozen times. That was when I noticed a second loon with a small chick on its back about eighty yards or so away. I'm assuming the adult that approached us was the male. It dove again as we paddled past and came up behind me and called a few more times before it mellowed out. That was one of the closest loon encounters we've ever experienced.

We reached the portage within only about fifteen minutes. It turned out not to be as bad as everyone described, so the slightly more than three-quarters of a mile went by quickly. The south side climb was naturally gradual. The north side was considerably steeper, but there were low-angle switchbacks, buffering what would have been a knee-jarring descent. The endeavor only took about twenty minutes, but there was definitely some sweat involved. Before directly exposing ourselves to the sun again, we did a cool-down at Duncan Bay prior to putting our life jackets on. I was pleasantly surprised that I didn't need to stop for a break during the portage. And I somehow didn't even feel fatigued. While we cooled down, Duncan Bay was quiet except for a seaplane flyover. I wasn't sure why they were flying over Duncan Bay because it wasn't on their normal take-off and landing routes.

We paddled over to the island right in front of the portage. At the east end, there was a rocky point with a sharp drop-off. Just the type of place I was looking for to fish. I put on my water shoes because casting from the stern of the canoe was difficult for me at best. Instead, I tried wading out and casting along the drop-off, but I had a difficult time throwing the large, weighted streamers. I couldn't cast them beyond about thirty feet. And even that wasn't pretty. I quickly got disgusted with myself! I typically spend most of my fishing time with my 7 ½-foot 4-weight rod and small to medium flies on small to medium streams. Out on Isle Royale, I was using a 9-foot, 6-weight rod and trying to chuck big, weighted streamers fifty feet or more, which obviously didn't go well at all. I didn't get hooked, and neither did Julie, but the overall outcome was still depressing. Despite my initial optimism, it was not proving to be a good day of fishing for me. I even tried casting a light-weight foam hopper to fish that were hitting the surface, but that wasn't working well either. It's hard to fish well when your attitude is swirling around the drain, so it was time to move on to something else.

As I switched gears and we paddled over to the portage to the Five Fingers area, a family was just coming off the portage. We exchanged quick pleasantries and began unloading our stuff. The short portage was easy, but it was still uncomfortably hot, which certainly didn't help my attitude. Paddling out into the Five Fingers area, we were surprised by two other canoes as we came around the first finger. Seeing another canoe obviously surprised them as well.

We paddled into the next narrow bay and ran into a trio of otters at the far end. They played hide-and-seek with us for a bit, then they ditched us by hiding in an old beaver house. We could hear them making grunting noises inside, and periodically, one would come out and peer at us through some sticks. While we paddled away, we could still hear them grunting at us from somewhere in the jungle of sticks surrounding the lodge.

As we made our way through Stockly Channel, we took advantage of some shade along the south shore to take a short break, because the sun was getting hotter. The portage to Lane Cove was very short and easy, but still a little draining because of the heat. We didn't spend much time in Lane Cove because there were quite a few people at the camp and a sailboat anchored at the west end. Instead, we ventured out into the open water area near Belle Isle, going out as far as Captain Kidd Island. Julie took reference pictures of several small islands in the area and a couple of large white pines standing tall on two different islands. After making a relaxing, casual loop of the neighboring islands, we decided it was time to begin making our way back to our cabin. The afternoon was waning, and the sun was draining.

All day, loons had been calling near and far, which added to the wilderness atmosphere of the northeast region. On our way back, we explored more of the fingers in the Five Fingers area. Then, as we were leaving Lane Cove, a merganser hen was guiding five rambunctious chicks. The chicks were frantically diving and skittering around. I don't know if they were actually catching and eating things when they dove or if they were just being a bunch of hyperactive youngsters.

Throughout the day, I was trying to savor our time out in the northeast islands because, for the most part, it was relatively quiet and relaxing. Other than my failed attempt at fishing, it was as close to peaceful solitude as we had experienced since arriving at Isle Royale. Also, I was trying to savor our time because I didn't know if we would ever be back in that area or not. In a way, it felt like when we leave the Minnesota Boundary Waters to return to civilization. We're reluctant to leave because we know we're going back into the busyness of modern life.

The portage back into Duncan Bay was not only easy, but it was thankfully not all that hot. We went around the west side of the big island just to see new territory, then headed for the portage to Tobin Harbor. Even with starting on the steeper side, the portage over the Greenstone Ridge was not that difficult, thanks to the switchbacks. I peeked out from under my canoe umbrella quite often in the hope of seeing another moose, but my peeks were unfruitful. We were able to make the ridge crossing in one shot again, which made me feel good and lifted my spirits. At the end of the portage, we met a lady sitting and waiting for her husband, who was taking a hike up to Lookout Louise — he was taking the long way via the portage instead of the Lookout Louise Trail. We had a nice conversation about the island and how our day tripping from a cabin was working out. I don't know where her and her husband were staying, but she seemed a bit envious of us having a cabin, and interested in giving it a try.

Afterward, we quietly paddled across Tobin Harbor once again, with loon calls coming from all around. We reached the dock about 7:30 pm, thankful for another busy day of canoeing. Not a good fishing day, but a good day of paddling and exploring. As we were unloading the canoe and portaging back to our cabin, I made a mental note that I needed to learn to cast big, weighted streamers. Or maybe I just needed to learn to cast my 9-foot, 6-weight rod better. I needed to learn something. That was for sure.

Roaming around the outskirts of the lodge area the next day, I realized that I was getting used to our Isle Royale life. It was beginning to feel normal. Distractions like motorboats and seaplanes didn't seem as much of a bother as they were at first. Then I realized that that is part of the problem. We quickly assimilate to distractions and disturbances and no longer see them as problems. Exposure desensitizes us. I believe that is what has happened to many of the folks who work on the island. Their senses have been dulled, and they don't even notice the things that detract from the wilderness park experience. Those distractions and negative elements simply become normal to them.

During my thinking time, two people came down to the rocky shore for a swim near where Julie was painting. I heard one of them remark to the other about a current that he could feel in the water. It reminded me that I have heard there is a mild west-to-east current in Superior. That makes sense because there are many, many water inputs to Superior, but only two outlets. One is evaporation, which does not affect the flow. The other outlet is the St. Mary's River at the far east end of the Lake. So, the entire lake gradually moves to the St. Mary's River, causing a mild current in the lake.

As I was exploring the rocky shoreline near the lodge, I noticed algae on the rocks along a short stretch. I thought it was strange until I noticed a trickle of a creek flowing into Superior from a swampy area. Nutrients. The reason for the algae. As I was jotting these notes, three Canada geese flew over my head at a height of only about twenty feet. It looked like they were flying in slow motion. They seemed unconcerned about my presence, just like when they are walking around on the trails and lawn.

Sitting on shoreline rocks in a natural stone recliner, enjoying the mild breeze and morning sun on my face, I realized that we had finally been on the island long enough that I didn't feel like I needed to be doing something every minute. I was just watching the water and listening to the sounds of the day. And I was content. I could easily do those same things near home, but near home, I would be thinking about all the projects and chores I should be working on. So on the island, where home projects and chores are too far away to deal with, I was perfectly content just watching what the water was doing. I recalled getting chastised once by a magazine editor for including such activities, or lack of activities, in an article I submitted. The editor said that stuff like that was too boring for a magazine article. I understand his point, but to some degree, I disagree. I think many people have forgotten how to just relax and ponder things. I would even go as far as to say that most people have lost the understanding of the benefits of and need for just thinking and pondering on a regular basis. Maybe that is why people as a whole do so many stupid things. They just don't take the time to think. Einstein even noted it as being something everyone should do on a daily basis. That is where new ideas and breakthroughs come from. It's also where books come from.

I read a park sign on the Stoll Trail Half Loop stating that approximately a hundred years ago, the island was vegetated by mostly yew and mountain ash. When moose showed up (swam over), they ate the yew and ash to the point where thimbleberries, which were once rare, flourished. That got me thinking about how interesting and sometimes unpredictable ecological relationships are. Things change. Especially in time spans beyond our normal lifespan. Was Isle Royale better when it was populated by yew and mountain ash, but no moose or wolves? Should the park service have relocated new wolves to the island as they did recently, or just left things alone to see what would happen next? I didn't have any answers. Just questions.

Mid-afternoon, I took a stroll a mile or so down the Rock Harbor Trail. Wind and waves were increasing. Haziness was also increasing, taking the edge off the heat of the sun. I was glad it was not a paddling day. Casually roaming and thinking was proving to be a relaxing change.

The evening brought rain. Finally. The cool air that came in with it — or ushered it in — felt refreshing after four hot, sunny days. I began hoping it would get wildlife moving around, increasing the likelihood of another moose encounter. Maybe even tomorrow.

Island Immersion

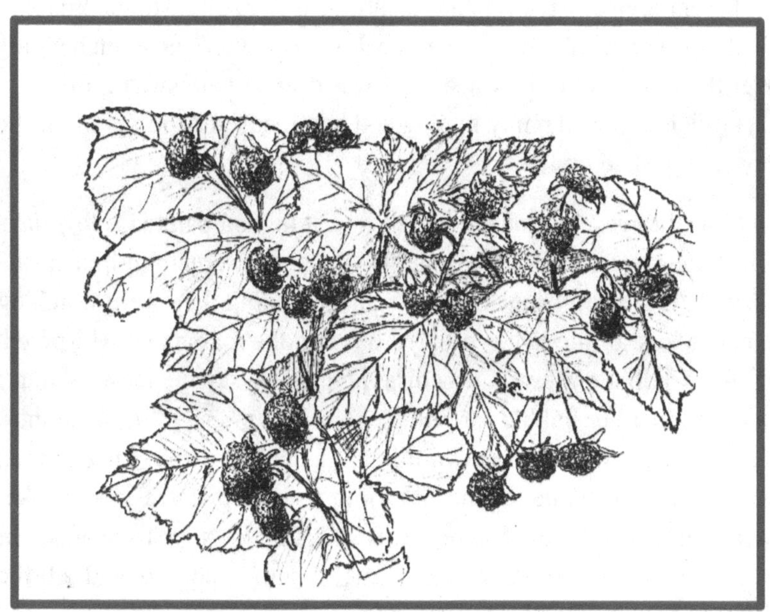

The morning was cool and foggy. It had rained most of the night until shortly before daylight. This was the day I planned to do a roughly sixteen-mile turn-and-burn hike to Mount Ojibway. Conditions were certainly not ideal, but I didn't have another day available. When I started at 8:30 am, I was literally walking in a cloud, so the humidity was probably close to a hundred percent. And it felt like it. With it not being very pleasant weather, I didn't expect to see many people, but that didn't turn out to be the case. Early on, I passed several people heading in to catch the ferry. After that, it was a random collection of hikers and backpackers who were probably in the same situation as me — this was the day they had available. I sweated off my bug spray within the first twenty minutes. Bugs were biting, but it didn't bother me much. Now that I think about it, most of the bugs probably drowned once they landed on me.

The mugginess really started hitting me on the Mount Franklin Trail. I was soaked mid-thigh and below from wet vegetation hanging over the trail. From the waist up, I was soaked with sweat. I did my best to ignore the clammy feeling and just focused on my goal for the day, and pushed on.

Near the west end of the marsh that Julie had painted a few days prior, there were two ladies intently watching something out in the marsh. As I quietly snuck up to them, expecting they were watching a moose, one of the ladies pointed out into the marsh and whispered, "Three sandhill cranes." I was disappointed, to say the least. I didn't want to burst her bubble for being excited by the sight of the cranes, but we see them in our backyard at home almost daily. I understood her excitement, though. The first time I saw a pileated woodpecker was on Isle Royale years ago. I was so excited! Now, I see and hear them all over our property all the time. I smiled politely and left the ladies to their excited bird watching.

When I reached Greenstone Ridge, three backpackers were coming up from Lane Cove and headed out along the ridge in front of me, so I took the opportunity to take a short cool-down and dry off break, letting them put some distance between us. Fortunately, up on the ridge, there was a mild breeze to keep things cooler. Like me, for instance. It was a misty, humid breeze, but it was much better than stagnant air with full humidity. Anyway, I cooled down, but there would be no drying off.

Greenstone Ridge is a patchwork of exposed rock, grass, trees, brush, and trees stunted by the elements, but the main scenery was fog. Several times during my hike, people appeared out of the fog, then soon disappeared again after they passed by.

At Mount Ojibway, I climbed the tower thinking that maybe there was something to see. But the view was the same as from the ground. Fog. I gave up sightseeing and ate my lunch snacks and a handful of fresh blueberries, then chugged a big drink of water. The three backpackers from Lane Cove were moving more slowly than I was, so I had passed them on the trail. They showed up at the tower as I was eating my blueberries. During our brief chat, I found out they were heading to Daisy Farm. After wishing them well, I headed east. Fog was still too thick to see much of anything besides ghosted trees. I didn't pass any other hikers until I started the descent from Mount Franklin. Even then, there were only a few people. At the Tobin Creek crossing, the creek was flowing away from the harbor again. I speculated that maybe it flowed into the harbor in the morning and out of the harbor in the evening or afternoon, but it would require a six-mile morning hike to verify my assumption. Maybe that would happen. Maybe not.

Back on the Tobin Harbor Trail, I encountered lots of people, including what looked like a high school group. Again, a lot of the people didn't seem like hikers or backpackers, but I had to give them credit for at least getting out on the trail. When I got back to our cabin about 2:30 pm, Julie was out and about with our key, so I had to go track her down in order to get into the cabin. While I was looking for her, I realized how much more peaceful the day had been without the seaplanes coming and going due to the fog.

After dinner, the fog thinned out considerably, so we paddled over to the Lookout Louise dock and hung around Hidden Lake for an hour or so in hopes of seeing another moose. We saw a pair of cranes fly over us, but no moose showed up. As we paddled back to what had become home, the entire harbor was quiet and still.

Julie had talked to someone earlier in the day who said they had seen both a moose and a wolf swim across Tobin Harbor the previous day. That made me think about the fact that we only had three more full days to hope for another major wildlife encounter. Then it dawned on me that I really had no room to complain. We probably had the best view of any of the cabins. We saw a big bull moose relatively close. We watched the Northern Lights. We had done a lot of paddling and experienced areas we've never seen before. We met Rolf and Candy Peterson and had a great visit. I explored several areas that were new to me. We encountered a number of otters and loons close up. And we also found out that Julie hasn't really missed anything by not being selected as a formal artist-in-residence on the island. Not to take anything away from a formal residency, but we were having just as good an experience with our own self-planned residency. Things were good.

The following morning was overcast and cool. Julie was working in the cabin for the morning, trying to get a few more mini paintings completed. I spent some time studying our island map, noticing that there was a lot of Isle Royale we had not yet explored, which left a big void in my island experience. There is an entry in my notebook that says: *I imagine finding quiet and solitude in some of these voids, these places I haven't been. It seems that I always envision great places being just around the corner: the next bay, the next lake, the next trail, or maybe the one after that. I'm constantly wondering, where to next? I'm envisioning interior Isle Royale via canoe: water taxi ride to Chippewa Harbor (explore Lake Mason and Lake Richie trails), Lake Whittlesey, Wood Lake, Siskiwit Lake, Malone Bay/Wright Island side trip, Intermediate Lake, Lake Richie, Lake LeSage, Lake Livermore, Chickenbone Lake, McCargoe Cove, Pickerel Cove, Belle Isle area, Five Fingers area, Duncan Bay, Tobin Harbor, Rock Harbor. Nine or ten days should do it. Plan for ten to twelve days in case of waves on exposed areas. That would include a lot of new trails and water. I'm thinking 2025.*

Julie and I took an early afternoon hike a mile or so along the Rock Harbor Trail toward Three Mile. It was reasonably cool when we set out, but the sun soon came out and warmed things up, so we stopped on a cobble beach to cool off in the breeze. Julie ended up lying in the sun with her eyes closed on an old plank board that had washed up on shore. I asked if she was pondering paintings. She said, "Yeah", in a "Whatever" tone of voice. As I investigated the beach, I was amazed at all the quartz or quartz-like variations I have seen on Isle Royale beaches. Many of them contain green, so they most likely have a copper component. I also thought about how surprised I was at the number of ripe thimbleberries along the trails. Even popular, heavily used trails. I would have thought they would be picked as soon as they ripen. I wasn't complaining because I was happy to pick and eat them. I was just surprised that more people didn't do the same.

Looking out at the water and the islands across the harbor, it felt strange not to stay in the backcountry at all during this trip. I felt like I needed to apologize to someone for it. Maybe myself. Or I felt I at least needed to explain my reasoning when I tell someone that we are staying in a cabin. In a way, we were privileged to be able to stay in a cabin for two weeks. But in another way, it made me feel like a softy. I consoled myself with a reminder that we at least still had a Minnesota Boundary Waters backcountry camping excursion coming up soon.

While we were cooking dinner in the early evening, a collared wolf supposedly stopped right in front of our cabin door. Our neighbor watched it and relayed the story to us later. I'm sure it was the smell of our bacon cooking that grabbed its attention. I couldn't blame the beast. The smell of bacon cooking grabs my attention, too. Particularly if I'm hungry to start with. We were just disappointed that we missed seeing the wolf ourselves. Especially since it was standing right in front of our door.

Later, we took an evening canoe cruise to Hidden Lake, in search of moose again. And again, we didn't see any moose, but the marsh and swamp were interesting, and the moose hunting itself was fun. On our paddle back to our cabin, a hen merganser and several chicks popped up from underwater about ten feet from our canoe. Unlike with previous surprise pop-ups like that, our presence didn't seem to bother them at all. Looking west down Tobin Harbor, layers of green-gray islands, water, and hills stretched out in front of us in the evening enchantment. In those conditions, even well-known areas look intriguing. It was that time of day when everything takes on a mysterious air.

Overcast and refreshingly cool conditions greeted us first thing the next morning. But the sun came out and warmed things up by about 10 am. Our plan was to launch our canoe from Snug Harbor and explore the rocky islands near the west side of the boat channel coming into the harbor. Attempt number two. It turned out to be choppier than we thought. We peaked out beyond the first row of islands protecting Rock Harbor, and Julie got nervous looking at the waves. So, we pulled back in behind the guardian islands and paddled east to the boat channel. That's where Julie got more nervous, but we had to cross the opening to even return to Snug Harbor. After a brief hesitation, I pushed us out into the relatively narrow channel. It turned out to be fine. One rolling wave splashed a small amount of water over the gunnel, but that was it.

On the other side of the channel, we took the boat out on a cobble beach near the western tip of Raspberry Island. The formal dock was a little farther east, but we decided to just get out where we were and explore the island, where we casually hiked the trails and investigated the rocky shorelines. In the middle of the island is a bog where we found a smattering of small tamaracks. Even though they were still summer-green, I could envision them soon lighting up the bog with autumn gold. The south side of Raspberry was all rugged, rocky shoreline. Julie spotted a pair of otters there, but we didn't get to spend any time with them because they headed out into open water and quickly vanished without a trace as soon as they saw us.

At the southwest end of the island, we decided to take advantage of a shady section of the cobble/boulder beach where we enjoyed a lakeside view of the channel, rocky islands (where we'd tried to explore earlier), and breaking waves, while we relaxed and enjoyed our sunny Isle Royale day. When we were ready to leave Raspberry Island, I was hoping to paddle east a little more, but Julie was still concerned about the minor rollers and choppiness. So we paddled east just to the dock area, then spun to quarter with the waves and made our crossing back to the main island, rounding the point at the old *America* Dock.

At the Snug Harbor beach, I began the familiar portage back up to our cabin. I had portaged to and from Cabin #210 almost daily for nearly two weeks. It was becoming a routine. Being near the east end of Isle Royale, with a small collection of trails available, our canoe had become our primary means of transportation. I don't know about Julie, but I had certainly settled into a paddling mindset. We did a considerable amount of hiking as well, but paddling was our primary means of travel. When you're in a watery world, you paddle. Isle Royale is certainly a watery world. Molded and sculpted by water. Guarded by water. Fed by water. Isolated by water. On the largest island in the largest freshwater lake in the world, paddling is the way to go. I know power boats, of which it seems like there are legions around Isle Royale, are faster and easier ways to travel, but nothing beats foot power or paddle power for intimate wilderness travel. It seems like when people come to the island, we want it to be wilderness, but then again, in some ways, we don't. We want to be able to get to the island quickly and easily, get around quickly, and get out quickly. We want comfy accommodations, meals prepared, and baggage hauled. Cell service and internet? Silly question. The introduction the National Park Service gives to arriving visitors asks, "How wild is it?" The honest answer is, in some places, "Not so wild". Especially around Rock Harbor. Sure, the animals are wild. The surrounding Superior waters are certainly wild. The terrain is no doubt wild. Still, we seem to be doing our best to tame the beast. To subdue it for our personal convenient enjoyment and amusement.

I overheard a guy talking on his cell phone, telling someone, "Man, we're like practically off-grid here." As he proudly made that declaration, he was using his cell phone outside a restaurant, surrounded by a large complex of buildings with running water and electricity. Overall, I think our society's idea of wilderness is getting watered down. In fact, I don't think most modern people could truly deal with real wilderness with no general conveniences or easy access. As a society, we tend to be a little spoiled, and sometimes, not very motivated. Everything needs to be powered — by something other than us.

What would Isle Royale be like without all the modern conveniences like seaplanes, motorboats, tractors, electric carts, generators, and the like? Well, peaceful for one thing. It would be quieter and cleaner. More natural. It would be, well, wilderness. The home of peace and serenity and solitude. Not that I'm suggesting we wipe the slate clean and eliminate all that modern stuff. It's just interesting to think about.

We took our usual evening paddle in Tobin Harbor, purposely waiting until the sun had lost its midday intensity. Instead of going straight to Hidden Lake and hanging around to see if any moose showed up, we first investigated some of the islands near the east end of the harbor. Even though we'd paddled around them before, islands are always intriguing. Besides, it was a good excuse to do a little extra paddling, just enjoying being on the water, before we paddled over to the Lookout Louise dock and pulled our canoe out. On the way over, we had a loon cruise past us at about twenty feet. I was hoping Julie got some good pictures. She's always our official trip photographer.

When we arrived at the dock, there was an aluminum rental canoe tied up there with fishing gear in it. We could only assume the paddlers were at Hidden Lake looking for moose, or up at Lookout Louise. Being that we were planning to make the climb to the lookout in addition to looking for moose, finding a canoe already there didn't exactly please me. Still, we hoped for the best and stuck with our plan. Hopefully, we would cross paths with the other visitors somewhere in the old burn area, where I highly doubted we would see a moose anyway. But the higher we climbed without crossing paths, the more I became concerned that the "competition" from the other canoe might screw up our wildlife viewing chances. I tried to stay positive and prayed that this situation wouldn't mess up our evening.

As we approached the lookout, I saw someone sitting there on a rock. It was a young guy who wasn't even taking in the view. He was just messing with his cell phone and gave no indication that he even knew Julie and I were there. Then I heard a cough from just up the trail at another vantage point. We enjoyed the view and cooling breeze from where we were for a few moments, then just quietly retraced our steps back down to Hidden Lake, where there still wasn't a moose, and out to our boat. The paddle back, just before sunset, was a peaceful way to end our day. Even the people gathered at the dock were all quietly taking in the sunset. One of them had taken a nice picture of us paddling in and offered to email it to us. We certainly appreciated the offer and were looking forward to receiving the picture. As usual, the outdoor adventure portion of my day ended with me portaging the canoe back to our cabin. Quietly, of course.

It was sunny and mild the next morning. Loons were calling, which is one of the things I loved about being on the island. We had been hearing loon calls throughout the day, every day. Around lunchtime, we took a stroll down to scope out where we could set up Julie's miniature paintings for a small public display. On the way down to the main harbor complex, we met the guy we'd been seeing hanging around a park bench with a big lens on his camera. He turned out to be a lawyer from near the Twin Cities, but in Wisconsin. And he did actually get a picture of the wolf that was hanging around. He showed it to us. The markings were certainly wolf, but the look on its face was just an exasperated dog. The caption I would give it is, "Oh great, another dang person. These things are everywhere!" The wolf was wearing a radio collar, so it had no privacy at all. I assume the island wildlife breathes a sigh of relief when the summer tourist season ends. Much like most of us living in tourist areas do. I say that, even though I'm a part-time tourist myself.

It was hard to believe we were already on our last full day of island life. Like all trips, even the longer ones eventually come to an end. And the end seems to come quickly. In some ways, our "old" life was still hanging around in the shadows. In other ways, our present life had become the new normal. Especially during the middle portion of the trip. That day, with only one day left, the cares, concerns, and responsibilities of my real normal life based in Deerton were beginning to take center stage again. I was beginning to write lists for when we got home. It seems to require a trip of about ten days or so to give your mind a chance to shift to a new normal. Minimum of a week for sure. Less than that, your body is present in the new location, but your brain is still back home, or at work, or wherever it normally primarily resides. So, where is our "real" life? Is it where we primarily live, at our mailing address? Or is it where we physically are at any given time? Well, being that our belongings are just temporary and really have no significance, I would tend to say that real life is where we currently are at any given time. But I'm sure that could easily be debated.

Wilderness gives us an opportunity to switch gears. To spend time in the life we were originally meant to have. To be the person we were designed to be. As human beings, our intended home was within nature. Somewhere, programmed into our brains, that connection still exists, whether we want to acknowledge it or not. Even diehard city dwellers have a natural streak buried somewhere. When we immerse ourselves in nature, that natural connection begins to come to the forefront. Time in the wilderness intensifies that connection and amplifies those hidden feelings. Some of us spend enough time in natural settings that our natural connections never get hidden. They stay in the front of our consciousness. We like it there. In fact, some of us love it there. And so, we take trips, relatively long trips, to places like Isle Royale. Places where our wilderness contact can be an immersion, not just a brief encounter. When we're on the island, especially for a long stay, this _is_ life.

Late afternoon, we hiked to Scoville Point via the Tobin Harbor side of the trail loop. Along the way, we met a park volunteer on the trail. A friendly guy we had talked with a few times already. He told us he had seen a cow and calf moose on the Rock Harbor side of the trail an hour earlier. So, we kept our eyes peeled, as the two sides of the trail loop are not far apart. We never saw the moose, and the hike took longer than we expected, which is not uncommon. It was also warmer than we thought, which seemed to have been a common theme throughout our stay.

Out at the point, Julie captured even more reference pictures. I poked around, as usual, and found a tadpole in a small pool atop the Scoville Point rock formation. It was small. Maybe a half inch long or so. It had both front and rear legs, as well as a tail. There was only one. Maybe only one egg had been accidentally transported to the puddle by a bird or something. Or maybe there were originally more tadpoles and only one remained. Regardless of how it came to be there in an isolated puddle, I left it alone.

After our visit to the point, we cooked and ate a quick dinner and headed out for a final evening paddle. During the paddle, Julie finally took a picture of an old, broken-down small cabin on an island in Tobin Harbor, not far from our cabin. It was nothing special. We had paddled past it several times without really giving it any thought. So, on our last evening cruise, I prompted Julie to photograph it while we had the opportunity. As Julie was taking the picture, I wondered about its story. There were quite a few old cabins, some still in use, some broken-down. They all have a story, but most of those stories will never be known by more than a few people. I thought about the fact that the stories of many of the older cabin remains may not reside in the memories of anyone still walking the earth. They're lost to time. During the evening, we also paddled around many of the Tobin Harbor islands, even though we had done it before on previous daily adventures, because we didn't know if or when we would have the opportunity again. Besides the fact that we're getting older, and we don't know what our health and abilities will be like in the future, we also have aspirations to visit other places. Even on Isle Royale. So, I find myself wondering more and more, if I will have an opportunity to revisit specific locations in the future.

As had become our evening practice, we stopped again at Hidden Lake to look for moose. At the landing, I saw my first non-minnow fish of the trip. A sculpin of about two inches. After our moose viewing stop, where we didn't see a moose — again — I spotted my second non-minnow fish during the final half hour of our cruise. That one looked like a small pike. Very small, as in six inches. Our cruise quietly ended, as usual, shortly before sunset. I began missing our evening Tobin Harbor cruises even before I hoisted the canoe onto my shoulders.

Our last day was again sunny and mild. Waves were mild as well. It was mostly a day of waiting. Waiting is difficult. Especially for me. I found myself ready to go home, yet eager to keep exploring the island. During our waiting wanderings — I don't sit around well — I read a sign near the old *America* Dock. The ship served Isle Royale from 1902 to 1928. It hit a reef and sank in Washington Harbor on July 7, 1928. The sign also noted that several frequent passengers later pushed to preserve Isle Royale. I couldn't help but think of how mere tourists helped preserve the island's wilderness. Maybe we have more clout than we realize.

While thinking about that, I contemplated our trip that was quickly coming to an end. In a way, we had the best of both worlds by staying in a cabin. Still, I missed truly being immersed in the backcountry. The day trips were fun and interesting, but we were not really part of the wilderness. We were just daytime visitors, so we missed a portion of the immersion experience. Things like venturing farther from civilization and its amenities than a single day allows. Sleeping out in the wilds, listening to the sounds of wilderness nights. And experiencing the serenity of wilderness mornings.

I wondered what the island would be like if it weren't a managed national park. How could it be better managed? Does it need to be better managed? As is often the case, there were many questions, but not so many answers.

I saw another sign that noted lodges flourishing until about 1930. I've seen pictures of the cabins and lodges from that timeframe, but what about the rest of the island? What did it look like? What condition was it in? I wondered.

We later boarded the ferry, sorry to leave, yet ready to get home and resume our daily life in the outside world. This adventure had come to an end, but many other adventures were still ahead. Like the Isle Royale plans we were formulating for the following year. That's what keeps me going.

CHANGING PLANS

Early August of the following year, we were back on the island. On our first full day on Isle Royale, we heard rain pattering outside the cabin early in the morning. Shortly after Julie's cellphone alarm went off at 5:30 am, we heard mild thunder rumblings and saw faint lightning pulses. No real bolts or bright flashes, just faint strobing pulses that you couldn't pinpoint to a specific location. About 6:30, we began hauling our gear down to the charter dock in hopes that the front would move through and our plans for a water taxi ride to Chippawa Harbor would still be feasible. After three trips from cabin to dock, we were sitting on some wooden lawn chairs, eating breakfast, and telling ourselves that things would work out fine, although I was struggling to convince myself. At 8 am, it began raining again. Lightly, but raining. Then the waves started increasing too, and our hopes began a downhill slide. When I spoke with Captain Bob, he told me that making it to Chippewa Harbor was not looking promising. Waves were running about two feet and building. Making it to Moskey Basin, where the other two passengers, Troy and Allen, were going, shouldn't be an issue, though. Captain Bob said that he'd try for Chippewa Harbor after dropping the other guys off at Moskey Basin if we really wanted him to, but said that it would not be a fun ride. So, we accepted a ride to Moskey Basin as Plan B and loaded our gear on the twenty-four-foot boat, otherwise known as a water taxi, with our bright red canoe riding up top. We had met Troy and Allen the previous day at the Bella Vista Motel in Copper Harbor and again on the Isle Royale Queen IV, so we basically just picked up our conversation where we had previously left off. They told us that Moskey Basin was their Plan B as well, but I don't recall them mentioning what their original plan was. Hard rain hit us as we were approaching the Moskey Basin dock, so after docking the boat, we all just hung out with Captain Bob for a while, waiting for the squall to pass through.

When things calmed down a bit, Troy and I took a recon trip to see if any shelters were vacant. The first three we checked were occupied by people looking like refugees who were waiting out a war. The occupants of the third shelter did say they would be leaving relatively soon, so one of our two groups could take that shelter. The fourth shelter was vacant, which was the second shelter that we needed. We would all have a relatively dry day and a dry sleeping bag, so we ended our search and returned to the boat with the good news. Julie and I ended up standing in the fourth shelter, lightening our food barrel while we watched a pair of loons diving right in front of us near shore.

A little later, during what I believe was round eight of the rain squalls, while Julie was preparing to paint in the shelter, a merganser hen swam by with six puffball chicks in tow. They were all sporadically skittering around and frantically diving. At the same time, several Canada geese were preening themselves on the point just west of us, where Troy and Allen were staying in the fifth shelter. They had moved over there once they realized that it was available, because it had a better view. The rain finally cleared up around noon, letting the sky brighten up, even though clouds still lingered.

With things looking a little more promising, Julie and I launched our canoe for an afternoon paddle around the end of the basin. In a small cove tucked into a corner across the bay, I noticed several bright white spots on a dark rock. As I focused on the spots, a group of mergansers materialized, resting on the rock. The darkness of the rock exaggerated the whiteness of their breast feathers. After noticing the mergansers, I also noticed that, to my dismay, the humidity was climbing.

After paddling along the south side of the basin to the first major point, we turned and crossed to the north side, cutting through waves that the increased wind was stirring up. The crossing was choppy, but at least it was dry. We ducked in behind a small island along the north shoreline to hide from the waves, then made our way into a creek at the end of the basin. As we paddled and poled our way up the creek, I noticed that we were traveling with the flow instead of against it. I assumed the flow direction must have resulted from a seiche, just like what we had seen happening in Tobin Creek the previous summer. By the time we got back to our shelter, the sky had clouded up again, and it looked like another squall was blowing through, which made me extremely thankful for the protection of the roof over our heads. After a hard, ten-minute rain, things mellowed back out again.

Later, while I was cooking dinner, a troop of twenty-six mergansers came by right along the shoreline. There was a lone loon just offshore, low in the water and looking like it had an attitude. At the sight of the loon, the mergansers all high-tailed it to the safety of nearby rock outcrops at water level. The group ended up split between rocks on both sides of the little bay by our shelter. After the loon left, the mergansers on our side of the little bay all scurried across the water to join the rest of their group. United again, they all settled in for a twenty-minute power nap. Then they all got back in the water and swam off down the shoreline.

By 6 pm, it was gray again, but dry. Two hours later, I was sitting at the picnic table on the dock, writing while Julie painted. The hen merganser and her brood of fluffball chicks were there. They all dove in unison whenever mom dove. I was wondering if the kids were chasing fish or just down there watching and learning. Whatever they were doing, it was comically entertaining.

It would have been extra relaxing to have a fire, but no fires are allowed at Moskey Basin. It also would have been relaxing to have a cup of tea or coffee, but we had opted not to bring those luxuries in order to trim down the bulk of food we were carrying on our ten-day venture. We turned in about 10 pm, surprised that we only had a couple of mosquito visitors. I really wasn't tired, so I just lay there thinking, not knowing exactly where my thoughts were going.

First, I thought about how well our new blowup sleeping pads worked. I also thought about our new water filters. Time would tell how well they work, but so far, so good. I also thought a lot about the rest of our backcountry venture and if I had made good plans and good choices. I was especially concerned about the two-mile-plus portage to Lake Richie. Pretty much everything sounds readily doable when you're planning things a year in advance. When it comes down to the wire, there seems to be a little more room for doubt. Again, we would see. With a full moon shining bright, I finally fell asleep sometime after … well, sometime.

After a comfortable sleep, we awoke to a calm orange sunrise, making me feel good about the day. As I was getting dressed, I realized that the new sleeping pads must have worked well if I slept comfortably on a hardwood floor. Julie was willing to do the Lake

Richie portage, and it sounded better to me again, too. Things just tend to seem better in the daylight. We hit the trail about 7:30 am with the air heavy and moist. The trail was a mud slog. My canoe pack with Julie's daypack tied on top likely weighed about seventy-five pounds. It pulled hard on my shoulders. Julie's canoe pack was probably around fifty pounds, so it wasn't a stroll for her either. We reached Lake Richie about 9 am, took a cooldown break to help dry my wet t-shirt, and headed back for our second load. During the trek back to Moskey Basin, we kept our minds off the conditions by focusing on the scenery and munching on thimbleberries whenever we could.

Following a brief visit with the two gals who were moving into our shelter after we left, we had a few snacks and a long drink on the rocks near the dock, then marched off again toward Lake Richie. With the canoe, portage pads, seat cushions, paddles, and my day pack, I was probably carrying about 75 pounds again. And it felt like it! By that time, it was warm and sunny, but not quite as muggy. Still, I set the canoe down and took a short break three times during the long portage. A stiff breeze kept trying to take control of the canoe as I crossed open areas, but it did help cool me down. While hoofing the canoe and full daypack across the long portage, it seemed like everyone we met along the trail either thought we were top-notch adventurers or just plum crazy. The verdict was still out in my mind.

We finally made it back to Lake Richie at 1 pm. A pair of swans and a loon greeted us when we arrived. The individual campsites were full, so we took the first group site, which was much more open and roomier than the individual sites anyway. Regardless, it felt good, and even a little triumphant, to set the canoe down at camp.

As soon as we cooled down and dried off a bit, we set up the tent and canopy. I also filtered three quarts of water, because our bottles were almost all empty. As I was filtering, four loons cruised by. It looked like a pair of adults with two grown chicks. They were soon serenading us with echoing calls out on the open lake.

While I was cooking dinner, one of our camp neighbors stopped by to look at our canoe. He said that a father-son group he passed earlier on the trail told him about a couple they saw portaging a canoe like that into Lake Richie. He told us that the father and son were both very impressed, which I took as a compliment as opposed to thinking we were plum crazy.

At about 6 pm, we continued the tradition we started the previous year when we stayed in a cabin and took an evening cruise in our canoe. West of camp, we found a small hidden waterfall back in the brush. I heard it as we paddled by, so we paddled over to investigate. Getting out of the canoe and poking around in the brush, I found a small stream, probably two feet wide, tumbling into a pool of flowering lily pads. Then it just quietly diffused into the lake with no apparent flow.

Just before we reached the designated canoe camp, we saw a pair of swans, just quietly being swans. At the canoe camp, there was a large, shed moose antler that we took a picture of. It was sitting at the base of the camp signpost. I would have loved to bring it home, but it's illegal to remove things like that from the island. So I just mentally drooled over it as we passed by.

Just past the camp, we saw a trio of swans and several loons, some of which I'm sure were youngsters. As we explored the long south arm of the lake, a large bird that looked like an owl took off from a shoreline tree and flew out across the water. It was mostly white on the head and breast/belly, with dark wings and back. I couldn't find an owl like that later in my bird book, so I wondered if it might have actually been an osprey, and I just didn't get a good enough look at its head.

On our way back through the main part of the lake, we passed a pair of cranes in a small bay, bathed in evening sun. They were not the moose we were hoping to see, but we enjoyed our evening cruise around the lake just the same. We also enjoyed a quiet evening in camp, except for the buzzing of mosquitoes once it got dark. Julie turned in about 9:30 pm. I followed about a half-hour later, when I got tired of fighting off the bugs.

Thankfully, it was a relaxing, bug-free night in the tent. Amazingly, we somehow only had one nature call. Clouds began moving in by morning. The lake was still, disturbed only by the dimples of feeding fish. The loon calls that serenaded us throughout the night continued into the morning. Bugs were even mellow during the morning calm. We were sore from the previous day's portaging, but relaxed. Getting out of the tent was noticeably more difficult than it used to be. I found myself thinking that tents must just be getting more difficult to get up in and out of than they used to be. I decided I should bring that to the attention of tent designers. We left camp about 9:30 am to explore our way down to Chippewa Harbor and back in order to see the lakes we missed because of not being able to begin our adventure at Chippewa Harbor in the first place. As we paddled past the Lake Richie canoe camp, a loon surfaced only about twenty feet in front of us, yodeled, then dove again. It soon popped back up right behind me and yodeled again. It was getting to be sunny and hot out on the water, but there was a mild, refreshing breeze. The world felt bright and new.

As we paddled toward the portage trail to Intermediate Lake, we noticed the actual portage is a little farther east than we expected. We thought we'd found it the previous day, during our evening cruise around the lake. I was glad that we only had a day pack and a canoe to carry because the trail went up, up, and up. I began wondering where the other side of the hill was. Once we finally reached a flatter section, there was a fresh big aspen lying across the trail, adding to the already ample deadfall collection. Bushwhacking with a sixteen-foot canoe on your shoulders is always a treat. Intermediate Lake looked larger than I remembered from our visit with our kids twenty-some years ago. It was certainly picturesque, though, like most Isle Royale water bodies.

The portage to Siskiwit Lake was a stroll through the open woods until we encountered another big aspen blow-down covering the trail. It fell into some older deadfalls, making for a challenging bushwhack to get around them all. On the upside, thimbleberries were plentiful. Even with the canoe on my shoulders, I managed to savor several berries as I passed by.

When we reached Siskiwit, it looked bigger than big. To paddle around it would likely be a day's journey. Fortunately, wind and waves were mild, so we didn't really need to tuck in amongst the east-end islands for shelter, but we did anyway, as it was a convenient route to the Wood Lake entrance. It took a bit of searching, but once we found the passageway behind the islands, it was obvious. While we were paddling through the islands, a lone loon popped up close to us, dove, and quickly popped up again, calling and carrying on like something was wrong. There wasn't another loon in sight, but we still just quietly moved on and let it be.

The Wood Lake campsite, which is right near the entrance channel, was traditionally marked with a shed moose antler near the signpost. It looked like a camp I would like to stay at sometime. Based on its location, I suspect that it doesn't get a lot of traffic, which would provide both solitude and serenity.

We stopped for lunch at the portage to Lake Whittlesey. It was a shady, breezy spot in a patch of ripe thimbleberries. Just the perfect remedy for a hot and humid sunny day. It felt cheery just being there. I wanted to stay longer, but I knew we still had a long excursion ahead.

Whittlesey was long, certainly not the caliber of Siskiwit, but plenty long when you know you'll be paddling the entire length and back again. Like all Isle Royale lakes we've seen and experienced,

Whittlesey is a beautifully tranquil wilderness lake. As we paddled eastward, wind and waves were beginning to build momentum, and I was sure the same thing was happening over on Siskiwit. Based on that and the time we had remaining in the day, we decided to leave our canoe at Whittlesey and just hike over to Chippewa Harbor to at least get a look at it, even if we couldn't paddle around it. The added bonus was that with my hands free, I could sample more thimbleberries. When we reached the harbor, part of me was disappointed that we were not able to get out onto the water and explore it. But, looking at a relatively large sailboat anchored out in it, another part of me thought that the wilderness characteristics and charm we were seeking might have been compromised there anyway, and it would be better to just imagine the beauty we were missing.

We got our exercise paddling back down Whittlesey straight into the wind and waves, but Wood Lake was relatively calm due to its smaller size. As we emerged into Siskiwit, the waves didn't look bad. As we got close to leaving the shelter of the islands, though, things looked a little different. Waves weren't terrible, but they were not exactly good either. They were not a serious threat, but they certainly deserved some respect and caution. I made sure we were quartering either with or into the waves as we paddled through open channels between islands, then quartered with the waves again until we rounded the last point and were able to ride them down the rest of the lake. Fortunately, the portage landing was sheltered just enough to prevent us from getting battered as we exited the canoe and pulled it out of the water. Overall, we took in a few rogue splashes on Siskiwit, but there was no harm done. Back on Lake Richie, we saw three other canoes and a pair of kayaks. Two of the canoes were sitting near the canoe-camp sign, where I was going to have Julie take my picture with the big moose antler there. Not wanting to look like a tourist, I decided to skip the picture.

We made it back to camp about 6:30 pm, much earlier than I originally expected. Dinner and camp chores were done by 8:30 pm.

After the sun set behind the ridge, we relaxed and waited for the onslaught of mosquitoes that typically began about 9:30 pm to push us into our tent for the night. There were a few loon calls and a swan that sounded like it was having issues, then all was quiet. I thought I heard a stick snap a couple of times. Maybe I did, maybe I didn't. It was a peaceful night despite all the human company we had on the lake. The three-quarter moon shone brightly as a night light.

Early morning was overcast, but the sun soon broke through. We hit the water at 8:30 am on our trek north to explore Lake LeSage and Lake Livermore. Maybe even Chickenbone. We were originally planning to paddle and portage all our gear up to Chickenbone and on to McCargo Cove, but with Julie's back acting up and weather concerns for getting from McCargo to Pickerel Cove in the open lake, we finally decided to revamp our trip once again. The new plan was to daytrip as far as Chickenbone, then back out through the Moskey Basin trail, and then through Rock Harbor over to Tobin Harbor and out to Merritt Lane. I was originally reluctant to give up on my plan to complete a big loop, ending back at the Rock Harbor ferry dock, but after a long night of contemplating the risks involved with physical issues and recent weather patterns, I concluded it was the right thing to do. So I readjusted my mental map with the new plan and hoped it proved to be a wise choice.

The trail to Lake LeSage was a typical Isle Royale trail, but the portage spur trail out to the water was a cross between a poor trail and a bushwhack. So we fought our way through the swamp and bog to find a beautiful, quiet lake. We were the only people on the hourglass lake. Just us and the birds and the breeze, along with a menagerie of ducks and loons. I had to mentally mark the portage from the lake, otherwise we would have a tough time finding it on our way back. We watched several loons while exploring the bottom half of the hourglass. One flew past us about ten feet off the water, then circled the lake a few times, passing us on each lap. Another loon surfaced right by us and did a quick emergency dive without any vocalization at all. Just a splash. A couple of minutes later, a turtle did the same thing, only without the splash. From what I saw, I was pretty sure it was a common painted turtle.

On the north branch of the hourglass, I looked into the trees to see the shear-cut boulders of the shoreline covered in luxuriously plush moss beginning about two feet in from the water's edge. The multi-colored carpet extended far up into the woods, giving the woods a pillow for a floor. Looking around, I noticed that haze from the Canadian wildfires was slowly flowing back in, continuing the hazy summer we had been experiencing at home.

The portage to Livermore was boggy in spots. There was also a big new aspen deadfall across the trail that had been hollowed out so you could climb through. Without a canoe on your shoulders, that is. I had to slide the canoe through on the lower small trunk, then climb through myself. I was happy to see and hear that Lake Livermore was peaceful and quiet, just as we had experienced on LeSage. The only other occupants that we could see were a pair of loons. The west end of the lake, where we entered, was under the command of a legion of water striders, randomly skating around.

At the east end of the lake, we came across a young bald eagle sitting on a large horizontal tree trunk, eating a fish. As we completed our tour of the lake, we saw a few painted turtles sunning on logs or rocks. I felt bad that our intrusion cut their sunning short.

As we approached the portage trail to Chickenbone Lake, we were debating whether we wanted to make the haul over or not. Darker clouds were rolling in, so we weren't sure if we wanted to continue on or head back. When we got to the portage, a family was spread out there, relaxing, and a boy was standing knee deep in the lake fishing, right where we would have needed to come in. We waited for a minute, but nobody looked like they had any intentions of getting out of the way so we could use the portage trail. Not being canoers, they were probably oblivious to the fact that it was a portage trail they were blocking. After a brief discussion, Julie and I decided to just move on and head back to camp. Dark clouds were still thickening anyway.

It began raining as we reached Lake LeSage, so right at the lake, I set one end of our canoe on a tree branch to create a makeshift lean-to shelter. It only rained hard for about two minutes, then the droplet rings on the water were replaced by tiny dancing shimmers on the lake surface. A few minutes later, we were back to raindrops again, then shimmers. We managed to find the portage out of LeSage through the bog and arrived back at Lake Richie about 2:15 pm. Dark clouds had cleared, and it was cheery and sunny with a welcome cooling breeze. Later, we were planning on an evening paddle to scout for moose, but rain clouds began drifting through again. Midway through the evening, a gap in the storm clouds allowed the sun to illuminate some big, puffy white clouds to the south. We sat on the rocks in front of camp, talking, planning, and trying to decide. About 8 pm, it started raining again, which finalized our plans, so I put away our canoeing gear. We mostly just relaxed by the lake for the rest of the evening. Until the mosquitoes came out.

We hit the trail back to Moskey Basin about 7:45 the next morning. Loons were taking off from Lake Richie, leaving wakes on the surface like tiny motorboats. Less than a hundred yards from camp, there was a collection of large wolf tracks in the muddy trail. It made me think about some of the noises I heard in the night. The first trek to Moskey Basin with our canoe packs was uneventful, except for finding more wolf tracks in the trail. I reached the shelter area about 8:50 am, and found Shelter #5 was open. Perfect! I wanted either #4 or #5, based on our earlier visit. Julie was only about fifteen minutes behind me, so we headed back for our second load together. About a half mile into the return two-plus-mile trek, Julie's back was bothering her. So, not wanting it to turn into a serious issue, I left the canoe by the trail and carried the food barrel for her, while she carried my lighter daypack. Later, I went back for the canoe on a third portage. At about

2:30 pm, I reached our Moskey Basin shelter to find a park ranger visiting Julie. As it turned out, he was just strolling by to say "Hi".

It felt good to have the work of the day done. Not long after we arrived, a group of five younger guys took up residence in Shelter #4. Once they arrived, they were the only thing anyone in the area could hear. Their voices echoed across the basin and back, really degrading a beautiful place. A place that should have been tranquil and relaxing. I gritted my way through, constantly wanting to go over and say something to them about it. Ever since the COVID debacle, people have been flocking to the outdoors. In one way, that's a good thing. People enjoying the outdoors is great! The problem is that most of these people are wilderness-challenged. They seem to think crowds and noise are normal, so they readily bring these things to the wilderness, which is killing many of the wilderness attributes that most of us love. I don't think most of them mean any harm. They just don't know any better. Unfortunately, some of them probably don't really care either.

About the time that I didn't think I could take anymore, the five mouths next door finally quieted down and went into their shelter. Within minutes, my attitude and outlook changed. I felt relieved and relaxed. Finally, I was able to enjoy the remaining fleeting moments of the evening. The world felt right again. The quiet evening ushered in a peaceful night.

We awoke to a tangerine horizon with two dominant stars in the southern sky. The morning was calm and hushed. Unfortunately, peacefulness and serenity are often fleeting, depending on who is with you, or even nearby. As I was quietly eating breakfast snacks out on the lakeside rocks in front of our shelter, absorbed in the morning, our neighbors emerged from their shelter. Serenity was no more. I tolerated it for a while as we packed our gear until I finally just couldn't deal with them stealing the wilderness from me anymore. I walked over and had a chat with them. I tried to be as nice about it as

I could, but I was sure they could tell I was struggling not to just unload on them. I knew anger was in my eyes. None of them even responded. They all just stared at me, wide-eyed. Everything was quiet as I walked back to our shelter. Within about five minutes, they were packed up and gone. Even though we were leaving soon ourselves, I felt like I had regained my morning, taking it back from a group of thieves. We launched our boat into a calm, tranquil basin, passing a trio of loons that were unusually quiet. Then, a lone loon, some distance away, let out a call. A long, serene call.

Looking down, I realized how much I like paddling through semi-shallow water, where bottom features are visible, but not so clear that they are pure fact. I like it when there is just enough haziness to leave some details to the imagination. Although in these situations I find that it's difficult to watch where you're going because you don't want to miss what you're going over.

It was tempting to stop at the Edisen Fishery and the Rock Harbor Lighthouse, but we wanted to get a shelter or campsite at either Tookers Island or the Rock Harbor Lodge area. I was also tempted to stop to ask Rolf and Candy why there are so few moose bones and antlers visible at the research cabin compared to the previous year, but again, timing was a concern. The other concern was that the breeze was increasing, and we were beginning to wonder how it would be crossing the open areas between protective islands. When we reached Tookers Island, the waves were not menacing, but they needed some respect. Due to the fact that we could possibly be stranded on Tookers if the waves increased much more, we decided to push on to the Rock Harbor Lodge area instead, which was only about another thirty minutes of paddling anyway. We arrived at Snug Harbor about 10:50 am to find that all the shelters were already occupied. Since no ferries had arrived with new people yet, and there is a one-night stay limit (so everyone there from the previous day should be leaving), I suspected that some people might be at least bending the rules. There was no way to prove that, and I don't think park staff actually check, so I took the first available campsite, which was campsite #1, and went back to help Julie with the rest of our gear.

The Rock Harbor Lodge area was a chaotic mass of people, many of whom had no idea what they were doing. Well, at least we had a place to stay that would give us a good start the next day. I ended up being pleasantly surprised at how quiet it was around the shelters and camps. It certainly wasn't what I expected.

Around 2:30 in the afternoon, I was sitting at the picnic table in camp, writing notes. Something caught my attention. I looked up to see a wolf staring at me from only about twenty feet away. Just beyond the edge of our campsite. It was wearing a collar, which seemed to detract from the novelty of the situation, but it was indeed a wild wolf. Once our eyes met, the wolf angled off into the brush between camps and disappeared. A few minutes later, it came strolling down the main campground trail, only about twenty feet away, to the other side. I wondered if it was the same wolf that someone spotted outside our cabin a year earlier, sniffing the aroma of the bacon we were cooking. The family in the camp next to us saw the wolf as well, and a young couple at another nearby camp said that when they returned to their camp, the pack that they carried their cook stove in had been dragged across their campsite.

That evening, we cheated a bit by eating a burger at the Rock Harbor Grill and taking a shower. Still, the campground was officially in the wilderness zone of the park, so I didn't feel too bad. I took a stroll as it was getting dark, just because that's what I do. As I was walking down the main trail through the shelters, I ran into the neighborhood fox. It ducked into a shelter trail and cut through the thimbleberries to avoid me. I just smiled and headed for our tent. There were always interesting things to see. Even in the campground.

AND MORE PLAN CHANGES

It was a quiet, uneventful morning at the Rock Harbor camp. I triple-portaged down to the seaplane dock to save wear and tear on Julie, keeping her back discomfort to a minimum. We loaded up and hit the water at 8:40 am, heading to Merritt Lane. Crossing the open area near Scoville Point, a few of the waves had white manes, but it was mostly just two-foot rollers. As we first paddled into the area, the waves were much smaller. The bigger rollers didn't hit until we were halfway across or more. At that point, it was safer to just push on a little farther than to try to turn around. We cruised into the Merritt Lane camp a little after 10 am. The shelter and campsite were taken by kayakers who had arrived about fifteen minutes before us. So, we ended up taking a make-shift campsite somewhat behind the shelter. It was perched on a small hill, so the view out through the islands in front of camp was nicer than being right down near the water. The kayakers turned out to be two couples that were related. Graham and Gretchen, who were from lower Michigan, have a camp near Munising, not far from our home. They also have connections with a friend of mine, Nick Simon, owner of Superior Outfitters in Marquette. John and Toni were from Idaho. They were paddling a tandem wooden kayak. Graham and Gretchen were paddling individual wooden boats. Graham had custom-built all three kayaks, beginning with kits. Beautiful boats. Of course, I have a thing for wood anyway.

By about 11 am, the sun was out, so we could dry out our tent and miscellaneous damp gear from the rain the previous night. The sunny, breezy day was comfortable, especially compared to most of the past week with temperatures in the eighties and muggy.

As we were sitting on the dock around 5 pm, a bald eagle flew over, which scattered all the gulls that were floating in front of us. Julie was painting a scene of the layered islands in front of camp. We could see at least five layers of islands, and Julie was trying to capture the depth of the scene. The sunny afternoon gave way to clouds, and the breeze intensified again as we watched a freighter silently pass by out past Blake Point, heading south.

A little later in the evening, Julie and I headed out to explore the islands near camp. We couldn't go too far south or east because we wanted to avoid the waves of the open lake. Julie collected a few reference pictures, then we paddled west through the sheltered islands into a hidden cove. It felt like a small oasis. The water was shallow enough to expose all of the bottom details. Faint water movements reflected the evening sun onto the surrounding trees with a soft disco ball effect. We could hear a hushed version of Superior waves through the trees surrounding the quiet little cove. The experience reminded me that serenity often isn't found where you expect it, but where you least expect it. It's often found in quaint little places, away from the grandeur.

As darkness was creeping in, I was standing on the dock once again. Julie was there as well. Something swirled in the water not far from the dock. Then the head of an otter appeared with a shiny fish in its mouth. It dove again, reemerging onto the shoreline rocks to eat its meal. After gulping down the fish, it disappeared back into the dark water.

I was in the tent at 9:50 pm to prep my sleeping bag, pillow, and blow-up sleeping pad. The tent floor had a slight slope to it, so water bottles and fuel bottles didn't stand up very well. Fortunately, the slope was toward our feet, so sleeping was comfortable. At least it was for me. I didn't think to ask Julie because I was too busy sleeping.

In the morning, we watched the sunrise from the Merritt Lane dock. Clouds were shifting around in the sky, sometimes blocking out the sun. After all the hot days over the past week or so, the morning coolness felt good for a change. My flannel shirt wasn't quite enough to keep me comfortable, which I appreciated.

Julie and I were contemplating yet another change in plans. I think it was "Plan E", which consisted of heading back to Rock Harbor the next day instead of waiting until Monday morning, to avoid the bad weather that was being predicted. Wind and waves are not your friends when you're in an open canoe. Rain either. Even though it would cost us a day in the wilderness, we still had a good visit and fun experiences. Learned a few things, too. I guess that it doesn't really matter if you're smoothly cruising along through "Plan A" or wrestling with "Plan ZZ". In the end, the only thing that really matters is God's plan, which is ultimately salvation through Jesus. As Solomon basically stated in the Book of Proverbs, everything else is just chasing after the wind. It can be fun, but not always very fruitful. It's pretty easy to understand those things when you're looking back, but I've found it's a lot more difficult to accept when you're out in the wilds and your best laid plans are crashing and burning like a bunch of mosquitoes in a bug zapper.

Shortly before 8 am, the sun went into hiding behind a bank of clouds. Roaming around behind our tent, I noticed a few moderate-sized paper birches mingled with the mossy spruces. Not that it mattered. I just tend to notice little details like that. By 10 am, the sun broke through the clouds and regained the sky.

Around 11 am I was surprised to see a wolf standing right next to our tent. It casually walked down to a small rocky bulge and prominently stood there for a few seconds, then strolled down through the thimbleberries and ended up standing right next to our canoe. It then walked out into the open about fifteen feet away from me. We stared at each other for a few seconds, then it turned away, walked past the wooden kayaks that were sitting near the dock, and slowly strolled away down the faint trail out toward Blake Point. It just acted like a big, disinterested dog making its rounds of the neighborhood. Julie took a picture of the wolf while it was standing by the kayaks Graham had built, so she promised to send him the image.

After our new kayak friends departed, heading for Rock Harbor, I suggested that we take a hike out to Blake Point, just to see it. We followed the faint trail that the wolf took toward the point until it petered out. Then we bushwhacked over to the shoreline and did some rock hopping until we reached the rock formation that continued out to the point. It may sound simple, but considering the surface angles, gullies, vegetation, and other features, it probably took us a good hour to reach the point. Of course, that included picture taking, note writing, and blueberry picking. The views of the Merritt Lane islands that Julie photographed were worth the trek. We ended up stopping just short of the navigational marker at the end of the point. The boulder-hopping and climbing route out to the marker was probably doable. For the trip back, though, there would have been a few dicey spots, and I decided the end of Blake Point was not a good place for a fall. Even though we didn't make it to the very end of the point, we still got a decent look at the Passage Island Lighthouse. We also got a look at the Sleeping Giant Provincial Park in Canada.

As we were heading back to camp, we saw a pair of canoes landing at the dock. It turned out to be four twenty-somethings heading for Duncan Bay. They were just stopping by for a late lunch. I warned them about Blake Point. Especially in an open canoe. I actually mentioned it twice because I was concerned for their safety. They said they were going out to take a look and would turn around if things didn't look good. A little while later, I saw them paddling by the dock with no life jackets on. I said a prayer for their safety. That was all I could do.

There was a cool afternoon breeze. Sun and clouds were alternating control of the sky as a blue heron appeared just down the shoreline. Neither of us knew where it had come from. Eventually, it simply disappeared into a small cove.

As we often do, we took an evening cruise in our canoe after dinner. After taking a few pictures right in front of camp and exploring part of one of the rocky islands where the cover of junipers and moss was thick and spongy, we explored a hidden channel that we had not even been aware of. It paralleled Merritt Lane. I thought we were just ducking behind a small island, but it turned out to be a long island that ran the length of Merritt Lane and tied into the open area near Scoville Point. It was peaceful and relatively calm. Too shallow for motorboat traffic, but perfect for our canoe.

At about 8:30 pm, a young man in a motorboat stopped at the dock for the night. He was from the Keweenaw and was working on the island. Having the weekend off, he was spending it away from the Rock Harbor busyness. After just making the voyage from Duncan Bay around Blake Point, he said it was his worst wavy trip ever. He also told us that wind and waves were predicted to be bad for the next couple of days, which wasn't good news for us at all. His plan was to just sleep on his boat and get up to do some fishing early in the morning. When he had first pulled up to the dock, Julie and I were afraid that the peaceful evening we were hoping for had just crumbled, but we were happy to find that he was a quiet, respectful neighbor. We extended the same courtesy.

Sometime during the night, we heard the wind and waves begin. It didn't sound good for our morning plans. Sometime around 5 am, I heard the engines fire up on the boat, then head off into the sound of the wind. Later, we found out that it was actually closer to 3:30 am when our boating neighbor left because the constant harsh bobbing of the boat broke one of the mooring ropes. When we got up around 6 am, the wind and waves still hadn't taken a break. We started packing, even though Julie was inclined to sit tight. The last forecast we had heard was predicting wind and waves to continue with rain added into the mix, so I wanted to make the crossing near Scoville Point before things got any worse. We hit the water at 7:20 with the promise that if the open stretch near Scoville Point looked too menacing, we would turn back and reclaim the shelter. We took advantage of the quiet, protected lane we had recently discovered to provide a smooth paddle to the open area of concern. In that sanctuary, wind and waves didn't exist. It would also provide a safe place to turn around if the need arose. The open area was choppy, with minor rollers. "We" decided to give it a go. At first, I quartered us into the waves to get out enough so that when we changed direction to quarter with the waves, we could make it all the way to the protection of the Tobin Harbor islands. The rollers turned out to be in the twenty-four to thirty-inch range. Not terrible, but big enough that I didn't want to make a mistake, because it could be costly. As we swung in behind the protection of the first island, I felt a slight sense of relief and said a thank-you prayer.

The trip down Tobin Harbor was relaxing, knowing that our little trial was over and we came out dry. Just before we reached the seaplane dock, I was surprised to see a loon with a tiny chick still in its charcoal gray fluff. I couldn't help but wonder if that chick would be ready when weather conditions necessitated a long flight south.

We were pulling our canoe out of the water by 8:30 am, thanks to a wind boost down the harbor. I quickly grabbed a pack and headed for the Rock Harbor Campground, hoping and praying for a shelter to be available. I said another thank you prayer when I saw that four of the first six shelters were open. I put our tag on Shelter #2, which came with a tree-filled view of the harbor. Later in the morning, after hauling all our gear to the shelter, we ran into a couple of our kayak friends from Merritt Lane, Graham and John. I gave them a rough time about the scratches on their wooden kayaks that were sitting on the public boat rack.

We settled into our new home and were out at the old *America* Dock site by 11 am so Julie could work on another small watercolor painting. Looking down the length of Rock Harbor, with a collection of small pinkish-yellow puffy clouds floating overhead, the world felt cheerful and friendly. We had paddled through that scene numerous times and hiked the edges of it. A "been there, done that, and want to do it again" feeling came over me. Any negative thoughts I had about Isle Royale and some of the people we had encountered there faded. Isle Royale is indeed a special place that seems to keep drawing people back, me included. It was the same semi-sunny, breezy, wavy day as it was earlier in the morning, but now that the somewhat iffy paddling was behind us, the day had a whole different feeling to it. The morning held a tinge of semi-nervous anticipation. Now, I simply felt relaxed. Whether the Isle Royale Queen picked us up the next day or not didn't really matter. Sooner or later it would. For the moment, it was time to just live in the moment. To absorb and experience what the island had to offer, including the people we were sharing it with. Later, as we enjoyed a pizza and beer visit at the grill with John, Toni, Graham, and Gretchen, it occurred to me that we truly do have some new friends.

To wrap up the evening, we enjoyed a glass of wine, which was actually in a mug, from what looked like an overgrown juice box, and watched the sunset from the Tobin Harbor Docks. Then we took a quiet walk back to our shelter for a peaceful night's sleep. Living simply felt good. There are two ways you can interpret that last comment. Both are correct.

First thing in the morning, it was still breezy. And wavy. After breakfast snacks, I strolled down to the boat dock to find out that the Isle Royale Queen IV was going to do one run that day to pick up passengers scheduled for the previous day. The plan was to then make two runs the following day to get everything caught up. We would be on the first trip the following day. So, we had a bonus day on the island. Even though it was yet another glitch in our plans, we took it as a blessing and embarked on the rest of our free day.

We purposely didn't make any big plans. It would just be a day to relax, at least somewhat, and live on island time. We took a short stroll along the Rock Harbor trail, ate some thimbleberries, and spent time poking around on a gravel beach, all just a fifteen-minute walk down the trail. Poking around in beach rocks is one of my favorite pastimes. I found a few interesting copper-quartz specimens that caught my interest, which was nothing new. I always seem to find rocks that catch my interest. Even along roadsides.

For lunch, we had whitefish sandwiches at the grill, then began exploring possibilities for a Windigo visit for the following September. About 5:30 pm, we set out on an evening paddle on Tobin Harbor, which ended up at Hidden Lake, looking for moose. Surprising, I know. Afterward, we hiked up to Lookout Louise and took in the panoramic view of Duncan Bay and beyond, one more time. The closest we came to seeing a moose was seeing fresh tracks up near the Greenstone Ridge. We did get to enjoy lots of fresh thimbleberries. And a few raspberries too. The northeast corner of Isle Royale was tugging on my mind. I had originally planned to paddle through that area, but that fell out of the picture a few plan versions ago. I think somewhere around "Plan D", but I couldn't be sure. Regardless, there, looking over the vastness from Lookout Louise, we had the magnificent view to ourselves. Nobody else had ventured up for the evening. Just us, thankfully. We could see Canada in the distance, and I think we could see a bit of Minnesota as well. We were quiet for the entire evening. Stealthy. Still hoping to encounter a moose. But to no avail. Just a few ducks and Canada geese. We arrived back at the dock a little after 8 pm, ready to relax one more evening in our shelter. It was time to wind down, maybe with a mug of wine, and prepare for tomorrow's departure.

The next morning, we leisurely waited for our ferry, while we kicked around plans for a visit to the west end of the island the following year. I never seem to tire of making plans for wilderness wanderings. I never seem to tire of the actual wanderings either.

BOUNDARY WATERS CANOE AREA WILDERNESS

When we took our kids to Isle Royale, one of them got sick on the ferry ride out there, and the other one got sick on the ride back. So, when I mentioned the possibility of another Isle Royale visit a couple of years later, I almost had a mutiny on my hands. That's how we started going to the Minnesota Boundary Waters. Because we could drive there. We've been exploring the Boundary Waters Canoe Area Wilderness (BWCAW) for more than twenty years now. This section follows a variety of those exploration adventures.

QUIET ADVENTURE

As we pulled our truck into the South Hegman Lake parking lot, the dreariness began splashing on our windshield. The early morning mist and mild sprinkles had now crossed the line, and I had to admit to myself that it was actually rain. Just the kind of day you want for the beginning of a five-day, early October canoeing excursion in the Boundary Waters Canoe Area Wilderness. We sat in the truck and ran the heater … just a little longer. I was wondering what was in store for us, but we finally accepted the challenge, hauled the two canoes and all our gear down the 80-rod portage, and launched into the rain-pocked waters of South Hegman shortly before noon. It felt good to finally be underway. The rain was actually more of an off-

and-on sprinkle by then, and it soon became just another part of the adventure.

My wife, Julie, and our fourteen-year-old daughter, Amy, paddled our well-used fourteen-foot Old Town Kingfisher. Our eleven-year-old daughter, Megan, and I commanded the new Kilarney Green Swift Algonquin 16, partly because this arrangement made for a pretty even balance between crew paddling strength and vessel speed, and partly just because I kind of liked paddling the new boat.

The 5-rod portage to North Hegman came up before we even had a chance to develop much of a paddling rhythm. Unloading and loading the boats for such a short portage hardly seemed worth the effort, so, testing our strength, we did it as a carry-over instead, which, in hindsight, was probably pretty stressful on the boats, but they came through without any known issues.

It was a good thing we decided to take pictures of each other as we paddled through the tiny, sheltered finger of water we launched into, because I discovered it was difficult to take pictures with my camera still sitting on the slab of rock between the two lakes. So we made an unscheduled stop at what was deemed to be a "good spot to get out of the canoe". After a short bushwhack, a near swim, and a scramble back through a tangle of deadfall and roots, the camera and I were back in our place in the stern seat.

North Hegman passed by nearly unnoticed in anticipation of the pictographs near the north end of the lake. We had seen them before on a day trip two years earlier, so we knew right where to look. On a small stretch of cliffs where the lake narrows, not far from the Angleworm Lake portage, there they were, still proclaiming their message from times past. The three canoes, the person with outstretched arms, the large antlered moose. I couldn't understand the message, but the pictures somehow had meaning nonetheless. This place was significant to someone else who had paddled these waters and walked the portage trails. The significance remained, just not the specific message. We lingered for a short while, then paddled on.

The longest portage of the week was just ahead, and I wanted to get at it. As we took a short lunch break at the rocky landing, hats and gloves went on and hoods went up in response to the misty breeze coming off the lake.

The trail was rugged with a lot of small ups and downs, soggy spots, and several blowdowns blocking the way. With the portage trail hike quickly warming us up, hoods and hats soon came back off. We made the 460-rod assault in three charges with the leapfrog approach. After the first 80-rod scramble, we decided to drop the gear and go back for the rest of the load, partly because we didn't want to get too far from any of our supplies in nasty weather and partly because walking back without carrying anything sounded appealing at that moment.

The original plan was for me to portage the heaviest canoe on one trip and my canoe pack on the second trip. Julie and Amy were going to take turns with the other canoe on one trip and carry their packs on the second trip. After getting reacquainted with slippery rocks, muck, and crawling over horizontal trees, we decided it would be better for me to take care of both canoes and let Julie deal with my pack. Fully loaded, the old red Kelty frame pack weighed as much as the heavier canoe but was a lot less awkward to carry.

When the last of our gear was finally deposited on the brushy shore of Angleworm, a celebration snack was in order. It was a short snack, though, as the portage took longer than expected and it was late in the afternoon with the sky still not looking very promising.

We paddled the length of Angleworm against a stiff, cold breeze. With the lake being narrow, the waves weren't significant, but the north wind felt like it was driving its chill into us clear to the bone. The time for enjoying scenery had passed somewhere along the portage. Now, as we paddled through the grayness, the only thing we were looking for was the end of the lake and camp. We found it about 6 pm, and scrambled to set up the tent and dig out more clothes. Tiny flames were just beginning to illuminate the fire grate as the grayness broke into crystals that pattered against our nylon tent. The joyful crackling of the fire was hidden by the monotone hiss of my old Svea stove, which we were using to cook with. After a rehydrated dinner (that only tastes good on the trail), we spent a short time staring at the small assembly of flames that were trying bravely to fend off the cold, but the call of warm sleeping bags was too much. We were in the tent before 9 pm, listening to the whisper of a northern Minnesota October night swirling amongst the trees, wondering what the morning would bring.

It came as no real surprise that our first morning in the wilderness was cold. Remnants of the previous night clung to the tent fly and pack covers. We had a quick breakfast of fruit bars and handfuls of stuff from an assortment of Zip-Lok bags, shook the ice off the tent, rolled it up soggy, and were launching the canoes into the promise of a new day by 9:30 am. The lakes and portages passed by in the grayness of morning and early afternoon with a lack of any real detail. Home Lake, Gull Lake, Gun Lake, Fairy Lake, Boot Lake, and the connecting portages were mostly passed and forgotten in our efforts to make progress and stay warm. By mid-afternoon, the sun began to fight its way through the overcast sky as we made camp on a tree-covered point on Boot Lake, which was the last camp before our portage to Fourtown Lake. We spread the tent on the yellowing bushes to dry in the breeze as we ate pre-dinner snacks and settled in. Our tent was soon dry and pitched on a mostly flat spot away from the fire grate. The wind faded along with the daylight as we boiled water for our one-pot meal, so we built a small fire. There's nothing like poking sticks into a fire in the backcountry ... for kids of all ages. Just before dark, a lone beaver patrolled the shore around the point. It slapped the water, apparently annoyed at our choice of campsites. We lost sight of it as it melted into the darkening bay on the backside of the point. Stars soon took over as the chill settled in. Julie and the girls turned in for the night after a short stint by the fire. I waited for the flames to die out in hopes of a northern light show. But I only lasted another half hour or so, then the promise of warmth pulled me into the tent, too. During the night, I awoke to the faint sound of wolfish howls drifting through the darkness. I smiled. The howls faded away. I did as well.

The third day dawned with the warm, yellow glow of a perfect October morning. It felt good to be alive and on a grand adventure. Our normal morning routine of breakfast snacks and packing ended with a 9:30 canoe launch, when we raced each other across the end of Boot Lake to our first portage. The short journey to Fourtown followed a small stream through a notch in the hills surrounding the end of Boot Lake. As I hauled the canoes, listening to the trickling stream, I thought of the Native Americans who had walked the same trail long before me. I imagined the sights and sounds had probably not changed much. Maybe one of those previous travelers painted the pictographs we saw earlier in the trip. There were plenty of things to think and wonder about, as there usually is in the wilderness.

The put-in at Fourtown was a large slab of rock divided by the stream we had followed over. Huge boulders were scattered about, likely deposited by a dying glacier. We took some pictures and had a snack on one of the large lakeside boulders. Soaking up the sun felt good, as it usually does on an Indian summer day in the north. Fourtown was a lake I wanted to return to when I had more time to explore. The multitude of islands, rugged shoreline, rocky ridges, and surrounding forest beckoned, but unfortunately, we were just passing through. Exploring the area would have to wait for another time on another visit. It was still early in the day, and we didn't know what adventures lay ahead or how difficult it would be to find a campsite. So, we made a somewhat precarious launch off the slab, leaving some telltale green marks to accompany the array of other colors previously deposited on the rock, and continued on our journey.

Across the lake, as we eased our way into the bay that housed our portage out of Fourtown, we discovered low water and beavers had created two obstacles not acknowledged on our map. Just before the first carry-over, we spotted a whitetail browsing along the shore. It was a stocky north woods buck that probably weighed two-hundred-plus pounds, with a stout, chocolate-colored eight-point rack. As we tried to close the gap for photos, he munched his way back into the shadows and melted away as only whitetails can.

At the first unplanned portage, the combination of rocks and mud caused much discussion between the captain and crew, but we ultimately decided it was a bit too treacherous for a carry-over, so we unloaded the boats. The little, no-name bay we entered was home to a beaver who slapped the water in protest to our intrusion. We just smiled at its indignant gesture and moved on.

The second obstacle was a beaver dam still under construction. The structure was mostly submerged and still had enough give to it to allow us to slide over without getting out of the boats.

We made camp on Horse Lake mid-afternoon, right across the lake from the mouth of the Horse River. The whole campsite opened onto a rippled slab of rock that sloped down to the water. Several dips in the rock made perfect seats for a comfy dinner spot. As we ate, two other canoes cruised past from Tin Can Mike Lake, apparently looking for a site, making me glad we stopped when we did.

As the flames flickered that evening, I pondered the portage trails, the water, the woods, and the feeling of this place. With the designation of "wilderness," it's now probably much like it was in the days of Native American trails and fur traders. Thanks to dedicated people like Sigurd Olson and others. As the evening chill settled in, another day faded to notes and memories.

Day four was meant to be our layover day just to relax, except we ended up planning an all-day side trip instead. Our destination was the pictographs on the lower end of the Basswood River. We had listened to wolves howling somewhere to the northwest before daylight. Now, as we readied the canoe at 8:30 am, we were treated to another chorus. Maybe it was a successful night of hunting, maybe a morning reunion, maybe for no particular reason at all. We enjoyed the serenade regardless of the reason.

Horse Lake was a mirror, but the peaceful feel of the lake faded as we negotiated the four surprise carry-overs before the first planned portage on the Horse River. Maps don't change as quickly as water levels and beaver projects. Fortunately, we had decided to take only one canoe — the sixteen-foot Swift — and a single daypack in order to keep things light and easy to manage, so the portaging wasn't too difficult or cumbersome.

We enjoyed a snack lunch on the rocks overlooking Lower Basswood Falls early that afternoon. Everyone wanted to linger there, but with the day more than half over, we soon pushed on to the pictographs. We had seen them once before, there on the low cliffs along the west side of the river. It was exciting to see them again. Some were familiar, others we had forgotten about. We gazed at them, trying not to miss anything as the current pulled us past. Then we slowly paddled back past them again, trying to soak in every detail. A man in a handcrafted wooden solo boat with a fishing rod hanging over the bow passed by and pointed out a handprint hidden beneath a low overhang on the south end of the cliffs. We hadn't seen it before. Looking at that handprint, I felt as if I could reach up and touch the past, but I didn't dare actually touch it for fear of speeding its decay. For some reason, I felt a strong bond with the person whose hand had left its print so many years ago.

The afternoon was quickly slipping by, with many miles and portages between our canoe and camp. Reluctantly, we dug in with our paddles and headed back toward the falls. About halfway back to camp, as we were watching turtles sunning themselves along the Horse River, I noticed long dark green water plants below the surface, waving in the current. They reminded me of a horse's mane waving in the wind. I wondered if they had anything to do with the river's name and wondered who named the river. Regardless, Julie nicknamed it the Horse Hair River. We still jokingly call it that even to this day. Another rock. Another turtle. My mind came back to the present, and we paddled on. We reached camp late that evening, tired, but feeling good about our adventure. After dinner, I built a small fire as an autumn sunset ignited the trees. We dabbled with the fire for a short while after dark, mainly because it felt too early to go to bed, but it didn't take long before we gave in. With the fire out, the stars and the cool breeze took back the night.

The next morning was bright and cool as we slid our canoes into the dark water of Horse Lake. It felt like we were on our way out of the wilderness all too soon. As I studied the shoreline features quietly gliding by, I already began to miss this place called the Boundary Waters Canoe Area Wilderness. Horse to Tin Can Mike to Sandpit. I wondered about the names as we passed through. Sandpit Lake; The name doesn't evoke much of a picture in your mind, unless you've been there, especially during autumn. Flat water, warm yellows, oranges, and reds mirroring the surrounding shoreline. Ripple-less except for the quiet, gentle wake of two green canoes. It felt like I was soaking in autumn, floating quietly through the world. As we neared the trail to Mudro Lake, we glided over a submerged birch tree, felled by some industrious beaver. Its white branches and newly submerged yellow leaves looked ghostly cold compared to the warm colors floating on the surface. The woods around the landing showed evidence of a very busy beaver. I examined some of the pale chips piled around a pointed stump, imagining the crash shattering the tranquil lake.

The trail out of Sandpit was steep, but fortunately not long. With the sun gaining strength as morning slipped into afternoon, we snuck off into the trees at Mudro to take off our now unnecessary long underwear. We enjoyed the sunshine and had our lunch snacks, which consisted of nuts, pretzels, Cheez-its, and dried fruits. Then it was time to push on.

The portage from Mudro to Pickett lay nestled at the end of a slow, winding creek. It seemed quite quiet and secluded until we walked onto the road leading to the parking lot of the Chainsaw Sisters Saloon. Civilization caught us by surprise. And after a few days in the autumn backcountry, the sight of several people and vehicles didn't really feel like a good surprise. Pushing the interruption aside, we crossed the road and slid our canoes into the waters of Pickett Lake. After putting some weathered trestle timbers and a few cabins behind us, we mentally glided back into the wilderness.

The portage from Picket to Nels was also tucked away at the end of a slow, winding creek. Unfortunately, there again were some beaver alterations not shown on the map. The navigable water stopped and started a couple of extra times. This led to an interesting 90-rod bushwhack that certainly added to the adventure. Once we made it to the planned portage, the going was smooth.

As the clouds thickened and the wind gained momentum, Nels turned into mostly just a succession of quiet paddle strokes. We did take notice of a couple of bald eagles and some interesting shoreline features, but mostly we just paddled. We found the landing at the Nels parking lot empty as a few droplets began to dimple the water. Our wilderness excursion came to a close quietly, the same way it began.

I reflected on the trip and pondered what the next adventure might be as Megan and I made the mile-and-a-half walk up the Echo Trail to get our truck. About halfway there, a lone, dark timber wolf trotted out of the tangle of trees thirty yards ahead of us. It paused in the middle of the gravel road just long enough to flash us an intense glance, then it dashed off to continue its eastward trek. I took it as a sign that our next adventure would be a good one

OF RIVERS AND BUGS

We launched our two canoes into the Island River late in the morning for a little different type of Boundary Waters trip than usual. Normally, we paddled mostly Boundary Waters lakes, with an occasional short jaunt in a connecting river or creek. This time, we would be primarily negotiating the Island and Isabella rivers, with intermissions on a couple of lakes. It was the very beginning of July, so the June biting bug madness hadn't yet died down. Our two daughters were still traveling with us at the time of this trip, so there were four of us for the bugs to dine on. Megan was a freshman in high school, and Amy was a senior.

The first stretch of the Island River was wide enough that it felt more like paddling a narrow lake than a river. That was where we saw a pair of bald eagles gliding overhead. We were still living in lower Michigan at the time, so seeing a bald eagle was noteworthy and reason to stare. Just around the first bend, the channel narrowed, and we came to our first set of rapids, marked by a huge boulder at the top end. As with every rapid, we beached our boats at the portage, and I got out to take a look. From atop the boulder, the short rapids didn't look at all menacing. After looking at the damp, shady portage trail and imagining the hordes of mosquitoes that I knew were lurking there, the rapids began to look even more like an inviting adventure. It was primarily one fast chute with an assortment of exposed rocks along each side. The chute looked to be no more than fifteen feet long, and the water wasn't really all that fast. When I announced that I thought we could readily shoot the rapids, nobody cheered, but they didn't openly balk either. Probably because their portage trail assessment was similar to mine.

Both boats glided through the rapids without a glitch. It was actually fun, so everyone was all smiles as we paddled around the bend to the next small rapids, where we eagerly repeated the same procedure. The only difference was that the smiles came as soon as I announced that I thought we could readily shoot those rapids, too. Again, it was fun and novel, making us all feel good about our little accomplishment, so we didn't care if our bug assessment was correct or not.

Shortly after the second rapid run, the Island River joined the Isabella River, where smooth paddling continued for a half mile or so. When we reached the 130-rod portage around a narrow run of fast water that was significantly longer than the ones we had paddled through, we knew a portage was inevitable, bugs or not. In anticipation, bug nets were put on before we even reached the portage, which proved to be a good idea. A heavy dose of bug spray didn't even seem to help keep mosquitoes off my hands once we got off the water. The portage was relatively flat and easy, and would have been enjoyable if it weren't for the onslaught of biting bugs.

When we reached the entrance to Rice Lake about a quarter mile later, we followed an eagle into the lake to see if either of the two campsites that were indicated on our map were available. As it turned out, both sites were open, but it was only early afternoon, so we decided to continue on and investigate the river campsite that wasn't far away. As we bobbed around in front of the vacant river campsite, looking at its swampy surroundings, with a pair of loons keeping an eye on us, we all agreed that the island site on Rice Lake would almost certainly host fewer bugs. With a unanimous decision, we followed another eagle – or maybe the same one as before – back into Rice Lake to claim the island campsite while we still had the opportunity.

As we explored the site and set up camp, bugs were promisingly mild, which I took as a good sign. There was a moderate breeze, which certainly helped, both at camp and later while we paddled around the lake. During that late afternoon exploration, we had a surprise when we nearly paddled right past a loon sitting on a nest on the far side of the island next to our camp island. It was sitting motionless, with its head and neck outstretched on the nest. As soon as we noticed the bird, we quickly backed off and left it alone. Even though it wasn't a long look, we were still excited to have experienced our first close encounter with a loon on its nest. Hopefully, the accidental intrusion didn't cause any problems for the loon or its offspring.

Our exploration of Rice Lake included a stop at the campsite that was on the main shoreline near our island. The site wasn't anything special, but someone had found a deer skull and left it at the edge of the tent site. It had a clean, symmetric set of antlers. Widthwise, it was only about thirteen inches, but it was relatively tall with long tines. I seriously considered keeping it, but eventually decided that as a complete skull it would be bulky and difficult to haul around during our trip. After showing it to Julie and the girls, I returned it to where

I found it, hopefully providing someone else with a good surprise. Still, as a long-time antler collector, it was difficult for me not to turn around to go back and get it as we paddled away.

After our lake cruise, we returned to our island campsite for dinner and an evening fire. The sky had spat a few scattered raindrops, but not enough to wet our firewood. That was a great blessing, because as evening progressed, mosquitoes increased. Significantly! In addition to providing warmth in the cool of the evening, the fire also helped ward off the bugs at least a little. I increased the smoke output with a few pieces of mildly damp wood specifically for that purpose. When we turned in that night, our tent had the ambiance of wood smoke mingled with the soothing scent of balsam fir.

In the morning, we found that head nets were an absolute necessity. Even while eating and brushing our teeth. Timing for quickly pulling open your bug net and inserting a bite of food was critical. While brushing her teeth, Megan completely forgot about needing to open her bug net while spitting out her toothpaste. Cleaning her bug net left it uncomfortably soggy, so it was a good thing that we had a spare.

It was still overcast with periodic light sprinkles when we broke camp. Ten minutes later, we were watching a cow moose with her calf along the Isabella River. As with the previous day, we paddled through a few small rapids to avoid portage trail bugs. We still needed to portage around four rocky rapids, but at least we were able to minimize our mosquito exposure. As a southern gentleman that we crossed paths with on one of the portages commented, "The bugs are mighty powerful here." Besides the powerful bugs, through the course of our paddling and portaging, we encountered quite a few waterfowl gathered in small flocks. We also saw two whitetail does come down to the river to drink, as well as four river otters that were curiously coy, as river otters tend to be.

As we paddled out into Bald Eagle Lake, we stopped and watched one of its namesake birds eyeing us from above. By mid-afternoon, when we were setting up camp along the eastern shoreline, the wind began to increase, which we were thankful for. It worked better than bug spray and didn't leave your skin feeling tacky. Of course, the wind meant no fire, but we could live with the trade-off.

The next morning was a mosquito's dream – dead calm. As a result, we spent most of the day just paddling around and exploring the shoreline from a distance. Anything to stay away from the buggy woods. At one point, we paddled over to the entrance to Gabbro Lake but decided not to shoot the rapids leading into the lake. We were pretty confident of our ability to safely make it into Gabbro, but we weren't sure about our ability to paddle back up through the rapids, and nobody wanted to do the short buggy portage. Open, bugless water had apparently spoiled us. At least for the time being.

There was an abundance of waterfowl on the water, including a few vocal loons, which added to the wilderness feel of the lake. I know loons migrate south for the winter months, but whenever I hear the call of a loon, I always think of north woods wilderness waters. We also spotted a couple of whitetail does along the shoreline. I wasn't sure if they were simply quenching their thirst or if they, too, were seeking solace from the biting bugs in a more open area.

Our own desire to stay away from the bug-infested woods was strong enough that we ate our lunch on a small rock slab island. I shuttled the girls to a nearby unoccupied campsite when they needed to use the latrine. Even then, the visits were as brief as possible.

When we finally went back to camp for the evening, head nets were still an absolute necessity. Even then, it was still annoying. Amy and Megan were considering a cool swim – possibly with bug nets on their exposed heads – until they noticed an eight-inch-long spotted leech in the shallows near camp. While they were hanging around the water's edge, they also saw two pike that were barely three inches long. I couldn't recall ever seeing a pike that small before, but I saw them myself, and I'm sure they were indeed tiny pike. Fortunately, it again cooled down enough near dark to allow us to appreciate a mosquito-repelling fire without sweating from the heat.

It was a quick breakfast and pack-up drill in the morning, as we were eager to get back on the water. We paddled back up through three or four Isabella River rapids, portaging around only when necessary. Still, it took six hours to make our return to Rice Lake, with our only wildlife encounter being a lone beaver. In hindsight, we probably should have either just taken one of the river campsites near Rice Lake and dealt with the potential of a few more bugs or paddled a little farther to Isabella Lake. Even if it wasn't less buggy, at least we could have explored another new lake. We weren't doing well with the bugs, though, so I'm sure that our thinking was a little clouded. Thinking aside, we returned to our previous Rice Lake island campsite, anticipating the attack of the little winged vampires.

The next morning, it was a relatively short trek out to the road. After the somewhat long portage on the Isabella, the day began to heat up, so we were happy to be able to paddle our way up through the two small rapids on the Island River. We just followed the lessons of a fish, paddling hard from one calm resting spot to another. After the second or third rest stop, we paddled out into the calm above the fast water, feeling triumphant.

As we were unloading our canoes at the road, I casually mentioned that I had read about some pictographs that were located not far upstream. It wasn't even noon yet, I reasoned, so we would have plenty of time for a quick visit and still be back in town by mid-afternoon. It wasn't until I noted that it didn't look like any portages would be involved that anyone even acknowledged my comments. After I promised that we would not do any portaging, even if it meant not making it to the pictographs, the crew reluctantly agreed to my trip extension. So, we loaded everything into our truck except our day packs, which contained water bottles and other assorted essentials, and paddled on upstream. After more than a mile of working our way through some shallow rock-infested areas, I was sure we were getting close to the ancient artwork. I speculated that somewhere around one of the next few river bends we would be there. As we rounded the next bend, I spotted it. Not the pictograph collection, but a shallow area of close-packed exposed rocks with fallen trees added to the mix. We would need to portage around them. But I had promised. As badly as I wanted to see the pictographs that I was certain were just up ahead, I wanted even more to maintain my integrity. Especially with my family. So, true to my promise, we turned our boats around and leisurely paddled downstream toward a shower and a bugless lunch.

Painting the Boundary Waters

Most of us who have visited the border country carry a collection of mental pictures reminding us of beautiful scenery, special friendships, and wilderness adventures. Many have the wherewithal to capture some of those cherished images with a camera as well. Only a relative few have the artistic gift to capture the wilderness and its inspiration on paper or canvas. My wife, Julie, is one of those fortunate few.

The majority of her work is focused on natural scenes from around our home in Michigan's Upper Peninsula, but our annual trip to the BWCAW allows her to apply her skills to a much larger wilderness landscape. In October of 2019, I was blessed to be able to do some writing as an artist-in-residence with the Listening Point Foundation in Ely. Accompanying me on this venture gave Julie an opportunity to more seriously expand her Boundary Waters artwork. The residency provided a place to stay at Sigurd Olson's house in Ely, access to his writing shack, and access to Listening Point, including the rustic cabin Sig had reconstructed there.

In addition to time at Listening Point and Sigurd Olson's house, we were beginning the venture with this seven-day backcountry trip to provide additional time to immerse ourselves in the border country wilderness and get more in tune with the world that Julie wanted to capture in her artwork.

So, our adventure starts near where the old Chainsaw Sisters Saloon once stood, as we slip our canoe into the creek connecting Picket and Mudro lakes. It's a typical October morning, thirty-seven degrees Fahrenheit with a non-descript grey sky. It's been a few years since we were last here. The area is familiar, but as things often are around water, some of the features are new. I remember some details of the creek, but with water running high, the creek doesn't quite match my memory. In one way, that is a good thing, because we are able to paddle right through two short portages that I remember having to scramble around on our last visit.

Paddling into Mudro on the first day of that wilderness journey, it is quiet, except for a slight whisper of wind and water. Peaceful. That's one of the reasons we come here. Hillsides are masked in bright golden birch and dusky-green spruce. I stop paddling for a moment and just look around, thinking how good it feels to be in our canoe again. At home in northern Michigan, we mostly hike and kayak.

Here we'll do our share of hiking across portage trails, but our primary means of travel is by canoe.

There is a light mist in the air. Not quite to the point where I would call it rain, but there's a hint of dimpling on the water. I peer back into the bay housing the portage to Fourtown Lake. We will be there in a week. But one of my goals on this trip is to do a better job of living in the moment, so I come back to now and paddle on toward Sandpit Lake.

The portage from Sandpit to Tin Can Mike is a mud-slog. A trailside swamp is no longer just trailside. Most of the swamp is already drably past its autumn prime except for a single red maple about four feet tall that is boasting peak color. As we're double-portaging toward Tin Can Mike, we meet a guy from Kansas double-portaging toward Sandpit. When we pass him on his way back for his canoe, he's carrying our food pack. Turns out that instead of walking back empty, he saw we had an odd number of packs and decided to haul one of them for us. We often meet nice people on portage trails, but this guy tops my list!

By the time we reach Horse Lake, the camp I wanted, right at the entrance to the Horse River, is already occupied, so we opt for the very next site north. Horse Lake tends to be pretty popular, so we don't want to waste time looking at other sites and risk not getting a good one or not getting one at all. After setting up camp, the late afternoon sun finally breaks through the greyness. Julie is a little too wired about being back in the Boundary Waters to be able to focus on painting. That can wait until we settle into wilderness mode. So, we set out paddling the north end of Horse Lake in search of photographs and firewood, and manage to find some of both. As we paddle back to camp about 6:00 pm, evening rays are lighting up the lake. It's funny how a little bit of sunlight lifts your spirits, even when they're not down, and puts a positive glint on everything.

After a small campfire that's a little smoky from damp wood, we finally decide it's late enough to call it a day and let the fire fade to a few smoldering embers. I'm not really ready to turn in, but I reluctantly douse the glowing coals and set my sights on tomorrow.

We awake in the faint grey beginning of day two with rain pattering on our tent. We quietly lay there for a bit, hoping the sound and its source will go away. Once the pattering at least weakens, we dress quickly, take down our soggy tent, and pack everything up before a hasty cold breakfast. Our day two plan is to follow the Horse River down to the Basswood River, then on into Crooked Lake to somewhere around Table Rock. That plan quickly begins to fall apart as we encounter sloppy trails and more Horse River portages than we remember from previous visits. Even though most portages are short, all the jockeying in and out, loading and unloading of gear, slipping, sliding, and splashing still eats up time and drains energy. Constant rain, running the gamut of intensity, makes everything feel like a lot of slow-motion work. It just will not quit. Even getting lunch snacks out without getting everything else wet seems like a chore that we're not sure is worth the effort. Although we normally don't wear rain pants, we are today, and we are certainly glad. We would be completely soaked and miserable without full rain gear and good waterproof boots.

About 4:15 pm, we finally reach Lower Basswood Falls. River, sky, and spirits are all sullen grey. Two soggy fishermen are preparing to launch their canoe at the top of the falls. Julie asks if any of the nearby camps are open. The guy carrying a hammer-handle pike announces that the two sites just below the falls are both open. Julie relays to me that we're taking the first one, so that officially becomes our new destination.

Fortunately, the first camp is a nice one, right at the base of the falls. Without much enthusiasm, we burn considerable time trying to decide which will be the least wet location for the tent, then hastily set up tent and canopy in a steady rain and throw something together for dinner by headlamp. Everything is too wet for a decent fire, so Julie turns in about 8:30 pm. I just can't. I am not tired enough to go to sleep, and I don't feel like lying in my sleeping bag, staring at the inside of our tent. So, I enjoy the lack of rain under our canopy until I finally feel I will be able to fall asleep. The dry sleeping bag feels good. Sleep doesn't come easily, but it finally comes after I get back up for one more nature call.

Sometime before sunrise, winds move in, pushing rainclouds out. The gusts sound strong at times, but we don't feel the effects in our sheltered campsite. We emerge from our tent to partly sunny skies and much sunnier attitudes. After enjoying a non-rainy breakfast while strolling around, catching a variety of views of Lower Basswood Falls, I string up a couple of para-cord lines to dry out our stuff. A good shaking of tent and canopy speeds them along in the drying process, too. Now, with mild sunshine brightening our outlook, it's easy to adopt the "It's only water" attitude, but we still decide that this drying out is going to take some time. So, not wanting to pack everything up while it's wet, we reluctantly decide to use our one layover day to dry out before moving on into the portion of our planned route that we've never experienced before.

As we finish munching on the last of our breakfast, we agree that this is a great place to hang around and do a little exploring anyway. We have front-row seats to rushing waterfalls, interesting rock outcroppings all around, and, looking down the waterway, a panorama of north woods spruce and pine with sun-lit autumn birch accents. Besides, this will give us time to appreciate the collection of pictographs a short distance away instead of just taking a quick look as we're paddling by to our next campsite somewhere around Friday Bay. We breathe in a dose of fresh, post-rain, pine-scented air and begin exploring near camp as our assorted collection of belongings dries in the morning sunshine. We're in the middle of the wild we came to experience, so we stay in the moment and just enjoy what we can. During times when we're not in physical contact with the wilderness, just knowing it is here is a comforting thought, but actually being here is what we dream about, so we try to make the most of this experience.

By lunchtime, everything feels dry. So, we toss it all in the tent, pack up some lunch snacks, and launch into Basswood River/Crooked Lake for a pictograph visit. As we approach the painted cliffs, we realize it is no longer sunny because of a thick bank of clouds that drifted in. By the time we are admiring the ochre artwork as we drift past, small droplets are dimpling the surface of the water. We paddle back to the south end of the cliffs, looking for the lone handprint that caught my imagination on our first visit years ago, but I fail to find it. Dimples are turning to small splashes, so we paddle back toward camp. Before we get there, it lets up, so we decide to venture over for a closer look at the falls. Near one of the foaming chutes, we find a quiet back-current that allows us to effortlessly hold there like a fish.

As we leave one of our tranquil vantage points, I get a little careless, sticking our bow out into the flow. Instead of the current gently spinning our boat into alignment with its flow, it grabs our upstream side and yanks it down to where water begins slipping in. I quickly shift my weight downstream enough to right the boat before we end up in the drink. I am amazed at how fast a slight miscalculation can turn ugly. By Julie's lack of reaction, I realize she probably has no idea how close we just came to a cold swim and a bad situation. That's exactly why we always wear our life vests anytime we're in our canoe.

Back at camp, rain is on hold again, and I boil water for tomorrow's drinking while Julie does some sketching near the falls. Boiling is certainly more work than most of the new filter devices, but I have more confidence in boiling. Besides, we're carrying the stove and fuel anyway, so there's not really any extra gear except for a little fuel. When boiling is done, I join Julie on an outcrop overlooking the churning falls. She is focused on creating her sketch, sitting on one of the canoe seat cushions we recently purchased. They provide a little padding and back support not only in the canoe, but also on the ground, or even on rock outcroppings like this that Julie often paints and sketches from. Listening to the rumbling falls, I am amazed at the thought that this volume of water has been rushing to some destination for probably thousands of years without ceasing. It just keeps flowing. There is no doubt in my mind that it's got to be part of a grand master plan, not just a freak happenstance.

A red squirrel is scolding me from a nearby white pine as I realize my stomach is talking about dinner, so I head toward our food pack to start making preparations. Looking around at evening rays igniting the autumn forest, I am glad Julie does the picture taking because I wouldn't even know where to begin to focus the camera. Everything looks like a picture that needs to be taken. Julie tends to have her compact Canon camera always within reach when we're in the backcountry. On this trip, she also brought her Nikon SLR camera so that she could take higher resolution images for reference. It means carrying more weight, but she considers the higher picture quality worth the trade-off.

Evening is spent ducking in and out of canopy cover, dodging small squalls as they come and go. Somewhere in the mix, a river otter swims out of the falls flow, arches and dives like a whale with its tail-end sticking up before disappearing. A pair of bald eagles are conversing in a white pine across the water as darkness settles in. After dark, the rain finally stops, stars are playing peek-a-boo with light clouds marching eastward, and a half-moon is casting silver streaks across the water. We climb into our tent with the Big Dipper just above the trees to the north, flat with the horizon, like it's holding water. Hopefully, it doesn't decide to pour it out on us.

Day four we emerge from our nylon dome to glorious sunshine. Julie and I both seem to have a little spark of excitement as we eat breakfast and pack up camp. Maybe it's the sunshine. Maybe it's the anticipation of exploring new water we've never seen before. Or maybe we are just really rested from our layover day. Regardless, it's a good, upbeat feeling.

We launch into the next leg of our journey at 9:10 am. It seems like no matter what we do, we almost always end up heading out between 9:00 and 9:30 am. No matter. As we paddle away, I make a mental note that we need to return to that campsite sometime. With access to falls, pictographs, and endless paddling opportunities, it's a great place to stay. Maybe we'll use it as a basecamp. For now, though, we're heading north into new territory. We can't resist another slow pass by the pictographs, just because we are here. As we wonder again about the painted figures, I realize that the cliff, with its fractured and carved surfaces, sporting colorings of red, pink, orange, green, and grey, is a piece of artwork itself, and it's in one of my favorite galleries.

As we glide past a small bay a little farther on, three swans stare back at us. Two come out toward us, looking like glowing angels in the morning sun, then they do a water walk as they take flight, honking their disapproval of our presence. Soon, sun and water interact, creating a disco-ball effect of bright spots moving across shoreline rocks and trees. We are looking everywhere, trying not to miss anything. As my eyes wander north and east into Quetico, I find myself wanting to follow. We have never ventured there, always content with the countless offerings of the closer-to-home BWCAW. I mentally put Quetico on my "someday" list.

As we approach Table Rock for a lunch break, a guy and his dog are just leaving, having done the same thing. We share a few honest pleasantries, wish each other well, and they head off in the direction we just came from. Looking at Table Rock and how it is balanced just right on those smaller rocks, I can't help but wonder whether it's actually just a chance occurrence, or if there is more to the story. By the time we finish lunch, I decide that it doesn't really matter because we will never know anyway, and I just accept it as an intriguing phenomenon. An afternoon breeze is picking up, so we decide we had better move on.

I always like keeping tabs of where we are on the map and following our progress as we paddle, but as we get into the collection of islands and bays up near Thursday Bay, I begin paying even closer attention than usual in an effort to remain un-lost, or so we at least don't get confused. My original plan was to explore the area on our way through, but with the afternoon wind increasing, I change plans and we skirt across the end of Thursday Bay. Julie is not very comfortable with wind or waves, but mostly waves. Fortunately, it's more wind than waves right now, but we press on toward Friday Bay to help Julie maintain a decent comfort level. As we approach Friday Bay, we feel the wind increasing, so we stop at an island campsite for a pick-me-up snack and to evaluate our options. The issue is still more wind than waves, though the bay is definitely choppy. Bright afternoon sunshine puts a positive edge on our situation, so we decide it is best to address the wind and moderate waves now and get to the bottom of Friday Bay, near our intended portage into Papoose Lake, instead of leaving it for tomorrow in case conditions worsen. Julie is a bit worried about the conditions, but not as worried as she is about worrying about them through the night. So, we paddle out of our island shelter and into the edge of the bay. It is indeed more choppy than wavy, and the wind direction is in our favor, making our venture more fun and energizing than concerning.

As we duck into the landing at the last camp on the east side of Friday Bay, we're greeted by an easy take-out and a glowing sugar maple that makes me glad I'm wearing sunglasses. Camp is well above water level with an abundance of smooth exposed rock. Afternoon autumn sunshine has us in its spell, and we feel at home even before we unpack. Previous campers have left us a nice pile of dry firewood. In appreciation, we set out to add to the pile so we can pass along the favor.

As I cook dinner, Julie is working on a small painting. If time and weather conditions allow, Julie captures scenes by painting directly on canvas right in the wilderness, which is referred to as plein air, in artistic circles. Other times, she may create a simple sketch or two on paper, which she will use, along with a photograph of the scene, to create a painting later in her home studio. Sometimes, Julie will also create small plein air paintings as a more elaborate form of a sketch and then use the initial small painting as a study for a larger, more formal canvas painting in her studio. Besides providing an artistic memory of the moment, these mini paintings can be readily completed in one sitting, which is a huge benefit when we're moving camp each day. Julie says her favorite part of plein air painting is that she is able to enjoy living and painting in the moment with the subject she is anxious to work on, while in the midst of inspiration. Thoughts and feelings from what she's experiencing are freshly clear, and she is immersed in that experience. That immersion means she can take in not only the visual effects of the scene, but what she is feeling as well.

Friday Bay shows barely a ripple, and our maple is dripping amber reflections into the water. Painting at the end of the day like this, as Julie often does, the light starts changing quickly, as does the temperature, forcing painting to be somewhat of a speed exercise, which is another benefit of smaller paintings like the one she is working on.

Later, the sun disappears below the horizon, leaving an orange glow to mark its exit. A faint north breeze brings in an evening chill as it lightly ripples our bay. We can hear the sounds of falling water from somewhere near the end of the bay. As we light our evening fire, the rest of the world doesn't exist except for a couple of old jet trails across the sky. Soon, early evening orange moonlight is painting a fiery strip connecting our camp to the dark island to the south. Our small fire is working hard to ward off the night chill. At 11:00 pm, we decide to trade fire for sleeping bags.

Next morning, shoreline trees are ablaze with sunshine. Julie is having a tough time deciding what to take pictures of because every direction is that photograph she's been looking for to paint from. Even though she is just taking pictures now, this is one of the problems Julie finds with wilderness plein air painting. That is, sometimes there are so many possibilities for subject matter that it becomes difficult to focus. Also, there are no clean boundaries framing the scenes, which makes it difficult to decide what to include and what to leave out. Having too many options to choose from may sound like a good problem to have, but when it interferes with your ability to actually make decisions and accomplish things, it can be frustrating. For taking reference pictures, the easy answer is simply to take plenty of pictures. For painting, Julie says she's found that the best course of action is usually to forget about it for a while. She just sits back and enjoys her surroundings, letting everything sink in and simmer in her mind. Sometimes this makes her feel like she's wasting time, but, like most good things, rushing plein air painting doesn't usually improve anything.

With our stay being so peacefully comfortable, we are hesitant to pack up and leave. In one way, we feel we have missed out by not exploring the Thursday and Friday Bay vicinity yesterday in anticipation of deteriorating weather, but this morning we are confident that pushing on to reach this camp was a great choice — exploring the bays goes on my mental list. I also make a note to give ourselves more time in the future to allow for changes in plans. We take our time packing up camp and check out some of the nearby scenery, including the small creek we could hear yesterday evening, before leaving Friday Bay. En route to Gun Lake, we quietly paddle through bog-lined creeks with golden tamaracks enhancing the morning's glow. Papoose and Chippewa Lakes look like they spilled out of the tamarack bog into the forest of pine, spruce, birch, and rock. This looks like moose country, but dark logs and big rocks are all we see. Still, we search portage trails hoping to find fresh tracks mingled with the amber birch leaves. Wolf scat is all we find, but it's still a tale of the wild.

We reach our intended five-star camp on Gun Lake mid-afternoon and happily find it empty. It doesn't look like it lives up to its rating, but we soon realize it's because of the mess left by previous campers. So, we clean up before we set up. There is not a lot of trash, but there is some. It's mostly a scattering of large rocks, charred wood, unburned logs, and a bunch of green brush someone just had to cut and leave in a "firewood" pile — I'll never figure out why some people are possessed to do that. Surveying our spacious camp all cleaned up with a large rock arm reaching into the lake for relaxing or casting, we agree with its rating.

As evening settles in, a lone loon appears. Its haunting cry echoes down the lake. We are surprised it's still here because most loons have already moved south. While enjoying our evening fire, we notice the sky is clear and the moon is out, so we douse the fire early and spend time lying on the rock out front, enjoying a celestial show before turning in for the night.

About 3:00 am I awake to hear a couple of simple two-note loon calls in the distance. Almost as soon as I wake, I am gone again into peaceful wilderness sleep.

As we eat breakfast, we hear one more farewell call from our loon friend, while I am being eyed suspiciously by an otter. We pack up and launch into another sunny autumn day, headed for our last camp on Fourtown Lake.

By the time we reach Fourtown, the wind has kicked in, making for a struggle as we use sheltering features to work our way closer to the south end, where we will portage out tomorrow. The camp we have our eye on is taken, so we opt for one just around the point from it in order to get out of the waves. After camp is set, Julie decides to do a little painting while I set out to explore the eastern hillside. She is taking some pictures prior to painting, which she finds helpful even for plein air work, because taking a number of pictures can help define exactly what would look best in the painting. Julie's outlook tends to be that you are far better off taking some unnecessary pictures and discarding them later than to later wish you had taken more pictures. Come to think of it, that's probably not a bad philosophy for outdoors excursions in general, not just painting expeditions. The approach Julie usually uses is to do limited plein air painting on small canvases or boards in the backcountry, accompanied by a variety of photographs, sketches, and notes to help capture additional scenes and things not yet incorporated into the paintings.

Meanwhile, I explore a mosaic of bare rock and oak brush, which gives the hillside the distinctive burnt-orange color we noticed from the lake. I flush a few grouse and find ample signs of deer and moose. This is a place I would love to hunt sometime, so I mentally put it on my list. On the other side of the hill, I look out over a vast swampy valley that I am sure is a wildlife haven. There is not enough time to go down and explore it, but I make another mental note and put a star by it.

Back at camp, we cook dinner and settle in, deciding to forgo a fire so we can enjoy the moon and stars again. Relaxing on the lakeside rocks, I am wondering about the large chain links cemented into bedrock. We saw some at Lower Basswood Falls, too. Part of the storied past and narrow escape of this wilderness. By nightfall, clouds have moved in, eliminating sky-watching. We never gathered firewood for "Plan B", which I mentally note as a mistake, so it ends up being earlier to the tent than planned.

In the morning, I'm standing lakeside, thinking of the old saying, "Red sky in morn, sailors be warned," glad we're not sailing today. For now, though, Fourtown is reflections on glass. Not the same lake as yesterday.

Today is a series of quiet, reflective paddles — figuratively and literally — separated by rocky, wet portages. Nearing Mudro Lake, I'm wading upstream because the creek has branched out and taken over the trail. Creekside colors are at their prime, and moisture in the air is accentuating their brilliance. Julie is working hard to capture what we're feeling in pictures until raindrops begin speckling her camera. On Mudro, as we approach the slow meandering creek where our journey began, a bald eagle soars past, barely above treetops, dipping a wing in what seems like a farewell gesture. This seven-day trip that seemed plenty long during planning slipped by way too quickly, and I'm not yet ready to leave. I stop paddling for a minute, realizing that I don't have nearly enough lifetime left to explore all of the places here that I want to explore. This is a place too wild, vast, and rugged to fully cover and comprehend, but it could be easily dismantled and destroyed if we're not careful. I'm thankful for all of the people like Sigurd Olson and others who have fought to keep this place intact and the many who are still in the battle. As I resume paddling, I nod to nobody in particular, saying farewell for now, as we set our sights on spending time at Listening Point.

There, we spend four days steeping ourselves in Sig's life and beloved point. Having read Sig's descriptions in *Listening Point*, we wander trails that feel familiar underfoot. We slip our canoe into Burntside Lake to explore Gusty Island and paddle quiet waters amongst other nearby islands, our only company being a northeasterly breeze and a scattering of raindrops. One full moon night, clouds break up for a few hours, giving us an opportunity to experience the magic Sig often wrote about. Quiet time is spent writing, painting, and reading Sig's words, while thoughts of our own listening points roll through our minds. That gets me to thinking about what might have been without special protections for the BWCAW, or more appropriately, how what we cherish today might not have been. Julie enjoys time in front of the large cabin window by the table, looking out over the entire border country wilderness and beyond while she paints. In a 1937 journal entry, Sig wrote, "Black and white is my canvas, my words my pigments, interpretation of the wild my theme." In the cabin where Sig often drew inspiration for painting so eloquently with words, Julie is now drawing inspiration for her Boundary Waters paintings.

Whether painted in the back country, a rustic cabin, or created in her studio by blending reference photographs and wilderness experience, some people are attracted to Julie's artwork because it brings back memories of wilderness adventures of their own, or inspires them to continue chasing their outdoor passions. Others simply appreciate the tranquil mood and soothing effects often associated with her work. Julie says the ultimate goal with her wilderness art is to connect people with the natural world they were meant to be a part of. She wants to rekindle the flame of their passion for wild places and remind them that the soothing effects and healing attributes of wilderness are out there waiting for their return.

Sidenote:

On this trip, with seven days in the wilderness and another four at Listening Point, Julie captured a little more than 1000 reference photographs. She created one 8x10 and three mini paintings (3x3 or 3x6), seven pen & ink drawings, and seven pencil sketches. After returning to her home studio, she created several larger paintings inspired by this Boundary Waters experience.

FIVE-STAR CAMPS

We pushed off into Clearwater Lake about 5:00 pm, with a stiff breeze stirring up foot-tall rollers. Fortunately, they were heading in the same direction that we were, so they were not bad company at all. Normally, we embark on wilderness adventures much earlier in the day, but we were planning to camp right there on Clearwater, and my wife, Julie, was finishing up a plein air painting workshop in Grand Marais that ran into the early afternoon. So, we spent our evening paddling east down Clearwater Lake, looking for a vacant campsite.

Each camp we passed was occupied, which didn't give me a good feeling about finding a campsite before dark, or even on that lake. As we rounded the point just before the last campsite on the lake, I visually picked out a possible makeshift site in some open pines while I was praying.

The last site turned out to be open — Thank You! — and it was an inviting-looking site. We pulled our canoe up to the shoreline rocks about 6:30 pm. Clouds were taking over the sky, and we could hear distant thunder. Thankfully, the threat was all we ever got. No raindrops ever fell, and the clouds blew out in time for the moon to rise above the wooded ridge right across the lake from camp. First, the yellow-white light lit up some random clouds that were lingering near the ridge. Then, the moon itself made an appearance, silhouetting a group of white pines atop the ridge. The trees looked like they were on stage for a show. And a grand show it was.

Our campfire died out about 10 pm, leaving me with the moon as my source of light and inspiration. I had split some of the firewood with the small axe that I have owned since I was fourteen years old, so our history goes back nearly fifty years. It's a satisfying feeling to use equipment that you've been using for a long time. It can be a little cumbersome to carry on my pack, and it certainly adds some weight, but I like having that axe with me and using it in the backcountry.

The full moon was keeping the forest awake, as it cast silvery shimmering swaths across the lake, straight at our camp. When there's a full moon, I feel like I should be outside doing something. Anything. It feels like I will miss out on something if I go to bed. It's a struggle to pull myself away from a full moon, because I always want to linger just a little longer.

I finally gave in at about 11 pm and slowly made my way to our tent, reluctantly going inside for the night, leaving the forest and lake to revel in the moonlight without me. Looking out of our tent door window, it felt like I was lying in bed at Dan's Cabin in the Porcupine

Mountains during our artist-in-residence there the previous year, looking out through the big picture windows. I enjoyed a peaceful, restful night of sleep, which was a fitting welcome back into the wilderness. We never got the overnight rain that had been predicted. Just a mild breeze blowing some clouds around.

The sun came up bright and cheery the next morning, with a light breeze still gently rippling the lake. The wilderness felt inviting, making me want to journey deeper into it. It felt like I belonged there. Looking around, I thought about how the previous day, while paddling Clearwater Lake, I had noticed that the surrounding area was basically one to twelve inches of soil perched atop boulders, cobble, and bedrock. It was a delicate balance, and I was surprised that the drought that summer hadn't killed off more trees due to their shallow roots. But bathed in the morning light, the surrounding forest looked alive and well. I also thought about how the previous night, I could see what looked like bands of mist angling up the hillside across the lake. Illuminated by a new day, I could see that those light bands were swaths of light-colored aspen trees poised on the steep hillside, adding variety to the wilderness landscape.

We pushed off from camp about 8:30 am. With the first portage within sight, it seemed like a lot of loading and lashing for not much gain. Although if we didn't lash everything down and we had an incident during the short paddle across the end of the lake, it would have resulted in a significant loss.

We pushed off again at about 10:30 am, this time into West Pike Lake. It was partly overcast and partly sunny, with a mild cooling breeze, but the overcast part seemed to be growing. The air was muggy to the point where rocks and boulders along the portage trail were wet with condensation, making footing somewhat precarious.

After our short paddle on West Pike, we made the climb up the portage trail to Gogebic Lake, after searching a bit for the trail because we paddled too far before we began looking for it. The portage wasn't as difficult as I remembered it to be from a previous visit, which is always a welcome relief. Usually, it's the other way around.

We had our camp set up by early afternoon, but there was a sizeable boulder surfacing in the only viable tent site, so I was a bit skeptical about our sleeping arrangements. Somebody had redesigned the fire grate area, eliminating the comfy rock-slab reclining chairs we had enjoyed during our previous visit. There was a large rock-slab table, though, which was certainly convenient. I tried fly fishing from the rocky point in front of camp, but the breeze had matured into wind, which was causing me difficulties. After less than an hour of fruitless — meaning fishless — casting, I decided to wait for the evening calm that often occurs. I probably should have switched from a Woolly Bugger that a guide in town had suggested to something else before I gave up, but the venture just seemed to have an unsuccessful feel to it.

Instead of an evening calm, we got an evening rain that started before dinner time. I stood there in my rain jacket, wishing I hadn't blown off setting up our rain canopy, regardless of the last weather forecast we had heard. By about 8:30 pm, my less-than-stellar rain jacket was getting saturated, so I retreated to the shelter of the tent, where I changed clothes and tried to settle in for the night. I had a feeling that I wouldn't last long in the tent, because I just cannot go to bed that early. The boulder bulge under my sleeping pad didn't help me relax either. After lying there restlessly staring at the top of the tent for about an hour, I began getting a bit stir-crazy, so I donned my cheap backup rain jacket and borrowed Julie's cheap rain pants that are too big on her and headed back outside to face the elements. Even though it wasn't exactly enjoyable, at least I could move around and burn off some more energy while I mentally steeled myself for a longer-than-usual night in the tent.

As I paced around in the rain, I couldn't help thinking about all the great firewood we had stashed under our canoe. I also promised myself that in the future, I would make the rain canopy work, even if there were no ideally situated trees to tie it to. At about 10:00 pm, I decided that it was late enough to give my sleeping bag another try. I still wasn't all that tired, but a slight chill at least made the sleeping bag idea sound inviting.

I finally fell asleep sometime before midnight. At least I think it was before midnight, but I didn't actually pull out my watch to verify the time. The rain had stopped by the time I had a 4:30 am nature call. Fortunately, I was able to go right back to sleep when I got back in the tent. When we emerged from the tent in the morning, the clouds still looked dense, with no sky-blue showing through. There was enough of a breeze, though, that our tent was relatively dry, which was a pleasant surprise.

We departed camp about 10:30 am. Instead of continuing our planned loop into Pine Lake, we opted to back-track to Clearwater, then decided to press on into Caribou Lake. On West Pike Lake, we talked with two guys heading to Gogebic for a day trip. They said they had fished it a few days earlier, with no success, which made me feel a little better about striking out there myself. On the portage to Clearwater, we met a hiker and a pair of backpackers, who I think were the first non-paddlers that we had ever encountered in the Boundary Waters Wilderness over the course of nearly twenty years.

Clearwater was sporting decent-sized waves again, coming down the lake toward us, so we were glad we were just doing a short stint across the end of the lake and not planning to paddle the length of it. The portage to Caribou was mild. I would even call it a little relaxing. Especially since we didn't have to fight waves on the portage trail.

The last campsite on the east end of Caribou was vacant, so we decided to take it. At first glance from the water, the site looked just okay. As we did our walk-around inspection, though, we realized just how nice it was. In fact, we were glad we would be staying for two nights. It had a gravel beach with a small stone break wall instead of the usual boulder or bedrock landing site. There were stone steps leading up to the campsite from the beach, and it was located in an open, airy pine grove that felt spacious and smelled like a fresh Christmas tree. As we set up our tent, rain canopy, and clothesline, a lone loon was calling out on the open lake, making it feel like a true north woods camp. Sun and clouds jostled for control of the sky for most of the afternoon, which sparked a few light sprinkles. We just stashed our firewood under the canopy, confident that we would be using it later.

I noticed that all the aspens across the lake had lightened to a yellowish green instead of their darker summer green. Some had already transitioned to true autumn yellow. Red maples were starting to show off their autumn colors here and there as well. Some trees had already lost most of their leaves and were mere skeletons. That made me think about the multitude of different trees with varying colors and shapes and sizes. I marveled at the fact that they all had a specific purpose somewhere in the grand plan, even though I didn't really know the details.

Loons were calling again just before we started out on an evening paddle. We quietly glided through sunshine and shadows, paddling in unison. Our paddling ended back at camp as the evening sky began to change colors from cool blue and white to the warmth of reds, yellows, and oranges. Clouds made the early stage of sunset look like the ridge to the west was ablaze, with smoke billowing out. Then, distant clouds became bathed in pinks and oranges. The entire eastern sky, at one point, took on the color of flames. We had front row viewing right along the shoreline. I was absorbed in the flow of the evening sky, but somehow still managed to look forward to an evening fire. A relaxing, peaceful fire to gaze into as I reflected on days past and present. It would be a damp-wood fire, but a backcountry fire nonetheless. Julie gave in to the call of her sleeping bag about 9:30 pm. I stayed out to coax the fire for another half-hour or so simply because my mind wasn't through wandering in the flames.

After fully dousing our fire, I moved out to the shoreline where I could see the full moon. The far shoreline was mirrored on the dead-calm surface of the water. A faint mist was rising from the surface, adding a sense of mystery to our wilderness lake. An owl had been calling earlier, as had a loon. But as I stood there by the motionless lake, all was silent. I wished we had experienced such a night on Gogebic so I could have done a better job of fishing for its brook trout. At least in my mind, I would have done better if the evening had been calm. I always fish well in my mind.

Standing by our fire, then out near the stillness of the water, I thought about past Boundary Waters adventures with our daughters, Amy and Megan. I recalled fun times and exciting adventures. Bugs, portages, paddling, family meetings, incidents, and wanderings all flowed through my head. Some wilderness laughter as well. Sometimes I miss those days of family activities and family vacations when the girls were growing up. I certainly love them and their families now, but part of me still misses those days of their youth. Maybe, in a way, what I'm missing is the days when I was younger, too.

Time only goes in one direction, though. So, we have no choice but to continue forward, into the future. Regardless, I went to bed that night with a smile and a warm glow long after the fire was gone. Fog began rolling in from the west as I headed for the tent.

Somewhere in the middle of the night, we woke to a squirrel on top of our tent. At first, I wondered what a red squirrel was doing out at night, and how it got on top of our slippery nylon tent. After closer inspection through the nylon with my headlamp, I realized that it was a flying squirrel. So, it likely glided in and landed on our tent, mistaking it for a big boulder. I gave it a gentle nudge from inside the tent to get it off before it did any damage.

I woke from a night of peaceful wilderness sleep to find that I couldn't see the other not-so-far-off side of the lake due to the fog.

The world was sullen gray. Fog was dripping from the trees, and the lake lay still and quiet as if it were still asleep. No morning bird songs. Just steady dripping.

As I was splitting a few pieces of old firewood, I got to thinking more about my old three-quarter-size axe. Mom and Dad gave it to me as a gift when I was in my early teens. I initially used it for trapping before branching out into other outdoor endeavors. We have a long history, me and my axe. I have a history with a lot of my outdoor gear. I've been using my backpacking stove for around forty-five years. The buffalo plaid wool shirt I often wear in the backcountry was my dad's. He bought it somewhere back in the 1970's. I like my vintage gear. Besides having history with me, it has classic style. At least I think it does. It's not just a collection of gadgets. It's important equipment that I know I can rely on, and I like the feeling of using it.

By mid-morning, the fog slowly melted away to reveal a sun-bathed wilderness world. Our response was to set out for Vale Lake, which was high on the ridge above Pine Lake, a couple of short portages away. There was still a faint mist rising from the water. A pair of swans glowed radiant white on the surface of Caribou Lake, over near the next camp to the west. There was a horde of water beetles along the shore, large masses of them looking like mini figure-skaters on the surface of the water. We quietly paddled along through the mist, enjoying the fact that the guys at the next camp were being quiet as well. A bald eagle soared overhead without making a sound. Beavers were busy. We watched three of them cruising near one lodge. The peaceful lake felt like it belonged to us and us alone.

We reached the portage to Vale shortly after noon, after paddling past a beaver sitting in the shallows eating its lunch. It swam out and circled our boat, then went back to its business. After our own lunch snacks, we began the climb to Vale. Besides being steep in sections, the trail obviously didn't get heavy use, so it was narrow and brushy, which made negotiating the trail while carrying a sixteen-foot canoe interesting.

There was already another canoe on Vale when we arrived. The three guys in that boat had a stringer of six brook trout. They told us where they caught them as they paddled by, heading for the portage trail. I fly fished the same area off of a small point for about thirty minutes without even a slight bump from a fish. I then cruised the shoreline, trailing a black Woolly Bugger fly. All I managed to catch was water. No fish. Not even the momentary excitement of snagging a log. As we paddled back to the portage, I comforted myself with the idea that maybe the other guys had the fish too stirred up, so they weren't biting anymore.

On our way back to camp, we passed the same three guys camping at the site I was hoping to get if we had camped on Pine Lake. They said it had taken them a couple of hours with worms to get things dialed in to where they started catching fish. I didn't feel so bad after that. It's hard to compete with worms.

Talking with those guys caused my mind to drift back several years to when we stayed at that same campsite. The early evening sun had accentuated autumn colors on the hillside across the lake, bathing everything in a warm amber glow. Just to the west of camp, a pair of points extended into the lake, mingling with the deep red-orange sunset sky. When the curtain fell on the last of the sunset show, we started our campfire while we listened to the sounds of the lake and surrounding forest. A gray owl started a conversation from its perch right behind camp. From somewhere down the lake to the west, what sounded like a great horned owl joined in. About 9 pm, northern lights made an appearance. Though the colors were not brilliant, a small curtain of yellow-green danced off and on in the northern sky. Green and red spires periodically jutted up from behind the black ridge across the lake. We were torn between dancing lights and dancing flames. Multiple times, the colors faded into the grayscale sky only to return for an encore. During the performance, a loon began its song out on the water, apparently inspired by the light show. After the last of the colors had been gone for an extended time, we doused our fire and climbed into the shelter of our tent, thankful that we had a campsite on the south side of the lake. Otherwise, we likely would never have seen the northern light show. We drifted off to sleep that night with aurora colors dancing in our heads. Julie later painted a picture of that place and titled it *Five-Star Camp*.

After my mental reminiscing, we finished our brief visit with the three fishermen, then paddled down to the portage to Little Caribou Lake. Before embarking on the portage, I recalled how on our previous visit to the area, we took a side trip to Johnson Falls. We had been there once before, when our daughters were still traveling with us, but it had been several years. On our first visit, we swam in the plunge pool below the falls, then hiked back to the lake. On our second visit, with the weather not conducive to swimming, we ventured a little farther along the trail and discovered that two additional falls, larger than the first, were just upstream. We took our discovery as a lesson that we needed to do a more thorough job of exploring when we visit somewhere — even if we've been there before.

Ending the day back at our camp on Caribou Lake, there was an orange-sky sunset without a hint of a cloud. Water beetle circles were visible as far out into the sunset reflection as I could see. The lake looked like it was covered with water beetle scrollings. I built a campfire — the last one of our trip — so I could sit and reminisce. Another peaceful night was unfolding.

The next morning was mildly foggy. But not nearly as foggy as the previous morning, because it wasn't dripping from the trees. Sometime during the night, I had heard a bull moose grunting as he passed by our camp. It sounded like he was up on the hillside behind us somewhere. Early in the morning, when it was just faintly light, I had heard, him grunting again near the portage at the end of the lake, as I stepped out of the tent.

Fog soon burned off to expose a clear, sunny sky. A pair of swans down the lake to the west were glowing in the low-angle morning light. We were packed up and headed out by 9:30 am, thinking about how quickly the past few days had gone by, which always seems to be the case when you're living an adventure that you had been planning for a long time.

Caribou Lake was smooth except for a slight blur in the reflections. Still, the depth of field in the reflections was surprising. We were alone on the lake except for a bald eagle perched atop an old snag on the island in front of the next campsite to the west. Reflections on the lake looked more three-dimensional than the real thing above the shoreline. It was like the world was upside down.

We quietly passed four canoes partway to the portage, ending our sole possession of the lake. They were all heading east. Shortly afterward, we passed a camp with seven tents and assumed that the four boats were from there. Gazing along the shoreline and surrounding ridges, it was amazing how noticeable each tree species was due to having its own unique shape or profile. It was most evident, though, with the white pines. Each white pine is a unique individual with a character all its own, which is probably why Julie loves to capture them in her artwork.

By noon, we were passing the Boundary Waters Canoe Area Wilderness sign, signaling our exit from the wilderness. Not that the surroundings changed any, but somehow, passing that sign made the world seem a little more civilized and less adventurous. For us, that wilderness exit usually initiates the planning process for our next trip. I had several possibilities in mind.

SAWBILL TRAIL

We decided to do something different. Over the course of twenty-something years, we have entered the Boundary Waters through a number of entry points from both Ely and Grand Marais. So, for a change, we decided to enter the wilderness from the Sawbill Trail, out of Tofte, to access an area we had never visited.

My wife, Julie, and I launched our canoe into a misty Baker Lake in mid-morning, surprised by how quiet the lake was even though there was a state forest campground right near the launch site. Paddling to our first portage, we discovered an additional portage thanks to unmapped beaver activity. As we quietly paddled through

Peterson Lake, relatively low water provided two more unplanned portages around boulder fields in the winding northern arm of the lake. In one case, I was able to get out and guide our boat while rock-hopping along the shore, but at the final portage into the south end of Kelly Lake, a guy coming out of the backcountry was already wading to guide his boat, so he graciously offered to guide our boat through the boulder maze while he was at it. Not wanting to unload our gear nor get soaked that early in the trip, we eagerly accepted his offer and heartily thanked him. Meeting nice people in the backcountry seems to be a common occurrence.

With beaver dams and boulder fields behind us, we paddled out into the relative openness of Kelly Lake. Julie was captivated by the stately white pines that dotted the shoreline, as they're one of her favorite trees to paint. The first open campsite that we saw turned out to be the best one — at least for us. We investigated two other nearby sites, but the tent pads were small, and they lacked an adequate place to hang our canopy.

At our chosen site, we hung our rain canopy first to provide shelter for us and our gear from the rain sprinkles that started as we unloaded our canoe. It was comforting to be in the protection of our little oasis from the rain, so we decided to enjoy our lunch snacks while we listened to the soft rhythm of the raindrops. During an interlude in the raindrop melody, we erected our tent and unpacked the rest of our belongings. With the needs for food and shelter satisfied, we began discussing options for the rest of the day and beyond.

The rain came to an end later in the afternoon, so we embarked on an exploratory paddle around what would be our home water for the next few days. As we ventured into the narrow north channel, we quietly passed a pair of swans. Pockets of white feathers scattered throughout the area told us that the swans had been hanging out there for some time. Shortly after our swan encounter, we passed four women in two canoes. They asked us if there were any available campsites ahead of them. Just behind them was a solo gentleman with a British accent who posed the same question. As we continued on our exploration, we were concerned that the peaceful evening we were looking forward to might have just evaporated.

We paddled on up into the north arm, past silent beaver lodges and small scattered collections of ducks. At the very north end of Kelly, near the portage to Jack Lake, we were quietly floating while Julie photographed lily pads for a possible painting. A hummingbird slowly worked its way past Julie's right shoulder, came down the length of our canoe, and hovered, beak to nose, right in front of my face as it was apparently evaluating the bright red bandana I was wearing on my head. That encounter seemed to heighten my awareness of the details of our surroundings. As we turned to paddle back toward camp, in my heightened awareness, I noticed a thick layer of clear gel that was on the pinkish underside of the lily pads Julie had been photographing. I had never noticed it before.

Back at camp in the early evening, we settled in for an alfredo dinner, then boiled lake water to replenish our water bottles. When we have had boiled lake water left in our bottles after leaving the wilderness, I've noticed that it typically tastes like lake water, with a faint aftertaste of dirt or silt. In the wilderness, though, on a quiet evening or during a portage workout, it tastes as refreshing as any water I've ever tasted.

As evening calm settled across the lake, we were relieved not to hear any of the fellow human residents we had encountered earlier. The only noise came from a red squirrel ravaging seed clusters in the small cedars around camp, leaving spent seed shells lying scattered on the ground. Kelly Lake was picture-perfect still, giving Julie an excuse to get out her camera and begin collecting more art reference pictures.

Nighttime brought hard rain. The next morning, the rain had stopped, but remnants were still dripping from trees and brush. The lake was unmarred, except for occasional drips along shore. Our resident red squirrel was frantically cutting clusters of cedar seeds again, throwing them from treetops with reckless abandon. A few clusters nearly landed on my hat.

Mid-morning, we paddled over to the Burnt Lake portage. Hiking along the portage trail, we encountered a pair of ruffed grouse all puffed up and tail fanning, apparently in competition to see who could put on the best show. I didn't see a female grouse anywhere around, so I wasn't sure who they were trying to impress, other than themselves. Shortly before Burnt Lake, we crossed a tiny creek that bubbled up from beneath a rock, then trickled down the trail and disappeared again beneath the mossy forest floor. From the end of the portage trail, several islands were visible on Burnt Lake. A misty rain was gently coming down as Julie painted a small painting of an island from within the shelter of the forest. Moose maples and other underbrush were transitioning to fall colors, but the rest of the north woods forest was still summer green. Even though it was rainy on our side of the lake, bright sunshine illuminated the far shoreline as Julie painted. When she completed her painting, we left Burnt Lake and points west for another day and headed back to Kelly, intent on exploring more to the north. On our way back to Kelly, we found the remains of a freshly eaten hind end of a snowshoe hare in the middle of the trail. It wasn't there earlier, and there was no sign of the diner. I was surprised that we didn't hear any noise from the hare during its demise, because rabbits and hares are known for letting out a loud, high-pitched squeal in those situations.

After a quick lunch break, we portaged up into Jack Lake, which was long and narrow like Kelly, then up into Weird Lake. We spent some time admiring the pretty creek and waterfall coming out of Weird Lake, then quietly paddled our way around the small lake under the surveillance of a bald eagle that was soaring overhead. A trio of what looked like young otters kept popping up out of the water to take a look at us. Apparently, we were not very interesting, because they soon went on their way, periodically raising up and looking back at us.

After our otter visit, we found a beaver lodge that was built up against a small cliff. As we quietly glided past, we could hear a beaver making noises inside. It sounded like grunts and squeaks from a guinea pig. We assumed that we were listening to a conversation between two beavers, but there was no way to know for sure. Regardless, it was the first time we had heard a beaver make noises other than a tail slap. There were lots of beaver houses in the area, but we still had not actually seen a beaver. We did see a number of kingfishers, though, and watched two of them apparently having a disagreement of some sort as we paddled past.

The sun finally broke through again about 5 pm, as we were paddling back to the portage to Jack Lake. Near the portage, a large painted turtle was sitting on a log, taking advantage of the late afternoon sun. We certainly appreciated it as well.

Back on Kelly Lake, we saw another bald eagle soar past as we were watching a lone otter that came half out of the water to get a better look at us. We left it to do whatever it was doing before our interruption and paddled back to camp as we contemplated our dinner options.

The evening sky stayed clear, letting the temperature drop lower than the previous night. At least it felt that way, but we didn't have a thermometer to verify the feeling. By 10 pm, stars were covering the sky in brilliant white dots, with the Big Dipper reflecting in the lake. I could hear fish splashing all over the lake as well. Some sounded rather large, making me wish I had brought my fishing gear. For a few minutes, I stood there on the shoreline, imagining myself fishing for the big splashers, wondering what kind of fish they were. Satisfied with my mental catch, I retired to the tent and my waiting sleeping bag.

The next morning, fish were jumping. I didn't know if it was again or still, but they were actively having breakfast when we emerged from our tent into the beginning of a cheerfully sunny day. We quickly ate our own breakfast so we could get out on the water and participate in the celebration.

Everything was bathed in the soft amber morning light. Early on into our explorations, we were quietly floating near a sun-drenched beaver lodge when we overheard a conversation going on inside, much like the previous day. It sounded like a youngster and a parent, but of course, we had no way to know for sure. We had no idea about what was being conveyed either, but it was recognizable as a dialogue, nonetheless. Nearby, a pair of swans silently floated in the morning glow on our postcard-picture wilderness lake — probably the closest I will come here on earth to seeing the glowing radiance of angelic beings. I tried to imagine the awe of a vast choir of even more radiant angels, but my mind fell woefully short of the task.

As we paddled onward, trying not to disrupt the surrounding events, I found myself watching the flow of water around my wooden canoe paddle, noticing the little details of the swirls and eddies. I saw it as a wild study of fluid dynamics in action. Engineers tend to do squirrely things like that.

On Jack Lake, we watched a bald eagle that was perched in the top of a tall white pine on an island as it watched us and surveyed the lake. The eagle raised its wings and ruffled its feathers, releasing a trio of fine, fluffy white feathers into the morning air. As Julie was taking pictures of rocks and fall colors along the edge of a small bay, we could again hear beavers conversing inside of a lodge on the other side of the bay. In all my wilderness ramblings, I had never heard beavers vocalizing before, and here I was listening to the audible communications for the third time in only a couple of days. I wasn't sure why it seemed to be becoming such a common occurrence, but I was happy to listen.

Not far away, a large painted turtle was basking in the relative warmth of the morning sun. The log it had chosen was leaning at a steep angle against a large rock face. I was amazed that a turtle had the coordination and balance to climb such a steep log. Farther on, in a shadowed bend near the north end of Jack Lake, there was a shaft of bright sunlight penetrating the shoreline forest, illuminating a lichen-covered boulder. Atop the boulder, a tiny tree was growing, highlighted in that perfectly placed shaft of light. That caused me to start thinking about all the scenes from that morning and the experiences we had enjoyed. I imagined that there must be an infinite number of beautiful scenes in an acre of Boundary Waters wilderness. It was difficult to decide if we should paddle hard to see all that we could possibly see, or if we should just slowly drift, soaking in everything that any given location had to offer. Anticipating the unknowns that awaited us up ahead, we quietly paddled on, but in no big hurry.

At the north end of Jack Lake, we saw a pair of otters. One was dashing and thrashing amongst the reeds in the shallows, presumably chasing a fish. The frantic display ended, and the otter climbed up onto the shore. A flash of silver in its mouth, followed by sounds of crunching and chewing, confirmed the reason for the frantic behavior.

The 240-rod portage to South Temperance Lake provided a nice reprieve from sitting and paddling, giving us an opportunity to stretch our backs and muscles while we did some dry-ground sightseeing.

On South Temperance, we saved island explorations for later and paddled directly to the winding east arm that connects with Brule Lake. In that narrow arm, we quietly glided past a pair of hen mallards that were sitting motionless on a matted tussock of grass, their drab green bills and coal-black eyes shining in the early afternoon sun. Around the next bend, we passed a painted turtle sunning on a log just before a trio of beavers exploded from the cover of amber marsh grass where they too had been enjoying the sunshine.

At the end of the winding arm, the water of Brule Lake trickled through a pile of boulders, becoming the water of South Temperance. A pair of loons were visible on the west end of Brule, sitting silently in the sunshine. On the upper side of the rock garden, off to the south side, an old barkless notched log lay submerged beneath a few feet of water, looking like a giant light-colored Lincoln Log from my childhood. Waves were increasing out on the open reaches of Brule, so we remained in the shelter of the islands and peninsulas at the west end. With waves continuing to build, we cut our tour of Brule short and made our way back across the 10-rod portage into the winding arm of South Temperance.

As we approached the bend where we had previously seen the turtle and beavers, we decided to quietly slide into position for Julie to photograph a pair of painted turtles, one of which was shedding its shell scales. As we softly bumped the bank, Julie whispered, "Beavers. Right here." Through the marsh grass and low brush, I could barely see reddish-brown fur about three feet from her. One beaver dashed under the canoe, right at Julie's feet. The other one sat motionless for a couple of pictures — that we later found to be blurry — before it scurried away through the tall grass. As we resituated to paddle on, a third beaver dove into the water across the channel from us. We could see it swimming underwater until it disappeared into the darkness of a deep hole.

Coming back into the main body of South Temperance, we hooked north to the short portage into North Temperance. We could hear a loon calling ahead of us as we negotiated the portage trail. Nearing the lake, we could see the lone loon calling out in a small bay. As we paddled out into the lake, the loon just disappeared into the water as loons often do. Being a common encounter on Boundary Waters lakes, we paddled on, not giving it any special notice. Moments later, the loon surfaced within a few feet of our canoe. With a panicked noise that I can't even describe, it hastily dove again, probably without time to take another full breath. We could see it swimming underwater away from us.

With the afternoon waning, we decided that North Temperance was as far as we would wander for that day. Paddling back across South Temperance, we were serenaded by the calls of another loon as we navigated through the central islands. On the portage out of South Temperance, we crossed paths with a group of six first-time visitors to the Boundary Waters. They were obviously fishing. Even so, we were surprised at the amount of gear they were hauling. The last guy in line was an older gentleman. Much older than the rest of the crew. He looked frail and a little pale in the face. Enough so that I turned around and watched him until he was out of sight, just making sure that he didn't collapse. I hoped his condition looked worse than it really was and that his buddies were looking out for him better than it appeared. There was really nothing that I could do but offer up a short prayer on his behalf, though I did think of him a few times later that evening.

On our way through Little Wishbone Lake to Weird Lake, we came across the mostly eaten remains of a young Canada goose lying along the trail. At the end of the portage, another young Canada goose was lying badly injured at the edge of some tall grass. I wanted to intervene and end its suffering, but I knew that it really wasn't my place to do that. I also knew that geese can get nasty if they need to, even when they're injured. Sometimes especially when they're injured. So, I ultimately left nature to take its course.

Our day ended with us relaxing by a small fire, reliving the events and encounters of the day, and planning for the explorations of the day to come. It felt good, like a wilderness campfire should after a long day of exploring.

The next morning, a ruffed grouse visited our camp during breakfast, making a brief appearance before fading back into the surrounding forest. It was sunny and calm as we launched into Kelly Lake, with our sights set on investigating the fire lakes to the west of us — Burnt, Smoke, and Flame. I could imagine that there was a story behind the naming of the lakes, as I'm sure there was with the naming of most border country lakes.

We found Burnt Lake full of suspended algae. I couldn't imagine how someone could camp on the lake in that condition. There would be no safe drinking water available. Flame Lake contained algae as well, but not nearly as much as the main body of Burnt. Even with the abundance of algae, we saw bald eagles and a lone otter that ducked underwater and disappeared as soon as it spotted us. There was also a large swath of water beetles creating an intricate, short-lived collection of "V's" on the water's surface. Like the otter, the algae didn't seem to bother them.

Smoke Lake had considerably less algae than Flame Lake. Just prior to entering a long, swampy channel to the north, we saw a mink swimming into shore from open water. I didn't see if it had ventured into open water and was returning to shore or if it was swimming across from another shoreline. Either way, I didn't realize how adapted they were to deep water. Once the mink departed, we paddled to the end of the swampy channel, then continued on into the small creek that came in from places farther north. We took each cautious stroke with anticipation, expecting to see wildlife close-up and personal at any moment. After at least a half mile of stalking our way up into the swamp, we came to a shallow two-foot-wide ribbon of water falling over an old beaver dam. With our only wildlife sighting being a pair of mallards, and paddling getting difficult, we turned back toward Smoke Lake. When we first entered the channel and creek, I was hoping to find a moose. After thinking through the situation a little more, though, I came to realize that surprising a moose in close quarters like we were in might not have ended well.

When we got back to Burnt Lake, we explored the south end and found it to have much clearer water than the rest of the lake. At the far south end, we stopped at a campsite where Julie worked on a small painting while I scribbled notes in the pocket notebook that I always carry. The campsite was on a hill in a stand of stately white pines. It was a beautiful location, but the actual tent site was not very large.

Later, as we paddled back to the portage to Kelly, the breeze had apparently moved more algae into the small bay. It reminded me of bright green pea soup. Any little disturbance left a pattern in the green sludge.

Back at camp, conditions were right for a good long campfire, giving us time to reflect on the past few days and to toy with ideas for potential future wilderness ventures. For me, the difficult thing about the last night in a wilderness camp is that my mind jumps ahead and begins focusing on the approaching departure. Still, that last night on Kelly Lake, I was able to rein in my non-wilderness thoughts and keep my focus on the surrounding woods and waters.

Our morning of transition back to the outside world was overcast but dry. The pack-up and trek out were uneventful, except for one short stretch in the boulder-strewn creek below Peterson Lake. There, to keep from having to unload our boat for a precarious ten-yard stretch, I decided to just launch our loaded canoe, unmanned, across an open pocket of water that was too shallow to paddle, letting it lodge itself in a collection of downstream boulders.

Thirty minutes later, we had loaded our gear in the car and were strapping the canoe on our roof racks as sprinkles began falling. We cozily enjoyed snacks in the car, listening to the music of the rain, refreshed from our time in the wilderness, and looking forward to our return.

ROSE LAKE RAMBLINGS

We launched our sixteen-foot Nova Craft canoe into West Bearskin Lake shortly before 9:00 am. The summer that was fading into fall had been busy, and even a bit trying. So it felt good to be out paddling, closing the year-long gap between Boundary Waters visits. The put-in was nestled in the middle of a group of cabins along Clearwater Road. At least that's what I call the road, because it ends at Clearwater Lake. The morning sky was overcast but clearing, allowing the sun to shine brightly on the middle of the lake while we were still in the shadow of the clouds.

Loons were calling from somewhere up ahead, which I took as our welcome back to the wilderness we were soon to enter. Cabins all around the lake were thankfully quiet, allowing us to enter the wilderness mindset before we physically crossed that invisible boundary. I love being in the wilderness, but I find that sometimes, wilderness is as much a state of mind as it is a physical place. A small inquisitive otter cautiously greeted us just before we paddled into the advancing sunshine, which helped close the door on the mental did-we-forget-anything check-list I usually find myself going through even after we leave the vehicle behind.

Even though the 75-rod portage into Duncan Lake wasn't really anything noteworthy, it felt refreshing to be formally entering the wilderness. We live in the north woods in Michigan's Upper Peninsula, but it still always feels like a homecoming when we first enter the Boundary Waters wilderness. The contoured hillsides around Duncan were just showing slight tinges of autumn yellow, with accenting sprinkles of red. Some of the camps on Duncan were occupied, but nobody was out on the water yet. We have plenty of people contact outside of the wilderness, so having the wilderness paddling to ourselves was just plain relaxing. As we unloaded our gear at the portage north to Rose Lake, I wasn't sure what to expect. Our Fisher map noted it as the *Stairway Portage*, but I didn't know exactly what kind of stairway we were going to encounter. Or how extensive it was. Being that the mapmakers considered it to be noteworthy, I was curious to see it.

The stairway turned out to be fairly extensive and was divided into three sections. The upper section dropped down to the waterfall between Duncan and Rose, which was an obvious stopover for a lot of people. The stairs themselves were built out of relatively flat rock slabs. Going down wasn't strenuous, but it was a little knee-jarring due to carrying extra weight. I carried our canoe for the first trip across the portage simply because I already had my hands on it from pulling it out of the water. At the put-in on Rose Lake, we could see a nice-looking campsite that had an open view of the most predominant of the palisades across the lake, on the Quetico side. I was surprised to find an inviting-looking campsite open, but we would have to investigate it later because I still had two more trips to make across the portage with gear. Normally, we double portage, but my wife Julie was having minor issues with her leg, and I didn't want it to turn into a more serious problem. So, I was triple portaging to relieve Julie of having to carry her canoe pack. Fortunately, all the heavy carrying for the day would be while I was going down the stairs, so it wasn't much of a strain. The workout of triple portaging our canoe and gear back up the stairs wouldn't be for another four days, on our way back out. At that point in the trip, I reasoned, food, fuel, and water weights would all be less, making the haul easier. That's also one of the benefits of doing a base camp, with daily excursions only involving day packs and the canoe. You don't have to haul all your gear around every day.

When I returned to our stash of gear at Duncan, several people were relaxing there before venturing down to see the falls. They told me they were camped on Duncan and were just exploring the area. One of them warned me about a bear that had been frequenting campsites on the eastern end of Rose Lake and had even recently visited a few sites on Duncan. We always keep a clean camp and hang our food barrel, so I wasn't too concerned, but as I headed back down the stairs with my canoe pack, I wondered if that news might be the reason for the open campsite near the portage. Regardless, at least we knew there was an available site on our destination lake, even if it did sometimes have a nosy visitor.

On my third trip down the stairs, I startled a ruffed grouse that was standing in the mist at the edge of the drop-off into the creek, staring at the falls. Instead of taking flight, it scrambled off into the nearby mix of underbrush and boulders. Once I reached Rose Lake, we ate a leisurely lunch while a cool breeze dried off the minor moisture from my portage efforts. While we ate, a bald eagle made a splashy dive into the surface of Rose. Its descent sounded like a mini fighter jet coming in for a landing. The big bird triumphantly flew away with silver flashing in the grip of its talons. Apparently, we weren't the only ones interested in lunch. After eating, we loaded our gear and paddled over to the closest campsite to take a look. Even though it commanded a good view of the main palisade, the tent site was small, and the overall campsite felt a little cramped for a four-night stay. So, we paddled east to see if we had any other options.

That next campsite was much roomier and more inviting for a longer stay. The tent site was also big enough to accommodate our five-person tent. I doubt our tent would comfortably sleep five, but it's great for the two of us because the extra room it affords allows us to bring most of our gear inside where it's protected and accessible. The site also provided a better view of the main palisade, along with the creek valley that leads up to Arrow Lake in Quetico. We doubted any of the other campsites would be better, so we ended our search and started setting up camp. Julie then began working on a painting of our view across the lake shortly after camp was set, while I collected firewood out along the low ridge that paralleled the shoreline. Wood was still wet from the previous day's rain, but I knew it would dry better if it were spread out in the open around camp.

Sun and clouds were taking turns, changing the appearance of the palisades as Julie painted. Both scenarios had endearing qualities, so Julie was having a difficult time deciding which variation of the scene to capture. If my memory is correct, I believe the melancholy, cloudy scene won the debate, but the painting isn't available to remind me because it was sold during the Grand Marais plein air painting competition the following week.

With the bear warning in the back of our minds, once the painting was mostly finished, we ate an early dinner and got the food barrel hung up in a tree well before dark. Then we settled in for the evening with rhythmic sounds of small waves lapping at the shoreline rocks.

Just after sunset, as light was fading and the evening chill was creeping in, a loon began calling from somewhere across the lake. Its mournful calls echoed down the lake to the west, causing me to notice that the calling of loons, breaking the quiet of the wilderness, seems to deepen the quiet between calls. We would have liked to have a campfire, but all the wood was relatively damp. If it had been an emergency, I certainly could have started a fire, but it wasn't, so I didn't.

No bears visited during the night, but an unexpected rain shower did. As a result, our slowly drying firewood was back to being wet. With the sky still heavily overcast, we stashed our wood collection under our canopy to start the drying process again. We should have done that the evening before, but a clear sky and dry predictions convinced us the wood would be fine.

After we settled into our breakfast routine, a large flock of Canada geese flew over, heading south. Even though fall colors were not yet in full swing, the geese confirmed that autumn had indeed arrived.

Rose was rippled, but not what I would call wavy, as we struck out to the west, intent on at least exploring through South Lake. If the sky held its moisture, we might even work our way up through the *Height of Land* portage into North Lake. We encountered numerous ducks as we navigated the narrow western offshoot of Rose Lake. About halfway to our first portage, we passed a pair of swans, white butts in the air as they dined on aquatic plants. They obviously were not bothered by our presence, because even after they came up and saw us, they went right back to their imitation of big white bobbers as they continued eating.

It took us ninety minutes to reach our first portage, which was just a 4-rod carryover to Rat Lake. It's often hard to tell where lake names came from, but Rat Lake did look like a good muskrat lake. The campsite that was located right at the portage to Rat was spartan. One of those camps that are welcoming in foul weather, but not your first choice in any other conditions. Rat was one of those lakes where you can readily see your next portage before you even start paddling. With only a canoe and a pair of daypacks in our possession, we were on the other side of that next portage and launching into South Lake in short order.

We circumnavigated South Lake, going in a clockwise direction for no particular reason. The only sign of autumn was a stand of birch, hinting at autumn gold. At the *Height of Land* portage, we sat bobbing in our canoe for a few minutes, contemplating taking the hike just to see the portage sights. With the sky still deeply overcast and the air laden with dampness, we opted to start our journey back to camp instead. Thinking back, though, it was a relatively short portage to a significant location where, on one side, the water flows toward Lake Superior and on the other side it flows toward Hudson Bay, so we should have gone ahead and made the hike while we were there. Rain or not.

As we neared the portage back to Rat Lake, an oddly shaped stump near the water's edge caught my attention. As I was staring at the stump, it turned its head, and an immature golden eagle materialized and eyed us intently as we paddled past.

At the Rat Lake portage, we encountered two couples heading west. Both were wading into the lake to launch their boats. As I watched water running off their shoes and pantlegs into their canoes, I wondered why so many people do that. I've always launched from rocks or ground to avoid having wet feet all day. They seemed content, though, so I opted not to mention that as we exchanged pleasantries and embarked on the portage trail.

While we were crossing Rat Lake, a pair of swans — presumably the ones we had paddled by earlier in the day — noisily flew over the 4-rod portage from Rose and continued past us, then looped around, crossing in front of us, and landed just north of us with an explosion of trumpeting. They were still noisily sorting things out as we crossed the short portage and launched into the western arm of Rose Lake.

On Rose, a misty sprinkle was beginning to fall. The farther east we went, the more it transitioned from mist to rain. We followed the northern shoreline in hopes of using its features to block the waves from the increasing breeze. Unfortunately, the wind seemed to be following the shoreline in the opposite direction, penetrating every would-be shelter. The open part of Rose was wavy enough that Julie took a couple of splashes over the bow as we paddled toward camp. Once we arrived, things didn't seem all that wet. Apparently, the trees were doing their job of buffering the weather. Still, it was nice having our rain canopy to cook and eat under. As light rain continued into the night, it was also nice to have someplace relatively dry to hang out before I felt tired enough to climb into the tent and nestle into my sleeping bag. Again, we skipped the evening fire. Even if I got one going with the damp wood, the wind would have blown any sparks directly toward our tent.

During our midnight nature call, it was still raining. Early morning hours, rain was still pattering on the tent. We finally awoke to a tent that wasn't dark. Not brightly lit, but not dark. There was a light grayish glow, with no pattering sounds. About an hour later, we emerged from our cocoon into a day with faint blue openings between clouds. Puffy white clouds, not somber gray ones. The sun broke through as we ate breakfast, illuminating the battle-worn white pine that marked our campsite. A pair of otters made their way by in the choppy lake as we finished breakfast and began cleaning up. Once dishes were done, Julie set up to paint a picture of the tattered white pine while I cut more firewood into campfire-size pieces to speed up drying. Then I took to exploring west of camp through remnants of an old pine forest. There were large white and red pine stubs taller than most of the current area trees, which were a mix of spruce, fir, birch, and maple, with cedars scattered throughout. The faint trail I was following petered out in a thick patch of young spruce. On the backside of the ridge, near the spruce thicket, was a fallen giant. Likely a red pine. It was nurturing a brood of tiny fir trees in pockets of orange-red rotting wood. The log was about forty feet long, pointing up the ridge. I climbed on top and carefully walked the length of it to the point of its former anchor to the earth, where the remains of its roots still slightly fanned out from the old stump. Small chunks of orange-red wood protruded from the soil that was reclaiming the tree.

When I returned to camp, Julie was in a good mood as she concentrated on her painting, so for once I decided not to interrupt her with my usual questions and comments, which typically just get me in trouble anyway. Instead, I headed east through a mix of trees dominated by cedars. The morning sunlight felt uplifting, even after only a day of gloom. Sometimes, I think we need a little gloom in order to fully appreciate the brighter side of things. I only explored as far as the next camp, where I found a note on the fire grate about recent bear visits. Someone had even sketched a picture and named the bear. Not being one to name wild animals, I didn't bother trying to remember the name. The campsite was definitely not as nice as the one we were staying at, so I headed back to see how Julie was doing, glad that we chose the site that we did.

Julie's painting was essentially done, so we decided it was time for a lunch break. After our lunch snacks, we both went exploring beyond the second camp east of ours. Near that second camp, we discovered a large burl growing on a white birch. I've seen lots of burls, but rarely on a white birch. We also found a fir tree growing in a full curl, like a sheep's horn. Away from the lakeshore, there was a small campsite right on the *Border Route Trail*. It wasn't much of a camp with respect to size, view, or amenities. Personally, if I were backpacking, I would rather make my way down to the lake for a much nicer campsite.

After our explorations and dinner, we finally had conditions for a relaxing campfire. It felt incredibly comforting after a couple of evenings of breezy, wet conditions. The night chill came in stronger than usual, making the fire feel even better. Relaxing by the warmth of the fire's flickering flames naturally led to a night of peaceful wilderness sleep.

The next morning, we were greeted by a misty fog shrouding the lake. For our daily excursion, we paddled over to the portage to Duncan to explore the connecting creek and waterfall. The falls drop probably thirty feet through a bedrock chute, then the creek tumbles through a ravine of rocks covered in well-dampened moss. Down in the ravine, it felt like being in a hidden, exotic paradise. One of the best things about wilderness areas like the Boundary Waters is that there are no railings or fences, so you're free to carefully explore any place you choose.

We then paddled over and cruised the north shoreline of Rose Lake. As we paddled around a Canadian island, we came upon a trio of otters playing in the shallows. They slipped into overhanging brush along the island shoreline and disappeared. As we continued our island loop, I could see the otters running through the trees along the minor ridge that spanned the length of the island. It looked like they were racing us, like a bunch of kids. When we again saw them in the water, they kept inching closer, popping up and "woofing" at us. At about twenty yards, they finally dove and reappeared quite a distance away. Then they moved on and left us alone. We did the same.

At the mouth of the Arrow River, a bald eagle watched us from its white pine perch while Julie took pictures. We also got a closer view of the main palisade, where we could clearly see rock features instead of just color variations. The slight breeze of the day subsided, leaving Rose's surface unmarred for our paddle back to camp.

There, Julie finished the afternoon touching up her painting of our camp tree while I poked around the water's edge, admiring the collection of palisades in front of me. The day ended with puffy white clouds scattered across the sky, except for directly overhead. There, it was nothing but blue. During my ponderings, I wondered about the prevalent evolutionary theory that this world, with all of its complexities and interwoven relationships, is purely a result of chance happenstance. Looking around, I highly doubted it. My ponderings continued periodically through our evening fire. Later, I crawled into the warmth of my sleeping bag even more convinced of my faith in a purposefully designed creation. That comforting thought led to another peaceful night of sleep.

Our last day in the wilderness dawned sunny and clear. It felt cheery. There was only one regret in my mind as we packed up our camp. I wished we had climbed one of the tall rock outcrops on the south side of Rose Lake to enjoy the panoramic view. As we unloaded our canoe at the stairway portage, I was anticipating a workout. My heart indeed got pumping during the triple portage up the three sets of stairs, but it didn't feel taxing. In fact, I came to appreciate the stairway portage and especially the labor that went into building it. I also appreciated the fact that, being in my early sixties, I can still make a trek like that with packs and a canoe and come out feeling refreshed.

For what it's worth, my plan is to keep enjoying wilderness experiences like that just as long as I possibly can! Regardless of my age.

TUSCARORA REVISITED

Julie and I had spent part of a day on Tuscarora Lake several years earlier and had decided then that the lake warranted revisiting when we had more time to explore the area. So, we launched into Round Lake, en route to Tuscarora, about 9:00 on a mid-September morning. The put-in was designed for motorboats, not canoes, so it was a bit of a pain launching from boulders and a wet log next to the formal launch structure. The short paddle straight across the lake was quick and unceremonious. We just wanted to get into the backcountry. In my haste to get packed up and underway, I neglected to remove my flannel shirt, so I was already getting hot when we arrived at the portage to Missing Link Lake.

Even though we had not needed to portage our canoe for nearly a year, we quickly picked up on the unloading routine and were heading out across the portage without giving it much thought. As usual, most of the thinking was done earlier as we were paddling away from our launch, and I was mentally reviewing my checklist one last time.

Shortly after passing the sign signifying the official wilderness boundary, I encountered five grouse on the trail. I spotted one at first. Then, as I raised the bow of the canoe on my shoulders, the count continued to grow. Julie said that when she came through behind me, three of the birds were back out in the trail again. As is our normal backcountry routine, we were double portaging. I hauled my daypack and our canoe on one trip and my big canoe pack on another. Julie hauled her canoe pack on one trip and the food barrel on another. It makes for safer portages than trying to haul too much gear at once. Regardless, the portage was muggy! Muggy, but it was behind us, and we were officially in the Boundary Waters wilderness once again. In a way, I felt at home because this was the type of place that I want to be, even when I'm not able to.

Missing Link was just a pass-through for us. We glided through the S-curve of the lake, focused on the shallow sandy take-out at the portage that would take us to our destination on Tuscarora Lake. I was looking forward to the portage because of what was on the other side. Although I wasn't really looking forward to the 428-rods of portaging, the only way to get to the other end was to pick up the gear and go. So, I hoisted my canoe pack and headed off down the trail. I had decided to haul the pack first so I could scout the trail without a sixteen-foot umbrella hampering my view. We met several people who were coming out of Tuscarora, which got us thinking that the lake would be pretty much empty when we arrived. The sun peeked out periodically, just to warm things up and add to the muggy feeling of the day. At about the halfway point, I set down the pack and waited for Julie so we could go back for our second load. On longer portages, we often deal with it in two stages. That way, we get a break to refresh partway through. It also keeps us from getting too far away from any of our gear in case we need something. There was a merciful breeze here and there along the trail, which thankfully helped combat the mugginess. When we returned to the Missing Link end of the portage, the crowd we passed on the trail had come and gone. It was just us and the breeze. Coming up out of Missing Link on the second leg of the portage, I noticed there were lots of leaves on the ground, releasing an herbal autumn aroma. Overall, the portage wasn't terribly difficult, just long. And hot.

With everything finally on the Tuscarora end of the trail, we loaded our canoe and set out to find a suitable campsite for the next several days. We ended up checking out several camps as the breeze intensified and the lake became choppier. Most were either occupied or crappy. One of the sites, being very small and wet, was the worst campsite I had ever seen. They say, any port in a storm, but we were not in a storm. At least not yet.

Mid-afternoon, we ended up at the island camp where we had stayed previously. I had to remove one star from my previous five-star rating due to a big White Pine right in front of camp that had succumbed to a windstorm and was lying on its side with a large root mat extending probably fifteen feet in the air.

After putting up our tent and rain canopy and unloading our gear, Julie took a short nap in the tent as I scrounged for firewood around the island. The waves that we were fighting as we searched for a campsite died almost immediately once we found our site. Without the breeze that accompanied the waves, the afternoon mugginess increased, making me wonder if it would be too uncomfortable for an evening fire.

After dinner, as evening settled in and we settled in as well, some guys in another camp started ramping up their conversation. It got louder as the evening went on. After a while, it didn't even sound like a normal conversation. I suspected that they were either drunk or high.

Their obnoxious noise completely killed the serenity and solitude I was hoping for. At first, I was annoyed and irritated. By 9 pm, my irritation had grown into anger. I wanted to either yell at them or go to their camp and physically shut them up. But I knew neither course of action would help the situation. So, I just stewed. Thankfully, by 10 pm things died down — both the noise and my anger. The incident showed me just how fragile serenity and solitude are and how easily they can be broken, making them all the more precious and desirable. The atmosphere of a nearly full moon overhead had helped me calm down once the noise subsided. So, ultimately, the night was peaceful, but to my sixty-two-year-old body, the ground was still hard. Even with double foam pads.

The next morning, we awoke to an overcast sky, but it was still warm. There was never even an evening chill the previous night. Autumn in the Boundary Waters, we usually wear a thin pair of long underwear and socks in our sleeping bag. Sometimes, even a pullover hat. Not that night. I never even closed or zipped my sleeping bag. Loon calls greeted us as we came to life that morning, which was what I needed. Part of what I had come to the wilderness looking for. No human-made noise. Small waves gently lapping shoreline rocks, the slight breeze through myriad branches and leaves, and loon songs. After breakfast, we hung our food pack, buttoned up camp, and set out on a cruise of Tuscarora, maybe even one of the small neighboring lakes. It didn't really matter. I was just ready to explore and quietly see what was out there to find.

As we paddled away from camp, distant thunder could be heard to the southwest. I estimated its location as somewhere around Little Saganaga Lake. As we paddled east, thunder became more frequent and sounded a little closer. We modified our plans accordingly. After all, we had no agenda. No necessary destination. So, we reduced our explorations to a closer proximity to our island camp. The morning calm had disappeared, but the bad weather didn't feel close at hand either. Soon, the thunder just abruptly stopped, so we continued our tour and ended up looking for the short portage into Thelma Lake. It was supposedly at the end of a small channel. We managed to paddle and pole our way to the end of the channel, but never found the portage. It looked like the water level was a little lower than usual, so I suspected that we just couldn't quite get as far as we needed to in order to access the portage. The end of the channel was not deep enough to take our canoe, but too wet to walk. Fortunately, the end of the long winding channel was just big enough to spin our sixteen-foot canoe around in. Not easily, but we managed. On our way back out to the main lake, Julie took pictures of three fresh white water lily flowers. I thought they would be gone by that time of year, or at least seriously faded and weathered. We accepted it as a little blessing and continued on with our exploring.

There were a few light sprinkles, but the dominating sunshine gave us confidence that the rain wouldn't amount to anything. We finished our tour of the south side of Tuscarora and ate our lunch snacks at the portage to Owl Lake. While we were eating, we met a guy coming from Little Sag who was in the middle of a sixteen-day paddling venture. He started at Sawbill Lake and was heading back there to wrap up his trip. He told us that a good portion of the weight he was carrying was food for his Golden Retriever paddling partner. I thought that going solo would be better and more enjoyable than carrying all that extra weight, but he seemed happy, so I didn't say anything. After he paddled off in search of a Tuscarora campsite, we hiked the portage trail as a reconnaissance for the next day. Afterward, we paddled a little more of the west end of Tuscarora, then headed back to camp for an early dinner and to watch and listen to another thunderstorm that was rolling our way. If nothing else, the cool breeze that was ushering in the clouds felt refreshing.

After barking for a while, the thunderstorm eventually bit, but just with minor showers. We just stood in the shelter of the white pine root mat standing in front of camp and watched it rain. With the coming and going of thunderstorms, we were able to watch a parade of interesting cloud formations throughout the day, which prompted Julie to take a considerable number of pictures.

After an early dinner, we planned to take an evening cruise in our canoe, but more thunder, wind, and waves kicked in and changed our minds. Instead, we roamed our island and watched a pair of loons close to shore. I was amazed at how quietly and gracefully they dove. It looked effortless. The sun went down behind yet more thunderstorm clouds, but it lit up a big cloud mass farther east, making it look like its inside was on fire. Later, a full moon was illuminating the eastern sky while lightning was lighting up the western sky. A cool breeze freshened everything, making the night feel vibrant.

We wrapped up the evening with a small fire. After all, a camp doesn't feel complete without a fire. Unlike the previous night, Tuscarora was at peace. The loud guys in the other camp were quiet for some reason. I assumed that they were either tired or gone. It was a selfish thought, but I figured that as long as they were quiet, why, didn't really matter to me. The moon and clouds were having a dance as I headed to the tent for the night. This was how things were supposed to be in the wilderness.

Nighttime lightning had disappeared to leave a mild sunny morning. It was quiet except for loon calls and bird songs. The lake was lightly rippled, but not a wave was in sight. After breakfast, a bald eagle flew in and landed in the top of a tall spruce on the island in front of us. As soon as we launched into our explorations, we paddled over and took pictures of the small island next to us so we could capture it in early morning light. We couldn't readily agree on which spot to take pictures from — we both had our own ideas — so we took shots from multiple locations. We then portaged into Owl Lake, where we slowly paddled into a sheltered grassy bay in hopes of seeing a moose. Instead, Julie got pictures of a tiny rock island that supported a trio of small spruces. There was nobody else on the lake.

Owl was ours to explore in the morning light and morning shadows that Julie is fond of for picture taking.

Five minutes after commenting that we had not seen an active beaver lodge on either lake we had explored, we found one. Fresh cuttings and fresh mud verified that it was being used. We sat and listened, but no noises came from within the lodge. Either nobody was home, or they were being very quiet. Large numbers of minnows were gathered amongst the fringe of branches in the water. While we were watching and listening, we heard noises in the woods. Our hopes for a moose sighting were dashed again when the noises turned out to be a red squirrel cutting loose pinecones from high in a nearby tree. Near the beaver lodge, we also encountered a loon with an adolescent chick. At first, I thought the young bird might be an odd color phase of a Common Loon, but we later saw several others that looked just like it.

As we portaged from Owl to Crooked Lake, I stepped into a mucky spot that turned out to be several inches deep. So, when we reached the lake, I washed off my boot and pant leg so as not to get black muck smeared everywhere. Not that I'm a clean freak when I'm in the backcountry, but I especially didn't want it to get all over my sleeping bag when I got undressed later that evening.

Just after launching, we paddled by a loon with a pair of mostly grown chicks that looked just like the light-colored one we had wondered about earlier. As we paddled past a collection of tall old white pines, I thought of how old white pines like that typically stand out above the rest of the forest. In fact, I often use unique trees like that — or collections of trees — to navigate and keep track of where I am.

The portage to Crooked Lake was short, but the day was warming up quickly, making any physical exertion a reason to sweat. As we made our way into Crooked Lake, we found the entrance to a long arm of the lake blocked by a small beaver dam. Exploring that area was my main attraction to the lake, so we got out of our canoe, onto the dam, and slid our boat over into the long, narrow channel that had caught my attention on the map. Based on the condition of the dam, it didn't look like anyone had made a crossing to explore that section of the lake any time recently. That made our venture all the more interesting. We paddled on with anticipation. As we reached a large island, we spooked several small groups of ducks. Together, they likely numbered close to fifty birds. Some didn't take flight to get away from us. Instead, they flapped and paddled, basically walking on the water, until they felt they were at a safe distance. A little farther along, we veered off into the east branch of the channel only to find it blocked by rocks and a small beaver dam. With the dam not being as solid as the first one, Julie was reluctant to climb out of the boat onto it. After a little coaxing from me, she eventually cautiously got out of the boat and made her way to one end of the dam, where we sat on a large flat boulder to eat our lunch. With the boulder being in the shade, it made for a relaxing break from the heat. It turned out that there wasn't a lot of water to explore on the other side of the dam, so we were soon back to cross the structure again. We found that the return crossing isn't always as easy as the initial crossing. The different views and perspectives can show or hide different features. Like rocks. We finished our tour of the rest of the long arm and paddled out into the breeze of the open lake. That breeze felt refreshing, but it did make paddling more of an effort. Crooked Lake has numerous arms and islands, so I had to keep a close eye on our map to track exactly where we were. I couldn't recall what the island campsite that we had stayed at on our previous visit looked like, but Julie and I both recognized it as soon as we saw it. It reminded me a lot of the campsite we were staying at on Tuscarora. With Crooked Lake still recovering from the Ham Lake fire, the scenery was not as enjoyable as that of other lakes, but it was good to see it recovering. Nature is certainly designed to be resilient.

Speaking of resilience, back at the portage to Owl Lake, I spent some time looking at an old, submerged log crib filled with rocks.

Obviously, there was once a substantial dock of some sort there, as is the case with many places throughout the wilderness. At one point, the hand of man had a pretty firm grip on the entire region. Left mostly to its own healing, the wilderness is recovering incredibly well.

At that point, we made our way back to camp to escape the heat of the day. Once again, the afternoon temperature was around eighty degrees Fahrenheit. Not at all what we expected when we packed mostly cold-weather clothing. The breezy shade of our island camp was a good cure for the unexpected heat.

Later, we watched the sunset from the rocks in front of camp until it was time to watch the moon rise behind camp. We had plenty of time to witness both because it was too warm for a campfire. As much as I love campfires, it was just too warm for a fire to even sound good. It felt good to just relax in the relative cool of the evening and think back through the roaming's of the day. Well after our day ended, I awoke in the wee hours of the next morning to the pattering of a light sprinkle of rain on our tent. Even though I couldn't feel it from within our nylon shelter, it sounded refreshing.

We awoke a little later than usual to a sunny morning. Maybe the sound of rain on the tent earlier in the morning relaxed me more than I had been on other nights. Maybe we just needed a little extra sleep. It didn't matter. We had no set schedule or deadlines. It was just another day to enjoy our current wilderness lifestyle. There was a relatively cool breeze rustling up the surface of the lake, making the morning feel comfortable compared to the heat and humidity of the previous evening.

After breakfast, which is usually just a collection of snacks, our plan was to portage into a series of small lakes east and northeast of Tuscarora. There was no special reason other than the lakes were there and we hadn't seen them. According to my map, the portage trail cut right across the first lake, which I assumed meant that it was not really a navigable body of water. After probably twenty minutes of brush scraping my arms and hands along the narrow portage trail, not to mention the noise of brush raking along the sides of the canoe, we reached a narrow channel of murky water across the middle of a swamp. It didn't look very inviting. I was already hot and sweating from the portage, and the day was quickly heating up as well. Revisiting my map, I reasoned that the small lakes ahead were closer to the edge of the wilderness and probably very swampy, which somehow diminished their original appeal. Especially in the heat. After a brief discussion, Julie and I agreed to backtrack and do a little more exploring on the open water of Tuscarora instead.

One of the areas we explored was a small island only about fifty yards from the island we were camped on. Adjacent to our island was a large boulder we had been photographing in different lighting conditions. Like a kid, I had to climb up on top of it. I don't know why, but it seemed important to do.

While I was standing on the boulder, surveying our island across the narrow channel, a bear emerged from our woods, strolled out onto a rocky point, and stepped into the water, obviously planning to swim over to the island we were on. My initial thought was to just stand still and get a good, close look at the bear as it came out of the water right near my perch. Then I thought about Julie, who was somewhere on the small island, but I didn't know where. Safety ruled. I clapped my hands at the bear so it would notice me standing on the boulder. The bear quickly changed its mind about swimming over and retreated to our camp island, then skirted around the east side, which I was happy was away from our campsite.

Just as the bear disappeared, Julie showed up. As I was telling her about my encounter, I glanced over and saw the bear swimming out from our island, perpendicular to where we were. Once it got about fifty yards into the lake, it turned and proceeded to swim past us, heading for the south shore of the lake, which I assumed was where it wanted to go in the first place, before I interrupted its island-hopping route. Several times, the bear looked our way, ears extended wide, keeping track of us as it swam by. It eventually faded from our sight as its black head melded with the dark shoreline.

We paddled back to camp not knowing what we would find because we had no idea of where the bear had been prior to seeing it. We reached camp shortly before noon, relieved to find everything intact with no signs of a visitor. So, it thankfully all turned out to be just an interesting wilderness encounter.

After lunch, the heat and blazing sun encouraged us to relax around camp to catch up on some writing and sketching. Hopefully, things would cool down enough to allow us to enjoy an evening fire for our last night on our private island.

While I was dipping water out of the lake to boil, I heard rushing air and splashing nearby. I turned around to see a small flock of mergansers landing along the shoreline about ten yards behind me. They lined up on the shoreline slab for a few minutes, their white necks glowing in the bright sunshine. Later, as I was washing dishes, they were back, completely ignoring me as I did chores right near them. Still later, as I was sitting near the water while I wrote notes of the day's adventures, the pack of eight mergansers swam past about twelve feet away. Apparently, I was considered to be just another natural feature. I took that as a compliment.

The days had been hot. Almost too hot to truly enjoy. We had spent lots of time seeking shade, but the mornings and evenings made the trip enjoyable. Even with the big white pine leaning on its side in front of camp, I still considered it a five-star place after all.

We decided to paddle out to watch the sunset from the vantage point of the open lake. Then we returned to camp to watch the moon rise from a perch on the north side of our island. The full moon rose large and bold orange. Almost as soon as it completely cleared the distant trees, it ducked behind a low bank of clouds. It peeked through the clouds in spots, and at one point, the cloud it was behind looked like it had a pair of burning orange eyes. Once it cleared the cloud bank and climbed into the open expanse above, it was more of a normal pale yellow ball, casting a streak of yellow light across the lake to us.

When we were done playing with the sun and moon, we lit our campfire and settled in to just relax and savor our last night in the wilderness. I was thankful that it wasn't too breezy for a fire. Conditions were perfect. Well, it would've been nice if it had been a little cooler, but the fire was still entrancing. After a couple of hours of quietly talking and tending our fire, we let it burn down and extinguished it before moving into the tent for one last night of wilderness sleep.

Knowing we were heading out of the wilderness and had things to take care of once we got out, I mentally switched back to business mode, so we were up at 6 am, packing. Somewhere in the midst of packing, we ate a quick breakfast of the same snacks we had been eating for the past four days for lunch. It was a breezy and bright start to the day. Despite the bright sky, the moon was still out as well. Packed and ready, we bid a quick goodbye to our island, knowing that we would likely never be there again. We launched our boat into Tuscarora about 7:45 am and were soon unloading at the portage to Missing Link Lake — the long portage, as everyone called it. We started portaging at 8:15. I hauled my canoe pack first, so I could get a good look at the trail and scenery before I had a canoe hanging over my head.

Partway across the portage, I encountered fresh, large moose tracks in the soft mud. Fresh, untrampled muddy clumps that had fallen off the hooves were scattered on the hardpacked trail beyond the muddy area. Red spots in the trail caught my attention. At first, I thought they were from birds eating red berries. Then, I recognized them as drops of blood. They continued on for probably a hundred yards, sometimes with several drops in one location. I touched one of the drops. The blood was still fresh. It dawned on me that I was probably following the trail of a bull moose that had been wounded in a fight. My senses went on full alert as I quietly slipped down the trail, scanning all around for hints of a large, dark, rut-crazed, wounded, pissed-off animal. I finally found where the bull had stood for a bit, leaving a good collection of larger red drops, before it veered off into the brush, up and over a small hill, leaving red smears on the thick foliage. At that point, my guard went down. A little. After that, our venture out, which consisted of three paddling stretches and two portages, was uneventful other than seeing a grouse sneaking through a spruce grove about ten feet from the trail. We arrived at Missing Link about 10:30 am and were at the takeout, unloading our boat at noon.

It was time to go check on Julie's artwork at the Johnson Heritage Post Gallery in Grand Marais, make a few phone calls, have a late lunch, and begin the trek home. Those thoughts made me realize how quickly we revert back to the hectic pace of modern life even after slowing down for a refreshing dose of wilderness. I took that to mean we need to enjoy wilderness slow-downs more often and savor them while we can. So I began thinking about options for our next adventure.

FOURTOWN

We entered the Boundary Waters at Mudro Lake, which means that we actually launched our canoe into the creek connecting Mudro to Picket Lake. Due to low water conditions, there were a few more portages between the put-in location and Mudro than the two that were shown on our Fisher map. So, what should have taken about an hour took two, and our expected two-hour journey into Fourtown Lake took four hours. The going wasn't difficult, just time-consuming. Though birch branches were already bare, the early October aspens were still in their prime autumn yellow attire, which glowed on the evergreen-dominated hillsides. Here and there, a scarlet bush accented the shoreline. A bald eagle flew ahead of us as we worked our way into Fourtown and was waiting for us on its perch when we first arrived at the lake. We saw a couple of grouse along the portage trails as well. One made a typical grouse departure, crashing through the branches as it flew away. The other contentedly sat in a leafless birch, watching us parade past.

Julie and I had passed through Fourtown with our daughters on a previous Boundary Waters visit several years earlier and were intrigued by its islands and highly contoured shoreline, but we had never stayed there to explore the area. This was our exploration visit. We found a prime campsite overlooking the largest of the central collection of islands. It was somewhat sheltered, yet we still had a view out into the main body of the lake, which was where we had paddled through once before. Julie's first task when we get to a new camp is to find and evaluate the latrine. Fortunately, it passed inspection, because I liked the camp and its strategic location on the lake. Besides the views, it wasn't far from the portages to Boot Lake or Horse Lake, making day trips convenient.

After setting up camp, we took an afternoon cruise to check out the creek up to Moosecamp Lake and to gather some wood for an evening fire. When we left camp, the lake was mirror-still. Cloud reflections on the water were so vivid that it felt like we were paddling through the sky, exploring cloud islands. Several times, we stopped paddling and just floated, not wanting to disturb the sky. Other than a few faint bird songs, the world was quiet to the point where my thoughts sounded loud.

When we reached the creek connecting to Moosecamp Lake, it looked navigable, so we ventured up into it until an old beaver dam blocked our way. It was getting late in the afternoon, so we decided to leave the creek exploration for another day when we had more time available, and then we retreated to Fourtown. There, we found a good place to leave the lake to search for firewood and soon had the center of our canoe loaded with campfire fuel.

Back at camp, we enjoyed a hearty backcountry dinner, then boiled enough water to replenish all of our water bottles. It had been sunny and unseasonably warm, so we went through more water than usual. After evening camp chores were done, we hung our food pack in a tree and settled in for our evening fire. The last weather prediction we had heard was that snow was coming within the next day or so. Just in case the prediction was right, we wanted to enjoy a relaxing campfire before foul weather had a chance to deprive us of the opportunity. Just as darkness was closing in, we were entertained by a snowshoe hare hopping around near our tent, its hind feet comically looking too big for its body.

In the morning, we ate breakfast bundled up to ward off the cold breeze as we watched thick clouds rolling in. We decided to spend the day around Fourtown exploring some of the interesting ridges and other features we could see from the lake. As we paddled past one of the vacant camps, I spotted something bone white sitting near the fire grate. Being a life-long hunter, I recognized it as an antler even from my quick glimpse. My priorities shifted, and I had to stop to investigate. It turned out to be a relatively heavy antler, sporting five points. It was a little weathered and had a few rodent chew marks, but holding it up in its natural position, I wished that I had the other half of the set to complete the picture. I had been collecting antlers since I was a kid — some by putting their previous owner in our freezer and others by picking them up as strays, like the one in hand — so I couldn't help putting it in our canoe.

After spending a few hours engaged in exploring a few ridges on foot, we ate lunch while floating in one of the bays at the north end of the lake. As we were finishing lunch, a strong wind blew in, driving a heavy cold mist. We scrambled into our rain jackets and began fighting our way back to camp into fifteen-inch rollers, some wearing white manes.

Cold and wet conditions continued through the afternoon. Julie finally resorted to working on a painting in the tent. Not wanting to be inside that early in the evening, I went for a walk along the swamp behind camp. After roaming for a bit, I got a little turned around in the edge of the swamp and decided to pull out my compass before turned around turned into lost. As I was working my way out to the lake, I stumbled onto a shed deer antler that looked like a newer match to the antler I had found earlier in the day. It was resting on a small mossy knoll right at the edge of the swamp. While I was admiring my treasure, I spotted the other side of the rack lying about eight feet away, slightly hidden by a fern. In my childhood, I would have probably wet myself from excitement over a find like that. Fortunately, I didn't have to pee, so it didn't turn into a test to see how much I had matured. I should have taken a picture of the antlers resting on their mossy forest bed, but that thought didn't register until I was back at camp, impressing Julie with my find.

Following my evening water boiling routine, I began making dinner, but before we had a chance to eat, snow began falling. A half-hour later, snow was blowing horizontally down the lake, making it look and feel like we had just made a time-warp leap into winter. We quickly put everything away, tied down a few things, and hung our food bag. After watching our resident snowshoe hare for a few minutes, Julie took to the shelter of the tent. I took a short walk, just to stay out of the confines of the tent a little longer. Even then, I entered the tent about three hours earlier than usual. Needless to say, there was no campfire.

After twelve hours in the tent, we emerged into wind, snow, rain, and sleet — pretty much everything but sunshine. We ate a hasty breakfast in the shelter of some thick evergreens, then decided our best course of action would be to stay active and make the most of the day we were dealt. We still wanted to explore the creek coming into the north end of Fourtown, so we decided to paddle our way up through Boot Lake, Fairy Lake, and Gun Lake, into Moosecamp Lake, then follow the creek back to Fourtown. It was a round-about way to explore the creek, but it would keep us active for a good share of the day and would require only one pass through the creek in case the going there was rough. As a bonus, we would also be paddling downstream through the creek instead of up.

While we were paddling to the Boot Lake portage, we briefly visited the huge boulder that our family had climbed up on to eat our lunch the first time we had passed through Fourtown. It had been a fun novelty for our kids. Unfortunately, snow and sleet made it too dangerous to repeat the climb that October day.

From what we could see through squinted eyes and the varying degrees of blowing snow, the scenery along our route was beautiful. There was even some autumn coloring still lingering, despite all the recent wind. Wildlife sightings were limited to a couple of bald eagles and a pair of loons. Apparently, everything else had the sense — or maybe just the instinct — to find some shelter and stay there.

We made good progress despite the weather and ate lunch on Moosecamp, then embarked on our creek expedition. In between the eleven beaver dam crawl-overs, the creek wasn't too difficult to paddle. Being that the entire creek was open and exposed to the elements, it worked out to be a perfect day for the venture. The dam-hopping would have been grueling on a warm, sunny day, but in the present cold, damp conditions, the extra work felt good.

By the time we arrived back at camp late in the afternoon, the wind and mixed precipitation had quieted down. While inspecting our camp for any damages, I found that something — presumably the resident red squirrel — had burrowed into our food bag and helped itself to most of our honey-roasted peanuts. I knew that red squirrels have to eat too and that, like most creatures, they are opportunistic, taking advantage of what they can find, but I still begrudged the little bandit for raiding our food bag. It was the first time in numerous years of

Boundary Waters outings that we had experienced any food-related issues with critters.

Our small campfire felt especially warm and comforting that evening. Sometimes it requires a little wilderness exposure to the elements without the luxury of hiding in a heated building or vehicle to help us appreciate basic things like simple food, fire, and shelter. I try to remind myself of that from time to time. Especially at home, where we have it pretty easy.

By morning, the wind had fired back up, and the thick cloud cover was still in place. Julie and I surveyed the lake, then looked at the map, considering our options. We ultimately decided to pack up and head out of the backcountry while our tent was still relatively dry and before the next wave of precipitation blew through. As we were digging through our food bag, considering breakfast options, I found that our pesky red squirrel neighbor had dug down near the bottom of our food bag and emptied an entire nine-dollar bag of pecans, which was something I was planning to include in my breakfast.

Wind had died down by the time we were ready to depart. Snow was back but limited to light now-and-then flurries. An eagle was soaring overhead as we paddled away from camp, giving me momentary thoughts of changing my mind. Our exit paddle through mild flurries, with patches of autumn colors still hanging on in the surrounding forest, felt peaceful, like we were doing the right thing. Even though we were leaving, it felt like a farewell, not a goodbye. I was confident that the Boundary Waters Wilderness would still be there to welcome us when we returned.

Shortly before we reached our official departure from the wilderness, we stopped for a minute to watch a mink hunting the north shore of Mudro Lake. Apparently, we were far enough away that our presence didn't bother the little hunter. When it casually left the lake, so did we as we soon crossed the invisible line separating wilderness from the man-made world. Speaking of the man-made world, before we left the area and headed for home, we bought a protective food barrel for our next wilderness journey.

On a subsequent autumn trip, we spent one night camped on Fourtown, just before leaving the wilderness. While we were there, I explored the hillside above camp and found a mosaic of bare rock and oak brush, which gave the hillside the distinctive burnt-orange color we noticed from the lake. I flushed a few grouse and found ample signs of both deer and moose, making it a place I would love to hunt sometime. On the other side of the ridge I found myself overlooking a vast swampy valley that I was convinced was a wildlife haven. There was not enough time to explore it, but I made a mental note to plan a return visit.

Four years later, we were finally back to explore that swampy valley. As we pulled into the Mudro Lake parking lot, I was disappointed to see twenty-eight vehicles already there. The morning fog had mostly burned off by the time we arrived, so our portage into the creek that fed into Mudro was just overcast and blah-looking. Still, it felt good to be underway and paddling again.

We soon came across two beaver dams blocking our way. The first one was fairly extensive, so we ended up going to one side where it was newer and lower. After getting out and pulling our canoe over the dam, I had to slide it through flooded grass and brush for about thirty feet before we were back afloat. The second dam was newer and lower, so we were able to simply do a pullover right in the main stream channel. Then there was a boulder field where we had to get out of the boat so I could pull it over a smooth, submerged rock. For the second boulder field, we were able to just carefully paddle through, with a few minor boulder bumps.

The three planned portages between Mudro and Fourtown were rocky and rough, but what made them difficult was the humidity. Of course, during the muggy portages, the sun came out so it could increase the temperature as well. After the sauna workout, paddling into Fourtown felt refreshing, but we still needed to find a campsite. With the full parking lot in mind, we began our search. The first camp on the east side was already being investigated as we paddled by. The next camp, which was one of the two I was hoping for, was vacant, so we stopped to allow me to take a look before deciding. It was the same place we camped during our previous trip when I wrote a Boundary Waters Journal article about Julie painting the wilderness. One of the benefits of that camp was that it had access to the big swamp I planned to explore in my quest for moose antlers. The stone wind-block around the fire grate held a set of ten-point whitetail antlers with a small portion of skull still attached. I took that as a good sign for my antler hunting plans and decided that when we left in a few days, those antlers were going with me.

It had taken us a little over four hours to reach our camp, which was longer than I expected, but not bad considering the humidity and beaver dam obstacles. After lunch and getting camp set up, we ate an early dinner and set out on an evening paddle, following the east shoreline. As we paddled along some low cliffs, the slightest movement of the water surface was causing the evening sun's reflections to pulsate and shimmer on the cliff face. It looked as if it would induce a trance if you stared at it for a while. Near the cliffs, we interrupted a kingfisher as we paddled by, sending it skittering away, apparently scolding us as it went.

Everywhere along the bedrock shoreline were huge boulders casually perched at random. I found myself marveling at the power it took to place them on their perch. We cut our tour short, limiting it to the southern end of the lake, returning to camp to watch the sunset and relax for the evening. The sun was right on the verge of disappearing when we arrived.

A half-hour or so after sunset, we started our campfire, which required quite a bit of coaxing due to semi-damp firewood. Within a half-hour of starting our fire, Julie noticed two slightly glowing areas in the northern sky that looked like someone was pointing a pair of dim spotlights into the air. But as the glow increased, it became apparent that the northern lights were flaring up. The aurora expanded into a mild arch across the northern sky with dim spires periodically rising from it. Over the course of an hour, the lights changed location, shape, and intensity continually. There were spires, moving sheets, and sometimes a greenish serpentine cloud trail. When the lights began to fade, Julie went into the tent, but I continued to watch for another twenty minutes or so as I tended the dwindling fire and waited for it to go out. Then, I followed Julie's lead, heading for the tent to blow up my sleeping pad and fluff up my sleeping bag. At that point, I was pretty sure the light show was over anyway, but I still couldn't help wondering about it as I slowly faded off to sleep. The lake was relatively quiet, even though most, if not all, the campsites were occupied. We heard just a few faint loon calls through the evening and into the night, making for a relaxing night of peaceful sleep.

We awoke just after the sun peeked above the eastern tree line, illuminating two identical worlds connected along the water's edge. There was not a ripple on Fourtown until a pair of canoes passed by, disturbing the lower world. In the stillness, the calling of swans and songbirds filled the morning air with vibrant notes.

After breakfast, we buttoned up our camp and embarked on another tour of the lake. Our whims took us to the first portage on the route to

Horse Lake. The map showed it as a paddle-through connection, but beavers and low water levels declared it to be a portage. The path looked well-used, so this was not a new thing. We stopped there at the small rapids to investigate. In one way, I wanted to cross the short portage and continue on to see what there was to see. Then again, we were planning to travel that route the next day, so I would see it soon enough. It was certainly an endearingly peaceful location with singing water and essentially a private lake most of the time. Still, our camp had an open view of Fourtown and more privacy than a portage route pass-through. We lingered for a bit, enjoying the quiet, then moved on. Farther along the eastern shoreline, we quietly passed a small painted turtle sunning itself on a small log, just above water level, in a quiet back bay. It was apparently enjoying the peace and quiet too.

We were back at camp by lunchtime. While we were eating, a pair of loons appeared just offshore in front of us. It was obviously an adult with a juvenile, which had a dull gray coloring instead of striking black. When the parent dove for food, junior looked lost, often putting its face in the water to watch what was going on down there. When the adult would call, junior would respond with a squeaky-sounding cry. When the adult came up with a fish, junior would go spastic, trying to grab the free meal. They eventually worked their way around the corner, where they were out of sight from our camp, ending our show.

After lunch, I decided to embark on my moose antler hunting expedition. Six years before, when we found the big swamp that was behind our camp, it was relatively easy to access. After my fourth attempt was thwarted by thick brush filled with downed, dead spruce trees that were covered with berry vines and guarded by sharp-pointed beaver-chewed stubs, Julie and I paddled over to the unoccupied camp across the small bay near us. That way, I could access the big swamp and surrounding ridges behind that camp. Unfortunately, I ran into the same issue there. It appeared that there was a recent spruce die-off, probably associated with a spruce budworm infestation, that caused most of the access problems. So, I decided to try accessing the swamp from the opposite direction when we paddled over to Horse Lake the next day. Surely, there was a way to access the swampy valley I wanted to explore. I envisioned moose antlers waiting for me there.

Following an early dinner, we set out on another evening paddle. After visiting with a pair of beavers not far from camp, we crossed the main body of the lake in choppy conditions to get a closer look at the fire-killed trees along the central area of the western shoreline. Even though I was sure we were looking at fire damage, most of the trees were not charred in any way, making me question my assumption.

Continuing on near the Boot Lake portage, we took a look at the big boulder where we ate lunch when we visited the area with our kids many years ago. Right in front of the boulder was a pair of swans, so we altered our course to give them their space. As we continued south down the shoreline, we passed a pair of beavers not too far from the big Fourtown island. It was a one-slap encounter, and they were gone.

Crossing the main lake back to camp, the water was still a touch choppy. Just enough to make it more of an adventure. We reached camp after sunset, just in time to greet the emerging bugs. I started our evening fire shortly after we arrived. An hour later, the bugs subsided, and northern lights began to show again. At first, it was just a greenish arch in the northern sky. Later, a second arch formed closer to the horizon. Some random spires were popping up now and then, but they never attained the level of the previous evening. About 10:00 pm, the light show faded, so I put out our fire and headed to the tent. It didn't take long for consciousness to fade into another peaceful, restful night.

We awoke again about sunrise — or what should have been sunrise — to an overcast world. The sun was a round orange ball just above the tree line. A few minutes later, it was gone, leaving the clouds in command of the sky. As we ate breakfast, a pair of swans noisily landed on the rocky point just west of camp.

We left camp about 8:30 am, intent on at least reaching Horse Lake. With the humidity, and Julie having a sore ankle from a minor sprain, I made a decision not to even attempt the twenty-two portages it would require for us to reach the lower Basswood Falls and Crooked Lake pictographs, then return to camp. Even though they were mostly short portages, it was still an ambitious plan. So, we just decided to make it an enjoyable day and leave it at that.

Right after our first short portage, the sun broke free of the clouds, adding more heat to the humidity. Throughout the route to Horse Lake, beaver activity was abundant, with all of the small rapids having a small beaver dam at the head. The longest portage, which was still less than a quarter mile, was an easy hike. About as relaxing as a portage can be. Unlike some of the other jumbled rocky portages of the past couple of days, it was more of an autumn stroll. Even with a canoe on my shoulders.

We reached Horse Lake shortly before noon. A brightly illuminated trio of islands and a busy red squirrel greeted us when we arrived. With a cool breeze coming from the lake and shade provided by a large white pine, we decided to linger there and eat our lunch. Afterward, I couldn't help exploring the creek feeding into the lake near the portage. Rock-hopping over to the mouth, I found the stream cascading through a bedrock chute. At the lake, rocks were piled up along each side of the creek like they were specifically placed there. The straight piles of rocks looked out of place in the wilderness. Then I realized that for many years, it was not a wilderness area and was not protected from development. I was pretty sure that the straight channel of rocks was a man-made reminder of activities before the wilderness protections.

Later, as we paddled around part of Horse Lake, we paddled past the campsite where we camped with our daughters a number of years ago. The loss of trees to spruce budworm had taken its toll. It was no longer the relaxing, picturesque site I remembered. It's now more open and spartan-looking. Still, some fond memories lingered there for me, momentarily pulling me into the past.

Then we paddled over to the entrance to the Horse River and worked our way into the first portage. It was at a boulder field. Based on the waterline marks on the rocks, most of them were submerged at one time, likely allowing a canoe to be paddled through, which is what I remembered from previous visits. Sitting there in the sun pondering things was getting hot, so we worked our way back across the lake and past the camp where we stayed with the girls, heading for a bay that borders the other side of the big swamp where I wanted to look for moose antlers. Along the way, we visited a huge beaver lodge in a small, shallow bay. It was a golden day for suntanning, but a bit warm for canoeing or portaging. Still, we paddled on, trying our best to ignore the heat and focus more on our surroundings.

The big swamp was penetrated by a tight, slow-moving creek. We navigated our way as far into the swamp as we could, but soon ran out of water to paddle in and never found a place where we could get out and explore on foot. So, another thwarted attempt at exploring the big swamp that I had planned the trip around. In fact, it was the last reasonable access route I could envision. I was defeated. At least until our next visit.

Back at the portage, we took advantage of the shade once again, relaxing with a snack and a cool drink of water. By 4:45 pm, we were back at camp and preparing dinner. It was ready just as the first of a few bouts of light rain hit. We had been hearing thunder for nearly an hour. Thankfully, the brief thunderstorms were not accompanied by much rain. The lack of lightning was also a good thing, as I was hurrying around camp, putting things away with a metal spoon lightning rod in my mouth from eating dinner.

After dark, we were entertained by a lightning show instead of northern lights. The frequent flashes over in the Horse Lake area went on for nearly an hour. During the show, we were able to enjoy a dry campfire that lasted past 10:00 pm. I finally put out what was left of the fire and relaxed in the dark for a while. None of the camps within sight of ours were occupied, so the only sounds were the sounds of the wilderness. Loons, owls, and scurrying creatures. Our neighbors. Just before going into the tent, I was standing on the point, close to the water, when I could faintly see the local pair of swans swimming out of our little bay, not more than twenty yards from me. When I turned to walk away, it must have startled one of the swans, because it let out an abrupt honk, which in turn startled me. At that point, I headed for the tent to tell Julie my new story.

We were up at daybreak once again, ready to embark on the day. Eight Canada geese flew in and landed right in front of me while I ate breakfast at the shoreline. Julie saw them flying in, but I didn't see them until I was startled by their noisy landing. We were packed up and on the water by 8:30 am. It was time to move on to the next segment of our Minnesota 2025 journey, which was an artist-in-residence with the Listening Point Foundation in Ely. I was disappointed that I wasn't able to find a moose antler, and still am disappointed, but I guess it's not that important in the grand scheme of things. A moose antler would have just been a symbol of the wild and the wilderness for me to take home, but I realized that I myself am already a symbol of the wild. A physical token of the wild would have been nice, but the wild and the wilderness are already part of me anyway. It's something that I carry with me all the time.

The first portage coming out of Fourtown was short and easy, as we already knew. Jumbled and rocky, but easy. The middle portage was, of course, still much longer, but it didn't really feel strenuous. It felt like a quiet stroll through autumn, with colored leaves scattered along the trail and more tumbling down with each faint breath of the light breeze. The herbal aroma of fall was already in the air. Shafts of sunlight filtered through the trees, highlighting portions of the forest floor and lichen-mottled cliff faces.

After the third portage, we had difficulty getting across a band of rocky rubble covered by shallow water. In frustration, I finally just stepped out of the boat in my LL Bean boots and pulled the canoe through, with only a tinge of dampness making it through the sewn seams.

After Mudro Lake, we were still able to carefully paddle through the first creek boulder field and pull the canoe through the second one. The first beaver dam required me to pull the canoe through twenty feet or more of flooded grass and brush, then over the edge of the dam itself. The second, smaller dam was already breached slightly around one end. Still, I had to pull the canoe through shallow water that was running through long swamp grass, then get it turned in the right direction and back into floatable water. It was a good backcountry workout. The reward was an easy paddle to the final portage and a simple carry back to our vehicle.

It was only about lunchtime as we were doing that final portage, reminiscing about our most recent brush with the wild. Just one of many, and hopefully just one of many more.

LISTENING POINT

I had picked up a copy of Sigurd Olson's collected works from his earlier writings many years ago. General curiosity attracted me to the book, but the words captivated my imagination. A few years later, while perusing the offerings of a small bookstore at the Isle Royale ranger station, my eyes caught the name, Sigurd Olson, on a book titled THE SINGING WILDERNESS. When we left the island, I was carrying a copy of that book. I've read it, or portions of it, multiple times since then. Each time I read it, new songs emerge. As a result, I naturally acquired and thoroughly read a copy of Sig's book titled LISTENING POINT as well.

Because of the book, Listening Point — both the physical point on Burntside Lake, near Ely, Minnesota, and the rustic log cabin that Sig built there — had floated through my imagination for years. I had read about the adventure of building the cabin, about the tranquility, the peace, and beauty of the place, and tried to envision what it was like to be there. The first time we had an opportunity to actually visit was in the fall of 2004. I'm not sure what I was more excited about, paddling the Boundary Waters Canoe Area Wilderness or visiting Listening Point. It was inspiring to be in the place where the eloquent words that eventually made it to paper stewed in Sig's mind. As an active conservationist, lifelong outdoorsman, and writer, I share many of Sig's values, aspirations, and struggles. Having built a north woods log cabin getaway from scratch in a remote area of Michigan's Upper Peninsula, I also felt a personal connection to Listening Point and its rustic cabin haven. It was hard to believe I was actually standing at the end of the point and looking at the views, feeling the feelings that flowed into the pages I had dreamed over. There was no doubt in my mind why the place was so special and still is. It fuels the imagination. It stirs the soul and kindles a restless flame inside. Standing there on a carpet of autumn color beside a young red pine, taking in the aroma of the woods, and looking out over the gently rolling lake, I could indeed see and hear and smell all the wild places I had ever been and places I dreamed of going. That first visit felt short, though, because the reality of being there just caught me by surprise and left me feeling a little awkward. I mostly just stared and pondered.

In October of 2019, I was blessed with the opportunity to be an artist-in-residence with the Listening Point Foundation to do some writing of my own. That residency allowed me to stay at Sig's old house, with access to his historic Writing Shack. It also provided access to Listening Point, including its historic cabin. Just visiting Listening Point and reading about it are fun and interesting, but life is built on experience. That artist-in-residence opportunity allowed me to immerse myself for a short time in Sig's life and experience it with all my senses, while adding my own experiences into the mix. My wife, Julie, who is an acrylic landscape painter, joined me in this venture.

Still feeling a bit star-struck with the place, I spent as much time as I could at the point, inside of the cabin and out, trying my best to simply live in the moment. One night, during the full moon, tightly packed snow-clouds finally broke up for a time. We quickly packed up at the house and ventured back out to the point to watch the moon following its appointed path across the night sky, keeping watch over Listening Point. Under its guidance, there was no need for headlamps or flashlights to find our way. The daytime slap of waves against rock had faded to a tinkling of rippled water like delicate windchimes dancing in a soft breath. We lingered in the chill and listened. Later, on our way back to our vehicle, we quietly passed by the cabin and its large guardian boulder, similarly grey in the soft moonlight. For a moment, I could see them both following the natural course of slowly melting back into the basic elements from which they came.

On our last of those four days at Listening Point, while Julie painted, I continued reading and listening. It occurred to me that Sig's descriptions of the point from the 1950's could have readily been written yesterday or even next year. Like the wilderness itself, Listening Point is a place governed by wilderness rhythms of days and seasons, not man-made clocks and calendars. It is a place for living in the moment, while listening to the past and looking to the future.

Then, all too soon, I had to lock the door as we reluctantly departed, not knowing if we would ever have an opportunity to return. I took something valuable with me, though. I left with a deep conviction to continue along my own life's path, weaving together the threads of conservation, wilderness adventures, and writing.

When we were blessed to be able to return in September of 2025 for another artist-in-residence stay to work on this book, like many people, I came to Listening Point looking for inspiration. Inspiration from the cabin and the physical attributes of the point itself. Inspiration from the outdoor recreation focus of the surrounding community. Inspiration from the nearby Boundary Waters Canoe Area Wilderness. And inspiration from the legacy of Sigurd Olson and his writing.

From my previous experience, I knew that the inspiration I needed was available there at Listening Point. Also, having been there before, I didn't need to spend time getting past the "Wow" factor of a first-time visitor. I certainly didn't know the point on an intimate level like Sig did, but I was at least familiar with it, and it felt good to be back. I felt like I could just relax and think, not feeling the need to run around trying to experience everything there is to experience all at once.

In his book LISTENING POINT, Sig wrote, *From this one place, I would explore the entire north and all life, including my own. I would look at the stars and feel that here was a focal point of great celestial triangles, a point as important as any on the planet. For me it would be a listening-post from which I might even hear the music of the spheres.*

And so can we all. For me, though, it goes beyond the natural attributes of the point. The cabin, too, is a listening-post. Sitting in the cabin, studying the details of design and construction, and visually following the patterns in the wood, I can see my own cabin that I hand-crafted from red pine logs more than thirty years ago. I find myself smiling at all the similarities in the two buildings and appreciating the unique differences. Sitting there in a rustic rocking chair, I can see my cabin being constructed with the help of family and friends and can relive thirty years of family adventures there. Bits and pieces of Listening Point and its rustic cabin take me not only to my own cabin, but to places across the country and around the world.

In the bedrock, trees, water, and wonder experienced at Listening Point, I not only found my needed inspiration, I also experienced the serenity, the reprieve from technology and chaotic busyness that we all need. In fact, what I found was that serenity enabled inspiration. It opened my senses, allowing the inspiration I needed to seep in.

In THE STORY OF LISTENING POINT, Robert Olson wrote about the point saying, ...*the goal of the (Listening Point) Foundation is to strive to preserve for all time the silence and serenity, which personify the wilderness experience and the place Sigurd loved.*

I found that Listening Point is indeed still that pocket of wilderness serenity. That place of respite. Like the wilderness it personifies, Listening Point is a place where we can let down our guard, brush aside burdens, be still, and listen.

The first day of our week-long stay, my wife and I wandered out to the end of the point. A lone adolescent loon was just off the tip of the point with its face in the water, surveying for fish below. The world was quiet, except for the drizzly breeze and the mumblings of a busybody red squirrel that was adding its two-cents-worth to the notes I was writing. Other than some dead pine branches and a fallen white pine, the point looked the same to me as it did when I was last there six years earlier. Just as it should be. Just as Sig wanted it to be. Timeless.

Looking around the south end of the lake, it appeared that there may have been some newer development in the area. Maybe it was new, or maybe it was there before, and I was just too enamored with the place to notice. Regardless, I suspect that Burntside Lake, like most lakes, tends to be considerably busier than in the early days. That day, though, it was quiet and peaceful. It could have easily been 1957, when the cabin was constructed.

Listening Point is a north woods haven. The cabin, too, is a haven. Not just from the elements, but from the cares and concerns and demands of life. From the drain of the modern world. There, things are still basic and simple. It's a shelter from anything you're needing shelter from. It's a sanctuary for the mind and body.

Later in our weeklong visit, we arrived at the cabin mid-morning, planning to just do some reading, writing, and thinking. As I was sitting in the cabin, writing, a loon began calling from somewhere out in the bay, prompting me to take a stroll out to the end of the point, then over to the dock. Once again, there were deer tracks in the trails from their wanderings the night before. I couldn't help wondering what the point looked like when Sig first found it. Based on his description, I envisioned much of the point being relatively bare bedrock, with trees primarily back near the cabin site. The cabin was constructed about sixty-eight years before my visit. A lot changes in that amount of time.

The next day, we went out to the point early in the evening, intent on watching the sunset. By the time we arrived, the sun was highlighting the point and penetrating the forest with an amber glow. It was just getting to be that magical hour when the world comes vividly to life. A trio of loons were diving near the point, almost looking like they were frolicking in the water. Maybe there was a school of fish causing the diving frenzy. Or maybe it was just an exhilarating time of day for them, too. As the sun set, there was a tall pine right in front of it. The big pine was on fire, and the perimeter of the blazing yellow-orange ball of sun was pulsating between yellow-orange and red. Once the sun had disappeared behind the trees across the lake, we could see a trail of woodsmoke emanating from a cabin across the end of Burntside. After the sunset show dimmed, we went back to the cabin. I could still see amber water glowing behind the forest through the cabin windows. I sat in one of the old rocking chairs, watching. As I watched, objects in the cabin were fading to shadows. We hurried back out to the end of the point as the faint oranges in the sky got bolder. Julie took a few pictures, then we retired to the cabin once more.

I turned on a battery-powered lantern and hung it on a nail on the main cabin crossbeam. Even though it cast a harsh blueish-white glow, it still illuminated the inside of the cabin to where I could visualize the glow of dancing flames in the stone fireplace and the yellowish light of oil lamps. That glowing nighttime cabin was even more inviting and inspiring than the daytime counterpart. The big moose antler above the mantle shined in the faint light. Oh, to have been there when the cabin glowed with the flickering of dancing flames. I was energized! My mind was alive with thoughts, memories, and ideas. Possibilities for future adventures stirred in my head. I could have sat there, rocking in that old chair through the night, waiting for and anticipating the sunrise. Alas, I knew that we needed rest for our coming adventures. So we collected our belongings, locked the door, latched the screen door, and made our way out to our vehicle and to the house, still anticipating the sunrise.

The following morning, the alarm went off early, allowing us to be at Listening Point well before daylight. With our headlamps, we walked out near the end of the point and watched in a relatively open area, where we had the best visibility. We watched the world slowly take on form. Black silhouettes slowly emerged from the night as bushes, trees, and boulders. Colors were then slowly revealed. As we waited and watched, two owls were conversing across the lake, and loon calls reverberated across the water. The eastern sky brightened, then orange and yellow hues took hold of the horizon. Ribbons of light fog were woven through the Burntside islands. Songbirds, then red squirrels awakened with the dawn. Still, the point, the nearby world in fact, waited for the glowing sphere to breach the trees on the eastern horizon. A bald eagle silently flew past the tip of the point as we too waited. The red-roofed cabin across the way to the west was basking in morning sunlight before the source of the light cleared the trees. It was like the builder of the cabin selected that site just for the sunrise. Finally, the long-anticipated source of the light broke free behind a stand of tall pines directly above a shoreline red maple adorned in crimson, bathing the point in light. Then we ventured over to the dock at the back of the bay and watched to the west as the sun illuminated the white pines and red pines near the tip of the point. An adolescent loon was quietly diving in the little bay, seemingly paying no attention. When we returned to the cabin, the other two loons joined the youngster in the bay to complete the trio we had seen the previous day. Julie took some pictures of the sunlit cabin, just because it looked too tranquil to ignore. While I was sitting in one of the rocking chairs in the cabin, reading Sig's essay titled *Laughing Loons,* one of the loons called twice from the little bay southwest of the point, bringing the story to life.

As I sat in that rustic rocking chair in the cabin a little longer, writing, I could again hear the calls of a loon coming through the open doorway, followed by the chattering of a red squirrel scolding something somewhere out on the point. The breeze, too, was speaking again. Its voice coming through the movement of aspen leaves and pine needles. A raspy blue jay joined the conversation, as did a chatty chickadee. All voices well-known to Listening Point, even before it was Listening Point. And so I sat in the old rocking chair, listening. Listening to the voices of the woods and waters. The voices within my own head. And the still small whisper of God. After relaxing in my new favorite old rocking chair for a short time, just mentally meandering, we quietly locked the door, latched the screen, and again bid the cabin farewell, hoping it was not a final goodbye.

Even though the point itself is beginning to get physically hemmed in by docks and cabins and homes, the spirit of the point can never be hemmed in or overrun. It remains wild and free. Likewise, while we're there at Listening Point, our spirits and dreams and ideals can always roam free, regardless of our current situation. Even when we are far away, places like Listening Point and our vast wilderness areas can help provide feelings of calm and serenity in the midst of this chaotically busy world we live in. We just need to take a deep breath and let the serenity seep in.

Spending time at Listening Point also allowed me to think about how I have been blessed with many personal listening points over my lifetime. Some were only available to me for a short time. Others have served me well for many years.

For instance, we bought a 110 acre farm when our daughters were young. We had no intentions of seriously farming. We just liked the 160-year-old farmhouse, the old timber frame barns, and the idea of working with the land. There were many things about that place that I loved, but one of the top-of-the-list things was my favorite hunting spot that I enjoyed there. It was more than just a great hunting spot. It was a listening point. One of my favorites.

Being in the farm country of lower Michigan, it had nothing to do with wilderness, but it was there that I dreamed of wilderness, planned wilderness ventures, and let my mind roam far and wide. Oh, and I hunted there, too.

It was near the junction of two farm fields, a wilding set-aside field, and a large swamp. A creek flowed into the swamp there as well. I had a trio of maple trees that I could sink into, so I was partially concealed. Surrounding trees around the edge of the swamp and along the creek helped conceal my presence and provided a wilderness atmosphere as well. I sat or stood there for countless hours during all the different deer seasons for twenty years. Even outside of hunting season, I would sometimes go there just to relax and think. It was my place to watch and listen, to think and ponder and dream.

One of my other long-term personal listening points is our family cabin. I hand-built it more than thirty years ago with red pine logs that I peeled with an old drawknife that I purchased at an antique shop. Much like Sig's old cabin at Listening Point, our cabin is short on modern amenities like electricity and running water, but long on attributes like character and atmosphere. An extensive collection of family memories lives there as well.

The cabin is nestled into the woods at the edge of a small meadow, in the middle of eighty acres. The property, in turn, is surrounded by thousands more acres of woods and meadows. As a result, distractions tend to be few, while peaceful thinking time tends to be plentiful. When I'm relaxing in my wooden rocking chair, either by the fire or out on the covered porch, my thoughts are free to roam far and wide. Ideas come easily. So do plans for future endeavors. Memories from family activities, along with a lifetime of outdoors adventures, are at my beck and call as thoughts new and old flow and intermingle.

The last sentence in Sig's essay about Listening Point states, *The adventures that have been mine can be known to anyone*. From my time there at the point on Burntside Lake, as well as my own listening points, I think I know those adventures. And I think I know, too, at least a little bit about what Listening Point on Burntside Lake meant to Sig.

Parting Thoughts

You've probably heard the term *Trout Bum*, pertaining to somebody who spends most of their time and energy just roaming around trout fishing. Well, as you've probably figured out by now, I'm somewhat of a *Wilderness Bum* in that I've been hanging around in wilderness areas since wilderness included the relatively small forests and fields around the neighborhood where I grew up. Vacations, especially the ones that I've planned, have always been focused on outdoor adventures. Visits to theme parks and such have thankfully been few and far between, regardless of who did the planning. I do have to admit that I have visited plenty of cities as part of my professional career, but not for personal trips. At least not if I could help it. Other than occasional family visits, most trips we take are outdoor adventures. And even when we're not traveling, wilderness-like adventures often take place right in our backyard. Or at least around our forest neighborhood.

Even though my heart has always been in the north woods, and probably always will be, over the years, I have been blessed to experience wilderness and wilderness-like areas across the country. Many states, in addition to my Michigan home, have hosted my wanderings over the years, including Minnesota, New Hampshire, New York, Wisconsin, South Dakota, Wyoming, Colorado, Arizona, Montana, Idaho, and Alaska.

Through these outings, I have been blessed to experience serenity in many situations and settings. Stirring sunrises and sunsets, peaceful lakes mirroring the world around them, grand scenic vistas, quiet hemlock cathedrals, mysteriously misty mornings, full moon nights, radiant autumn forests, softly singing streams, and many other settings along the way.

Often, it seems like when I am consciously seeking serenity, it's frustratingly elusive and leaves me wondering. Sometimes wandering. I tend to find serenity most often when I'm not really pursuing it. When I'm not trying to force the feeling. It certainly does not appear on cue or at a predetermined location. Serenity seems to subtly slip in and begin growing in your heart, until you finally recognize the feeling. Even close to home, serenity often finds me when I'm just quietly spending time at one of my personal Listening Points, not necessarily looking or listening for anything in particular.

Looking back over my years of explorations, I don't recall experiencing serene feelings as much when I was younger as I do now. Probably because when I was younger, I was often too busy just trying to accomplish things, checking locations and experiences off the list. The number of lakes reached, miles covered, or fish caught contributed heavily to the success of any given venture, so those things tended to be my focus. Over time, though, I have come to realize that numbers, although they're not bad, are not the primary measure of success. Visiting new places and experiencing new things are certainly fun and exciting, but I now try to focus more of my time and energy on the little things experienced along the way. Those intangible benefits, like the blessings of simply basking in tranquility when I find it, or gaining new insights from my experiences.

Sometimes, serenity comes bundled together with awe, while gazing out over grand vistas, or in the presence of colossal natural features. Other times, it's conveyed through a quiet, deeply personal encounter that may only last for a moment. Regardless of what inspires it, the feeling of serenity makes you wish that you could hold onto and savor it for the rest of your days. At least that's what it does to me.

Unfortunately, I think many people take our natural areas for granted and overlook the blessing that wilderness areas are, and how fortunate we are in this country to have so many wilderness and wilderness-like areas to enjoy. As we move into the future, I pray that our forests, fields, mountains, and waterways, where I, and hopefully you, truly feel at home, will not eventually be loved to death or exploited to death. If we destroy our wild places, or let them be destroyed by others, then serenity is one of the many things we will likely lose in the process. Peace and serenity come from God, quite often through that natural world that we, as human beings, were a part of in the beginning of time. The manmade world is just part of the chaos that we are currently living in. As good as some of it seems to be at times, it's still, unfortunately, just part of our chaotic modern world.

Serenity is most often found by stepping out of the mind-numbing chaos. Sometimes, it only needs to be a mental step, but I have found that physically stepping out of the chaos and into the natural world provides the atmosphere for taking that mental step. And it doesn't necessarily need to be a big physical step to put you in the right atmosphere. Compared to the busyness that normally surrounds most of us, even the flickering flames of a backyard campfire, a simple stroll in the woods, or a quiet cruise in a canoe or kayak can provide the comforting feelings of peace and tranquility. The serenity that is missing from the lives of many people today.

Even though the need for wild places is real, true wilderness may become more and more difficult to find as time goes on, because the pressures affecting our wilderness areas are growing. Increasing pollution, fluctuating weather patterns and catastrophic events, overuse, fragmentation, and development are just a few of the issues that are degrading our wild lands and waters. These are often difficult, and sometimes controversial, issues to deal with. But, somehow, they need to be addressed. Ignoring issues like these does not make them go away.

For example, here in the Lake Superior region, as we work to balance public demands for access with economics and wilderness health, protecting our wilderness heritage may mean things like limiting the number of people entering the Isle Royale backcountry on any given day to keep it from getting overcrowded. Just like we do in the Boundary Waters of Minnesota. Or it may mean removing seaplane traffic from Isle Royale to protect the wilderness atmosphere. Again, just like we protect the relatively nearby Boundary Waters Canoe Area Wilderness from the noise and disruption of aircraft traffic.

I hope and pray that we, as a society, have the wisdom to address these and other pressing issues, to preserve the integrity of our vast wild areas so that my kids and grandkids, along with all of our future generations, will have opportunities to explore and enjoy our natural heritage. And not just in pictures. Future generations need to have real access to the peace and tranquility found in our wild lands and waterways. The blessings of wilderness serenity need to be available to everyone willing to quietly accept and appreciate them.

Just as I have been blessed with a lifetime of adventures around the Lake Superior region and beyond, I hope that you, too, have enjoyed many similar experiences. May our wild lands and waterways not just survive, but thrive, continuing to inspire us, and those that come after us, by providing the timeless peace and tranquility from above, here on earth.

Enjoy the blessings of our natural world whenever you can. And I hope you are able to find peace and tranquility, that comforting sense of serenity, whenever you need it.

John Highlen

ABOUT THE AUTHOR

For more than five decades, John Highlen has been enjoying pursuits such as hiking, hunting, fishing, backpacking, canoeing, kayaking, exploring, and climbing, as well as many others. Though John's wanderings and outdoor adventures have taken him across the country, the north woods have always been his home. The many years spent absorbed in the outdoors, experiencing nature from numerous perspectives, has given him a deep appreciation of, and respect for, our natural world. As a degreed mechanical engineer, John is able to recognize and understand the details of what he sees and how those details work together in the grand scheme. Overall, this eclectic blend of skills and experience allows him to see and interpret the natural world through a unique set of eyes. John strives to use those skills and experience in his writing to help connect readers with the natural world everyone is meant to be a part of, and all the intrinsic benefits that flow from that connection.

In 2016, John was blessed to be able to turn his attention full-time to outdoor adventures, writing, volunteering for conservation organizations, and being the support crew for his wife, Julie's, art studio.

In 2019, John had the privilege of being an artist-in-residence with the *Listening Point Foundation*, in Ely, Minnesota. There, he focused his writings on Sigurd Olson's beloved Listening Point and the nearby Boundary Waters Canoe Area Wilderness.

In 2020, he and Julie were each blessed with an artist-in-residence with the *Friends of the Porkies*. Having an opportunity to live a simple life in the Porcupine Mountains wilderness for more than a month that year, focusing on interpreting his outdoors experiences, helped solidify John's desire to write.

In 2025, John once again was blessed with the opportunity to be an artist-in-residence with the *Listening Point Foundation*. That time in the Ely, Minnesota area was invested in further developing this book.

In addition to a number of outdoor-related articles, John has published three other non-fiction outdoor adventure books, *Touching the Wild UP*, *Porkies Wilderness Wanderings*, and *Chasing Traver's Magic*. All of John's books are available through Amazon, as well as most local bookstores.

John and his wife enjoy living in Deerton, Michigan, in a home surrounded by woods, less than ten minutes from the wonders of Lake Superior. From this vantage point, they paint the wilds of the north woods and waters to share nature's inspiration with others—Julie with brush and canvas, John with pen and paper.

The author may be contacted at jlhighlen@gmail.com